iPad®

FOR DUMMIES®

A Wiley Brand

6th Edition

by Edward C. Baig
and
Bob "Dr. Mac" LeVitus

iPad® For Dummies®, 6th Edition

Published by: **John Wiley & Sons, Inc.,** 111 River Street, Hoboken, NJ 07030-5774, www.wiley.com

Copyright © 2014 by John Wiley & Sons, Inc., Hoboken, New Jersey

Published simultaneously in Canada

For general information on our other products and services, please contact our Customer Care Department within the U.S. at 877-762-2974, outside the U.S. at 317-572-3993, or fax 317-572-4002. For technical support, please visit www.wiley.com/techsupport.

Wiley publishes in a variety of print and electronic formats and by print-on-demand. Some material included with standard print versions of this book may not be included in e-books or in print-on-demand. If this book refers to media such as a CD or DVD that is not included in the version you purchased, you may download this material at http://booksupport.wiley.com. For more information about Wiley products, visit www.wiley.com.

Library of Congress Control Number: 2013949066

ISBN 978-1-118-72306-7 (pbk); ISBN 978-1-118-72755-3 (ebk); ISBN 978-1-118-72783-6 (ebk)

Manufactured in the United States of America

10 9 8 7 6 5 4 3 2 1

Contents at a Glance

Table of Contents

Introduction

As Yogi Berra would say, "It was déjà vu all over again": front-page treatment, top billing on network TV and cable, and diehards lining up for days in advance to ensure landing a highly lusted-after product from Apple. The product generating the remarkable buzz this time around is the iPad Air. We hope you bought this book to find out how to get the very most out of your remarkable device. Our goal is to deliver that information in a light and breezy fashion. We expect you to have fun using your iPad. We equally hope that you have fun spending time with us.

About This Book

We need to get one thing out of the way right from the get-go. We think you're pretty darn smart for buying a *For Dummies* book. That says to us that you have the confidence and intelligence to know what you don't know. The *For Dummies* franchise is built around the core notion that everyone feels insecure about certain topics when tackling them for the first time, especially when those topics have to do with technology.

As with most Apple products, iPads are beautifully designed and intuitive to use. And though our editors may not want us to reveal this dirty little secret (especially on the first page, for goodness sake), the truth is you'll get pretty far just by exploring the iPad's many functions and features on your own, without the help of this (or any other) book.

Okay, now that we've spilled the beans, we'll tell you why you shouldn't run back to the bookstore and request a refund. This book is chock-full of useful tips, advice, and other nuggets that should make your iPad experience all the more pleasurable. We'd even go so far as to say that you wouldn't find some of these nuggets anywhere else. So keep this book nearby and consult it often.

Foolish Assumptions

Although we know what happens when you make assumptions, we've made a few anyway. First, we assume that you, gentle reader, know nothing about using an iPad or iOS — beyond knowing what an iPad is, that you want to use iOS, that you want to understand your iPad and its operating system without digesting an incomprehensible technical manual, and that you made the right choice by selecting this particular book.

And so, we do our best to explain each new concept in full and loving detail. Perhaps that's foolish, but . . . oh, well.

One last thing: We also assume that you can read. If you can't, please ignore this paragraph.

Icons Used in This Book

Little round pictures (or *icons*) appear in the left margins throughout this book. Consider these icons as miniature road signs, telling you something extra about the topic at hand or hammering a point home.

Here's what the five icons used in this book look like and mean.

These are the juicy morsels, shortcuts, and recommendations that might make the task at hand faster or easier.

This icon emphasizes the stuff we think you ought to retain. You may even jot down a note to yourself in the iPad.

Put on your propeller beanie hat and insert your pocket protector; this text includes the truly geeky stuff. You can safely ignore this material, but if it weren't interesting or informative, we wouldn't have bothered to write it.

You wouldn't intentionally run a stop sign, would you? In the same fashion, ignoring warnings may be hazardous to your iPad and (by extension) your wallet. There, you now know how these warning icons work, for you have just received your very first warning!

We put a New icon next to anything that's new or improved in iOS 7 or with the iPad.

Beyond the Book

We wrote a bunch of things that just didn't fit in the print version of this book. Rather than leave them on the cutting room floor, we've posted the most useful bits online for your enjoyment and edification.

Here's where you'll find them:

✓ **Online articles covering additional topics are at**

`www.dummies.com/extras/ipad`

You'll find a fairly complete list of phrases Siri understands; an essay on cameras, megapixels, and image quality; making sense of the alphabet soup of cellular data networks (EDGE, 4G, LTE, HSDPA, GSM, CDMA, and more); why your computer offers a shopping mall for content while your iPad doesn't; and much more.

✓ The Cheat Sheet for this book is at

`www.dummies.com/cheatsheet/ipad`

Here, you'll find tips for mastering multitouch; a list of things you can do during a phone call; managing contacts; and where to find additional help if your iPad is acting contrary.

Where to Go from Here

Why, straight to Chapter 1, of course (without passing Go).

In all seriousness, we wrote this book for you, so please let us know what you think. If we screwed up, confused you, left out something, or — heaven forbid — made you angry, drop us a note. And if we hit you with one pun too many, it helps to know that as well. Because writers are people too (believe it or not), we also encourage positive feedback if you think it's warranted. So kindly send e-mail to Ed at `Baigdummies@gmail.com` and to Bob at `iPadLeVitus@boblevitus.com`. We do our best to respond to reasonably polite e-mail in a timely fashion. Most of all, we want to thank you for buying our book. Please enjoy it along with your new iPad.

Note: At the time we wrote this book, all the information it contained was accurate for all Wi-Fi and Wi-Fi + 3G and 4G iPads with the exception of the first-generation iPad, which we no longer cover. It's also based on version 7.0.2 of the iOS (operating system) used by the iPad and version 11.1 of iTunes. Apple is likely to introduce new iPad models and new versions of iOS and iTunes between book editions, so if you've bought a new iPad and its hardware, user interface, or the version of iTunes on your computer looks a little different, be sure to check out what Apple has to say at `www.apple.com/ipad`. You'll no doubt find updates on the company's latest releases. When a change is very substantial, we try to add an update or bonus information that you can find at `www.dummies.com/extras/ipad`.

Part I
Getting to Know Your iPad

In this part...

- Get basic training for getting along with your iPad.

- Enjoy a gentle introduction to your iPad with a big-picture overview of what's in the box (if you haven't already peeked).

- Take a peek at your iPad hardware and software and explore the way it works.

- Discover the joys of synchronization over USB and Wi-Fi and how to get your data — contacts, appointments, movies, songs, podcasts, books, and so on — from a computer onto your iPad, quickly and painlessly.

1

Unveiling the iPad

Congratulations! You've selected one of the most incredible handheld devices we've ever seen. Of course, the iPad is a combination of a killer audio and video iPod, an e-book reader, a powerful Internet communications device, a superb handheld gaming device, a still and video camera, and a platform for over 850,000 apps at the time this was written — and probably a lot more by the time you read this.

There have been seven iPad models so far: The original iPad (2010), the iPad 2 (2011), the iPad third generation (Spring 2012), the iPad fourth generation (Fall 2012), the iPad mini (Fall 2012), the iPad Air (Fall 2013), and the iPad mini with Retina display. Yes, the 2010 and 2012 iPads share the same moniker and are both named iPad. To avoid confusion we refer to them as the first-, second-, third- and fourth-generation iPads throughout this book. Note that we're not covering the first-generation iPad in this book, because the latest operating system (iOS 7) doesn't run on it. If you're the owner of an original iPad, you can still find a lot of handy information, but some things might look or work differently. You might want to rummage around for a previous edition.

In this chapter, we offer a gentle introduction to all the pieces that make up your iPad, plus overviews of its revolutionary hardware and software features.

Exploring the iPad's Big Picture

The iPad has many best-of-class features, but perhaps its most notable feature is its lack of a physical keyboard or stylus. Instead, it has a super-high-resolution touchscreen — 132 pixels per inch (ppi) for second-generation iPad and 264 ppi for the third and fourth generation — that you operate using a pointing device you're already intimately familiar with: your finger.

And what a display it is. All four generations have beautiful screens, and the third-generation, fourth-generation, iPad Air, and iPad mini with Retina display sport Apple's exclusive high-definition Retina display, which is easily the most beautiful screen we've ever seen on a tablet.

Other things we love include the iPad's plethora of built-in sensors. It has an *accelerometer* to detect when you rotate the device from portrait to landscape mode — and instantly adjust what's on the display accordingly.

The screen rotates — that is, unless the Screen Orientation Lock is engaged. We tell you more about this feature shortly.

A light sensor adjusts the display's brightness in response to the current ambient lighting conditions.

In addition to the aforementioned sensors, iPads have a three-axis gyro sensor that works in conjunction with the accelerometer and built-in compass.

Last, but definitely not least, the latest iPads (all but iPad 2), running at least iOS 6, come with Siri, a voice-controlled personal assistant happy to do almost anything you ask.

In the following sections, we're not just marveling about the wonderful screen and sensors. Now it's time to take a brief look at the rest of the iPad's features, broken down by product category.

The iPad as an iPod

We agree with the late Steve Jobs on this one: The iPad is magical — and without a doubt the best iPod Apple has ever produced. You can enjoy all your existing iPod content — music, audiobooks, audio and video podcasts, iTunes U courses, music videos, television shows, and movies — on the iPad's gorgeous high-resolution color display, which is bigger, brighter, and richer than any iPod or iPhone display that came before it.

Here's the bottom line: If you can get the content — be it video, audio, or whatever — into iTunes on your Mac or PC, you can synchronize it and watch or listen to it on your iPad. And, of course, you can always buy or rent content on your iPad with the iTunes Store and iBooks apps.

Chapter 3 is all about syncing, but for now, just know that some video content may need to be converted to an iPad-compatible format (with proper resolution, frame rate, bit rate, and file format) to play on your iPad. If you try to sync an incompatible video file, iTunes alerts you that an issue exists.

If you get an error message about an incompatible video file, select the file in iTunes and choose File➪Create New Version. When the conversion is finished, sync again. Chapter 8 covers video and video compatibility in more detail.

And here's another tip at no extra cost: The free HandBrake application (http://handbrake.fr) often provides better results than iTunes when converting movie files to an iPad-friendly format. It has a preset for the iPad, so it's simple to use, and it can often convert movie files and formats that iTunes chokes on.

The iPad as an Internet communications device

But wait — there's more! Not only is the iPad a stellar iPod, but it's also a full-featured Internet communications device with — we're about to drop some industry jargon on you — a rich HTML e-mail client that's compatible with most POP and IMAP mail services, with support for Microsoft Exchange ActiveSync. (For more on this topic, see Chapter 5.) Also onboard is a world-class web browser (Safari) that, unlike what's on many mobile devices, makes web surfing fun and easy on the eyes. Chapter 4 explains how to surf the web using Safari.

Another cool Internet feature is *Maps,* a killer mapping application that's much improved in iOS 7. By using GPS (3G or 4G models) or triangulation (Wi-Fi–only models), the iPad can determine your location, let you view maps and satellite imagery, and obtain driving directions and traffic information regardless of where you happen to be. (See Chapter 6 for the scoop on Maps.) You can also find businesses, such as gas stations, pizza restaurants, hospitals, and Apple Stores, with just a few taps.

We daresay that the Internet experience on an iPad is far superior to the Internet experience on any other handheld device.

The iPad as an e-book reader

Download the free iBooks app and/or any of the excellent (and free) third-party e-book readers such as the Kindle and Nook apps, and you'll discover a whole new way of finding and reading books. The iBooks Store and Newsstand app (covered in Chapter 10) are chock-full of good reading at prices that are lower than what you'd pay for a printed copy. Better still, when you read an e-book, you're helping the environment and saving trees. Furthermore, some (if not many) titles include audio, video, or graphical content not available in the printed editions. Plus, a great number of really good books are absolutely free. And best of all, you can carry your entire library in one hand. If you've never read a book on your iPad, give it a try. We think you'll like (or love) it.

The iPad as a multimedia powerhouse

The spectacular screen found on second-generation iPads is superb for personal video viewing, and the Retina display on the third-generation and later iPads make it even more extraordinary. Add an adapter cable, as discussed in Chapter 17, and it turns into a superb device for watching video on an HDTV (or even a non-HD TV), with support for output resolutions up to 1080p.

You won't even need an adapter cable if you have an Apple TV ($99), a marvelous little device that lets you stream audio and video to your HDTV wirelessly.

And all iPads include a pair of cameras and the FaceTime video-chatting app, taking the iPad's multimedia acumen to new heights. Chapter 8 gets you started with FaceTime.

The iPad as a platform for third-party apps

The App Store offers more than 1,000,000 apps for the iPhone, iPad, and iPod touch at the time of this writing, in categories that include games, business, education, entertainment, healthcare and fitness, music, photography, productivity, travel, sports, and many more. The cool thing is that most of them, even ones designed for the iPhone or iPod touch, also run flawlessly on the iPad.

Of those 1,000,000+ apps, more than 400,000 are designed specifically for the iPad's larger screen, with more arriving daily.

Chapter 11 helps you fill your iPad with all the cool apps your heart desires. We share our favorite free and for-sale apps in Chapters 18 and 19, respectively.

What do you need to use an iPad?

To actually *use* your iPad, only a few simple things are required. Here's a list of everything you need:

- An iPad
- An Apple ID (assuming that you want to acquire apps, videos, music, iBooks, podcasts, and so on, which you almost certainly do)
- Internet access — broadband wireless Internet access is recommended

In previous editions of this book, we said you *needed* a computer with iTunes to sync your iPad. We've since amended our advice. Because iOS now lets you activate, set up, update, back up, and restore an iPad wirelessly without a computer, you don't technically *need* a computer to use with your iPad. But it's still nice to have a computer; many tasks are faster and easier on a computer with iTunes than on your iPad.

If you decide to introduce your iPad to your computer (and we think you should), here's what's required for syncing (which we discuss at length in Chapter 3):

- ✓ A Mac with a USB 2.0 or 3.0 port, Mac OS X version 10.6.8 or later, and iTunes 11.1 or later

- ✓ A PC with a USB 2.0 or 3.0 port; Windows 8, Windows 7, Windows Vista, or Windows XP Home or Professional Edition with Service Pack 3 or later; and iTunes 11.1 or later (free download at www.itunes.com/download)

Touring the iPad Exterior

The iPad is a harmonious combination of hardware and software. In the following sections, we take a brief look at the hardware — what's on the outside.

On the top

On the top of your iPad, you find the headphone jack, microphone, and the Sleep/Wake button, as shown in Figure 1-1:

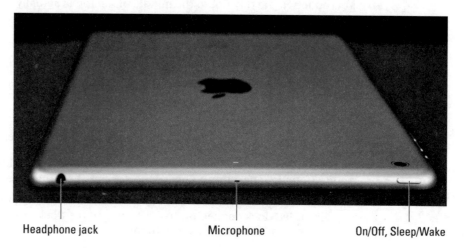

Headphone jack   Microphone   On/Off, Sleep/Wake

Figure 1-1: The top side of the iPad.

✔ **Sleep/Wake button:** This button is used to put your iPad's screen to sleep or to wake it up. It's also how you turn your iPad on or off. To put it to sleep or wake it up, just press the button. To turn it on or off, press and hold the button for a few seconds.

Your iPad's battery will run down faster when your iPad is awake, so we suggest that you make a habit of putting it to sleep when you're not using it.

When your iPad is sleeping, nothing happens if you touch its screen. To wake it up, merely press the button again or press the Home button on the front of the device (as described in a moment).

If you use an Apple Smart Cover or Smart Case (or any of the third-party cases that use the Smart Cover mechanism), you can just open the cover to wake your iPad and close the cover to put it to sleep.

In Chapter 15, you can find out how to make your iPad go to sleep automatically after a period of inactivity.

✔ **Headphone jack:** This jack lets you plug in a headset. You can use the Apple headsets or headphones that came with your iPhone or iPod. Or you can use pretty much any headphones or headset that plugs into a 3.5-mm stereo headphone jack.

Throughout this book, we use the words *headphones, earphones,* and *headset* interchangeably. Strictly speaking, a headset includes a microphone so that you can talk (or record) as well as listen; headphones or earphones are for listening only. Either type works with your iPad.

✔ **Microphone:** The tiny dot in the middle of the top is actually a pretty good microphone.

On the bottom

On the bottom of your iPad are the speaker and dock connector, as shown in Figure 1-2:

✔ **Speaker:** The speaker plays monaural (single-speaker) audio — music or video soundtracks — if no headset is plugged in.

✔ **30-pin dock connector (second and third generation) or Lightning connector (fourth generation):** This connector has three purposes:

   • *Recharge your iPad's battery:* Simply connect one end of the included dock connector–to–USB cable to the dock or Lightning connector and the other end to the USB power adapter.

   • *Synchronize your iPad:* Connect one end of the same cable to the dock connector and the other end to a USB port on your Mac or PC.

   • *Connect your iPad to cameras or televisions using adapters:* Such connectors include the Camera Connection Kit or the other adapter cables discussed in Chapter 17. Make sure to use an adapter that is appropriate for your dock or Lightning connector.

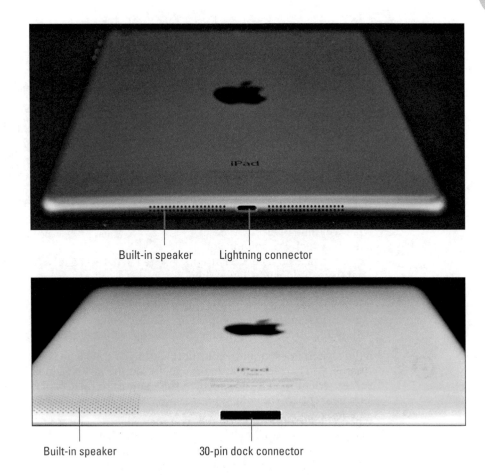

Built-in speaker   Lightning connector

Built-in speaker   30-pin dock connector

Figure 1-2: The bottom of the second- and third-generation iPad (bottom) and iPad Air (top).

If you connect the USB cable to USB ports on your keyboard, USB hub, display, or other external device, or even the USB ports on an older Mac or PC, you may be able to sync, but more than likely can't charge the battery. For the most part, only your computer's built-in USB ports (and only recent-vintage computers at that) have enough juice to recharge the battery. If you use an external USB port, you probably see a Not Charging message next to the Battery icon at the top of the screen.

On the right side

On the right side of your iPad are the Volume Up/Down control and Mute switch, as shown in Figure 1-3:

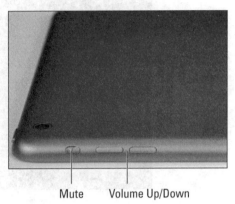

Mute   Volume Up/Down

Figure 1-3: The right side has two buttons.

✔ **Mute switch:** When the switch is set to Silent mode — the down position, with an orange dot visible on the switch — your iPad doesn't make any sound when you receive new mail or an alert pops up on the screen. Note that the Mute switch doesn't silence what we think of as *expected* sounds, which are sounds you expect to hear in a particular app. Therefore, it doesn't silence the iTunes or Videos apps, nor does it mute games and other apps that emit noises. About the only thing the Mute switch mutes are unexpected sounds, such as those associated with notifications from apps or the iPad operating system (iOS).

If the switch doesn't mute your notification sounds when engaged (that is, you can see the little orange dot on the switch), look for a little Screen Orientation icon (shown in the margin) to the left of the Battery icon near the top of your screen.

When you flick the Mute switch, you may see this icon for two possible reasons. The most likely reason is that you've selected the Lock Rotation option in the Settings app's General pane. Another, far less likely reason is that your iPad is running an older version (version 3 or earlier) of iOS. Turn to Chapter 3 right now to upgrade to a newer iOS.

✔ **Volume Up/Down control:** The Volume Up/Down control is a single button that's just below the Mute switch. The upper part of the button increases the volume; the lower part decreases it.

The Camera app uses the Volume Up button as a shutter release button as an alternative to the onscreen shutter release button. Press either one to shoot a picture or start/stop video recording.

On the front and back

On the front and back of your iPad, you find the following (labeled in Figure 1-4):

✔ **Touchscreen:** You find out how to use the iPad's gorgeous high-resolution color touchscreen in Chapter 2. All we have to say at this time is . . . try not to drool all over it.

Application button

Front camera

Rear camera

Touchscreen   Home button

Figure 1-4: The front and back of the iPad: a study in elegant simplicity.

- **Home button:** No matter what you're doing, you can press the Home button at any time to display the Home screen, as shown in Figure 1-4.

- **Front camera:** The front camera is serviceable, and delivers decent-enough video for video chats and such, but it's not particularly good for taking still photos.

- **Application buttons:** Each of the 20 buttons (icons) shown on the screen (see Figure 1-4) launches an included iPad application. You read more about these applications later in this chapter and throughout the rest of the book.

- **Rear camera:** iPads have a better camera (than the one in front) on the backside, just below the Sleep/Wake button. The iPad 2's rear camera captures decent video at 720p and shoots fair-to-middling stills; all other iPads have better rear cameras that shoot nice HD video at 1080p and very nice stills.

Status bar

The status bar, which is at the top of the screen, displays tiny icons that provide a variety of information about the current state of your iPad:

- ✈ **Airplane mode:** Airplane mode should be enabled when you fly. It turns off all of the wireless features of your iPad — the cellular, 4G, 3G, GPRS (General Packet Radio Service), and EDGE (Enhanced Datarate for GSM Evolution) networks; Wi-Fi; and Bluetooth — so you can enjoy music, video, games, photos, or any app that doesn't require an Internet connection while you're in the air.

  Tap the Settings app and then tap the Airplane Mode switch so it says "On." The icon shown in the margin appears on the left side of your status bar whenever Airplane Mode is enabled.

  Disable Airplane mode when the plane is at the gate before takeoff or after landing so you can send or receive e-mail and iMessages.

  There's no need to enable Airplane mode on flights that offer onboard Wi-Fi. On such flights it's perfectly safe to use your iPad's Wi-Fi while you're in the air (but not until the captain says so).

LTE

- **LTE (Wi-Fi + 4G models only):** This icon lets you know that your carrier's 4G LTE network is available and your iPad can use it to connect to the Internet.

3G

- **3G (Wi-Fi + 3G models only):** This icon informs you that the high-speed 3G data network from your wireless carrier (that's AT&T, Verizon, Sprint, and T-Mobile in the United States) is available and that your iPad can connect to the Internet via 3G. (Wondering what 3G, 4G, and these other data networks are? Check out the nearby sidebar, "Comparing Wi-Fi, 4G, LTE, 3G, GPRS, and EDGE.")

O

- **GPRS (Wi-Fi + 3G and 4G models only):** This icon says that your wireless carrier's GPRS data network is available and that your iPad can use it to connect to the Internet.

E

- **EDGE (Wi-Fi + 3G and 4G models only):** This icon tells you that your wireless carrier's EDGE network is available and you can use it to connect to the Internet.

🛜

- **Wi-Fi:** If you see the Wi-Fi icon, your iPad is connected to the Internet over a Wi-Fi network. The more semicircular lines you see (up to three), the stronger the Wi-Fi signal. If you have only one or two semicircles of Wi-Fi strength, try moving around a bit. If you don't see the Wi-Fi icon on the status bar, Internet access with Wi-Fi is not currently available.

◉

- **Personal Hotspot:** You see this icon when you're sharing your Internet connection with computers or other devices over Wi-Fi. Personal Hotspot is available for every iPad except for iPad 2 and may not be available in all areas or from all carriers, and additional fees may apply. Contact your wireless carrier for more information.

Comparing Wi-Fi, 4G, LTE, 3G, GPRS, and EDGE

Wireless (that is, cellular) carriers may offer one of three data networks relevant to the iPad as of this writing. For now anyway, only the third-generation and later iPads can take advantage of the speediest 4G or LTE networks the carriers are rolling out as fast as they can. The second-fastest network is called 3G, and there are older, even slower data networks called EDGE and GPRS. Your iPad starts by trying to connect to the fastest network it supports. If it makes a connection, you see the 4G or 3G icon on the status bar. If it can't connect to a 4G or 3G network, it tries to connect to a slower EDGE or GPRS network, and you see EDGE or GPRS icons on the status bar.

Most Wi-Fi networks, however, are faster than even the fastest 4G cellular data network — and much faster than 3G, EDGE, or GPRS. So, because all iPads can connect to a Wi-Fi network if one is available, they do so, even when a 4G, 3G, GPRS, or EDGE network is also available.

Last but not least, if you don't see one of these icons — 4G, 3G, GPRS, EDGE, or Wi-Fi — you don't currently have Internet access. Chapter 4 offers more details about these different networks.

 ✔ **Syncing:** This icon appears on the status bar when your iPad is syncing with iTunes on your Mac or PC.

 ✔ **Activity:** This icon tells you that some network or other activity is occurring, such as over-the-air synchronization, sending or receiving e-mail, or loading a web page. Some third-party applications also use this icon to indicate network or other activity.

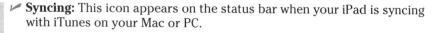 ✔ **VPN:** This icon shows that you're currently connected to a virtual private network (VPN).

 ✔ **Lock:** This icon tells you when your iPad is locked. See Chapter 2 for information on locking and unlocking your iPad.

 ✔ **Screen Orientation Lock:** This icon appears when the Screen Orientation Lock is engaged.

 ✔ **Location Services:** This icon appears when an app (such as Maps; see Chapter 6 for more about the Maps app) is using Location Services (GPS) to establish your physical location (or at least to establish the physical location of your iPad).

  ✔ **Do Not Disturb:** This icon appears whenever Do Not Disturb is enabled, silencing incoming FaceTime calls and alerts. See Chapter 15 for details on Do Not Disturb.

✔ **Play:** This icon informs you that a song is currently playing. You find out more about playing songs in Chapter 7.

✔ **Bluetooth:** This icon indicates the current state of your iPad's Bluetooth connection. If you see this icon on the status bar, Bluetooth is on, and a device (such as a wireless headset or keyboard) is connected. If the icon is gray, Bluetooth is turned on, but no device is connected. If the icon is white, Bluetooth is on, and one (or more) devices are connected. If you don't see a Bluetooth icon, Bluetooth is turned off. Chapter 15 goes into more detail about Bluetooth.

✔ **Battery:** This icon reflects the level of your battery's charge. It's completely filled when you aren't connected to a power source and your battery is fully charged (as shown in the margin). It then empties as your battery becomes depleted. The icon shows when you're connected to a power source, and when the battery is fully charged or is currently charging. You see an onscreen message when the charge drops to 20 percent or below, and another when it reaches 10 percent.

Discovering the Delectable Home Screen and Dock Icons

The iPad Home screen and Dock display 20 icons, with each icon representing a different built-in application or function. Because the rest of the book covers each and every one of these babies in full and loving detail, we merely provide brief descriptions here.

To get to your Home screen, tap the Home button. If your iPad is asleep when you tap, the unlock screen appears. After your iPad is unlocked, you see whichever page was on the screen when it went to sleep. If that happens to have been the Home screen, you're golden. If it wasn't, merely tap the Home button again to summon your iPad's Home screen.

In the following sections, we tell you briefly about the icons pre-loaded on your iPad's first Home screen page, as well as the icons you find on the Dock that are always accessible from each Home screen.

Home is where the screen is

If you haven't rearranged your icons, you see the following applications on your Home screen, starting at the top left:

✔ **FaceTime:** Use this app to participate in FaceTime video chats, as you discover in Chapter 8.

✓ **Calendar:** No matter what calendar program you prefer on your Mac or PC (as long as it's iCal, Calendar, Microsoft Entourage, or Microsoft Outlook or online calendars such as Google or iCloud), you can synchronize events and alerts between your computer and your iPad. Create an event on one device, and the event is automatically synchronized with the other device the next time the two devices are connected. Neat stuff.

✓ **Photos:** This application is the iPad's terrific photo manager, which just keeps getting better. It lets you view pictures from a camera or SD card (using the optional Camera Connection Kit), screen shots of your iPad screen, photos synced from your computer, saved from an e-mail or web page, or saved from one of the myriad third-party apps that let you save your handiwork in the Photos app. You can zoom in or out, create slideshows, e-mail photos to friends, crop, do a bit of image editing, and much more. And it's where you'll find the Camera Roll album with photos and videos you've taken with your iPad. To get started, see Chapter 9.

✓ **Camera:** This app is for shooting pictures or videos with your iPad's front- or rear-facing camera. You find out more in Chapters 8 (videos) and 9 (camera).

✓ **Contacts:** This handy little app contains information about the people you know. Like the Calendar app, it synchronizes with the Contacts app on your Mac or PC (as long as you keep your contacts in Address Book, Contacts, Microsoft Entourage, or Microsoft Outlook), and you can synchronize contacts between your computer and your iPad. If you create a contact on one device, the contact is automatically synchronized with the other device the next time your devices are connected. Chapter 12 explains how to start using the Calendar and Contacts apps.

✓ **Maps:** This application is among our favorites. View street maps or satellite imagery of locations around the globe, or ask for directions, traffic conditions, or even the location of a nearby pizza joint. You can find your way around the Maps app with the handy tips you find in Chapter 6.

✓ **Clock:** The Clock app includes alarm clocks, timers, and more. You hear more about this nifty new app in Chapter 13.

✓ **Videos:** This handy app is the repository for your movies, TV shows, and music videos. You add videos via iTunes on your Mac or PC or by purchasing them from the iTunes Store using the iTunes app on your iPad. Check out Chapter 8 to find out more.

✓ **Notes:** This program enables you to type notes while you're out and about. You can send the notes to yourself or to anyone else through e-mail, or you can just save them on your iPad until you need them. For help as you start using Notes, flip to Chapter 13.

- **Reminders:** This app may be the only To-Do list you ever need. It integrates with iCal, Calendar, Outlook, and iCloud, so To-Do items and reminders sync automatically with your other devices, both mobile and desktop. You'll hear much more about this great app, but you have to wait until Chapter 13.

- **Photo Booth:** This one is a lot like those old-time photo booths, but you don't have to feed it money. You discover details about Photo Booth in Chapter 9.

- **Game Center:** This is the Apple social networking app for game enthusiasts. Compare achievements, boast of your conquests and high scores, or challenge your friends to battle. You hear more about social networking and Game Center in Chapter 13.

- **Newsstand:** This app is where you find iPad editions for magazines and newspapers that you subscribe to. Shop for subscriptions at the aforementioned App Store; you read more about Newsstand in Chapter 10.

- **iTunes Store:** Tap this puppy to purchase music, movies, TV shows, audiobooks, and more. You find more info about iTunes (and the Music app) in Chapter 7.

- **App Store:** This icon enables you to connect to and search the iTunes App Store for iPad applications that you can purchase or download for free over a Wi-Fi or cellular data network connection. Chapter 11 is your guide to buying and using apps from the App Store.

- **Settings:** This is where you change settings for your iPad and its apps. D'oh! With so many different settings in the Settings app, you'll be happy to hear that Chapter 15 is dedicated exclusively to Settings.

Sittin' on the dock of the iPad

At the bottom of the iPad screen are the final four icons, sitting on a special shelf-like area called the *Dock*.

The thing that makes the icons on your Dock special is that they're available on every Home screen page.

By default, the Dock icons are

- **Messages:** This app provides a unified messaging service dubbed iMessage to iPads, iPhones, iPod touches, and Macs. You can exchange unlimited free text or multimedia messages with any other device running iOS 5 or later (the iPad, iPhone, and iPod touch) or Mac OS X Mountain Lion. Find out more about iMessages in Chapter 5.

- ✔ **Mail:** This application lets you send and receive e-mail with most POP3 and IMAP e-mail systems and, if you work for a company that grants permission, Microsoft Exchange, too. Chapter 5 helps you start e-mailing everyone you know from your iPad.

- ✔ **Safari:** Safari is your web browser. If you're a Mac user, you know that already. If you're a Windows user who hasn't already discovered the wonderful Safari for Windows, think Internet Explorer on steroids. Chapter 4 shows you how to start using Safari on your iPad.

- ✔ **Music:** Last but not least, this icon unleashes all the power of an iPod right on your iPad so that you can listen to music or podcasts. You discover how it works in Chapter 7.

Apple puts four icons on the Dock, but it can hold up to six. Feel free to add icons to or remove icons from the Dock until it feels right to you. To rearrange, add, or delete icons from the Dock, press and hold the icon until all the icons wiggle. Then drag the icon to where you want it. Press the Home button to save your arrangement.

There are two last things:

- ✔ iOS 5 introduced the totally useful Notification Center, which got even better in iOS 6 and iOS 7. We wanted to mention it even though it doesn't have an icon of its own. You hear much more about it in Chapter 13; to see it now (we know you can't wait), swipe your iPad screen from top to bottom to make it appear. Then swipe from bottom to top to put it away again.

- ✔ Last but not least, iOS 7 introduces the even more useful Control Center, with useful controls for Wi-Fi, Bluetooth, audio playback, and more, all available from any screen even when an app is running. You'll learn much more about Control Center in Chapter 14, but if you just can't stand the suspense, put your finger at the very bottom of your iPad screen and swipe upward to check out Control Center (and then swipe downward or tap the Home button to put it away).

2

iPad Basic Training

*B*y now you know that the iPad you hold in your hands is very different from other computers.

You also know that these slate-style machines are rewriting the rulebook for mainstream computing. How so? For starters, iPads don't come with a mouse or any other kind of pointing device. They lack traditional computing ports or connectors, such as USB. And they have no physical or built-in keyboard.

iPads even differ from other so-called tablet PCs, some of which feature a pen or stylus and let you write in digital ink. As we point out (pun intended) in Chapter 1, the iPad relies on an input device that you always have with you: your finger.

Tablet computers of one form or another have actually been around since the last century. They just never captured the fancy of Main Street. Apple's very own Newton, an ill-fated 1990s personal digital assistant, was among the machines that barely made a dent in the market.

What's past is past, of course, and technology — not to mention Apple itself — has come a long way since Newton. And suffice it to say that in the future, tablets — led by the iPad brigade, of course — promise to enjoy a much rosier outlook. Indeed, since the iPad burst onto the scene, numerous tech titans (as well as smaller companies) have introduced their own touch-enabled tablets; many rely on the Google Android mobile operating system, some on versions of the Microsoft Windows operating system, and a few on other operating systems. Some solid machines are among them, but the iPad remains the market leader and a true pioneer in the space.

If you got caught up in the initial mania surrounding the iPad, you probably plotted for weeks about how to land one. After all, the iPad, like its close cousin the iPhone, rapidly emerged as the hippest computer you could find. (We consider you hip just because you're reading this book.) You had to plot in advance to get the subsequent versions as well.

Speaking of the iPhone, if you own one or its close relative, the Apple iPod touch, you already have a gigantic start in figuring out how to master the iPad multitouch method of navigating the interface with your fingers. If you've been using iOS7 on those devices, you have an even bigger head start. You have our permission to skim the rest of this chapter, but we urge you to stick around anyway because some things on the iPad work in subtly different ways than on the iPhone or iPod touch. If you're a total novice, don't fret. Nothing about multitouch is painful.

Getting Started on Getting Started

We've always said that you needed the following four things to enjoy your new iPad, but starting with iOS 5, you don't *need* a computer (and the connection to iTunes and whatever program you use to store your contacts) to use an iPad. You see, iOS 5 was the first operating system to allow you to activate, set up, and apply iOS updates to an iPad wirelessly, without having to connect it to a computer. And iOS 6 and iOS 7 continue the tradition. We show you how to get your iPad set up without a computer in the next section; in Chapter 3, we show you how to set up your iPad with your computer.

Because even though you don't, technically, *need* a computer, we think you'll prefer using your iPad with one rather than without one. So we don't recommend using your iPad totally unplugged unless you really don't have a computer available to use.

In our experience, many tasks — such as iOS software updates and rearranging application icons, to name just a couple — are faster and easier to do using iTunes on a Mac or PC than on the iPad.

Now, here are those four things you need to use your iPad:

✔ **A computer:** This can be either a Macintosh running Mac OS X version 10.5.8 or later, or a PC running Windows 8, Windows 7, Windows Vista, or Windows XP Home or Professional Edition with Service Pack 3 or later. That's the official word from Apple anyway.

The iCloud service has higher requirements: Mac OS X Mountain Lion, Lion (10.7), Mavericks, or higher for Macs; or Windows Vista or Windows 7 and 8 for PCs. Flip to Chapter 3 for details about iCloud.

✔ **iTunes software:** More specifically, you need version 10.7 or later of iTunes — emphasis on the *later* because by the time you read this, it probably will be later.

That is, unless you're a fan of the popular TV show *Mad Men* and can't remember what decade you're living in. All kidding aside, Apple constantly tweaks iTunes to make it better. You can go to www.itunes.com/download to fetch a copy. Or, launch your current version of iTunes and then choose iTunes (Help in Windows)⇨Check for Updates.

For the uninitiated, *iTunes* is the nifty Apple jukebox software that owners of iPods and iPhones, not to mention PCs and Macs, use to manage music, videos, apps, and more. iTunes is at the core of the iPad as well, because an iPod is built into the iPad. You can use iTunes to synchronize a bunch of stuff from your Mac or PC to and from an iPad, including (but not limited to) apps, photos, movies, TV shows, podcasts, iTunes U lectures, and of course, music.

Syncing is such a vital part of this process that we devote an entire chapter (Chapter 3) to the topic.

✔ **An Apple ID account:** Read Chapter 7 for details on how to set up an account, but, like most things Apple, the process isn't difficult. You'll want an account to download content from iTunes, the App Store, or to take advantage of iCloud.

✔ **Internet access:** Your iPad can connect to the Internet in either of two ways: Wi-Fi or cellular (if you bought an iPad with 3G or 4G capabilities). You can connect your iPad to cyberspace via Wi-Fi in your home, office, school, favorite coffeehouse, bookstore, or numerous other spots.

At press time, 3G (third-generation) and 4G (fourth-generation) wireless data connections were available from many carriers in countries too numerous to mention; in the United States, you can choose among AT&T, Sprint, Verizon Wireless, and T-Mobile. Those wireless carriers are still building the zippier *4G* (fourth-generation) networks across the USA, with Verizon in the lead with the fastest variety called *LTE,* shorthand for Long Term Evolution. While the others play catch-up on LTE, the latest iPad on AT&T and T-Mobile makes nice with other pretty fast networks, including something known as *HSPA+.*

Unlike with the cellphone contract you may have with your cellular carrier, no long-term service commitment is required to connect your iPad to the network.

As this book goes to press, data rates (no contract required) are reasonably priced as long as you don't stream or download a lot of movies or watch tons of videos while connected over 3G or 4G. For as little as $5 in some instances, you can purchase a day pass for data instead of opting for a monthly plan.

And T-Mobile, a latecomer as far as selling Apple tablets, is even dishing out 200 megabytes (MB) of monthly LTE data gratis for people using the iPad mini with the Retina display or the iPad Air. That translates to about 800 Instagram photos, more than 2,500 e-mails, or 200 minutes of streaming music. You can start paying if you need a bigger allotment. The following are plan highlights from other carriers:

- *AT&T:* $14.99 a month for 250 megabytes (MB), 3GB for $30, and 5GB for $50

- *Sprint:* $14.99 a month for 300 megabytes (MB), 3GB for $34.99, and 6GB for $49.99

- *Verizon:* $20 for 1GB, $30 a month for 2GB, $50 for 5GB, $80 for 10GB

A friendly warning pops up on your iPad when you get close to your limit. At that point, you can pay more to add to your data bucket or start from scratch next month. Keep in mind that with 4G, you're likely to consume more data in a hurry.

Find a Wi-Fi network if you want to buy, rent, or watch movies.

Turning On and Setting Up the iPad

Unless your iPad is brand-spanking-new and fresh out of the box, chances are good that you've performed the steps that follow. We cover them here because if you choose to use your iPad computer-free, these steps comprise the entire setup process.

Apple has taken the time to partially charge your iPad, so you get some measure of instant gratification and can go ahead and set it up right away by following these steps:

1. **After taking your iPad out of the box, press and hold the Sleep/Wake button on the upper-right edge.**

An arrow appears near the bottom of the screen, flashing messages in many languages. We're pretty sure they all say, "Slide to Set Up," because that's what the English rendition says.

2. Swipe the Slide to Set Up arrow to the right.

The first thing you see on your shiny new (or freshly restored) iPad is the Wi-Fi screen.

3. Tap to choose a Wi-Fi network, provide a password (if necessary), and then tap the blue Join button or tap the blue Next button.

While you *can* skip this step by tapping the blue Next button without selecting a Wi-Fi network, we suggest you select your network now if you can. (If you do wait to set up your Wi-Fi network, turn to Chapter 15 to find out how to do so via Settings.)

The Location Services screen appears.

4. Tap to enable or disable Location Services.

Location Services is your iPad's way of knowing where, precisely, you are geographically. The Maps app, for example, which is covered in Chapter 6, relies on Location Services to determine where in the world you are.

You can turn Location Services on or off globally or for individual apps in Settings, as you discover in Chapter 15.

The Set Up iPad screen appears.

5. Tap Set Up as a New iPad, Restore from iCloud Backup, or Restore from iTunes Backup.

See Chapter 16 for the scoop on restoring from iCloud or iTunes backups. For these steps, we'll tap Set Up as New.

The Apple ID screen appears.

6. Tap Sign In with an Apple ID, Create a Free Apple ID, or Skip this Step.

If you have an Apple ID, sign in with it here; if you don't have one, tap the Create a Free Apple ID button. If you tap Skip This Step and proceed without supplying an Apple ID, you can't take advantage of the myriad excellent and free features described in this and other chapters. Obtain an Apple ID if you don't already have one, because you need it to take advantage of iCloud. See the end of this chapter for an introduction to this service.

Note that if you skip this step now, you can sign in later by tapping Settings⇨iCloud⇨Account.

The Terms and Conditions screen appears.

7. **Tap the blue Agree button in the lower-right corner, and then tap the Agree button in the Terms and Conditions alert box that appears in the middle of the screen.**

What happens if you disagree? You don't want to know. And, of course, you won't be able to use your iPad.

Find more info about iCloud at the end of this chapter, or tap the About iCloud link on this screen for the party line from Apple.

The iCloud screen appears.

8. **Do one of the following:**

   • *If you want to use iCloud:* Good choice! Tap Use iCloud.

   • *If you don't want to use iCloud:* Tap Don't Use iCloud.

   Don't worry: If you choose not to enable iCloud now, you can enable it at any time in the Settings app, as described in Chapter 15.

   The Find My iPad screen appears.

9. **Tap either Use Find My iPad or Don't Use Find My iPad.**

If you misplace your iPad, you can use Find My iPad to display its current location on a map. You can also choose to display a message or play a sound, lock the screen, or erase contents on your missing iPad.

Find My iPad won't find your iPad if the battery is drained, the iPad is turned off, or no network connection (Wi-Fi or cellular) is available.

The iMessage and FaceTime screen appears.

10. **Tap the e-mail address(es) (and/or phone numbers for iPhone users) you want people to use to contact you via iMessage and FaceTime, and then tap the Next button in the upper-right corner.**

The Create a Passcode screen appears.

11. **Type a four-digit passcode to unlock this iPad.**

The Re-enter Your Passcode screen appears.

If you choose a commonly used passcode (such as 1111, 1234, 0000, and the like) before the Re-enter Your Passcode screen appears, your iPad will warn you that the code you typed can be easily guessed. You can either change it or use it anyway — it's your choice. If you're at all concerned about keeping what's on your iPad safe from prying eyes, we suggest you change it.

12. **Type the four-digit passcode again.**

The Set Up Siri screen appears.

13. **Tap Use Siri or Don't Use Siri.**

    If your iPad is third-generation or later, it offers the extremely desirable option (at least in our humble opinion) of using your voice to control your iPad, as well as the capability to dictate (speech-to-text) text in any app that displays an onscreen keyboard.

    You can find out more about using Siri and Dictation in Chapter 14, but for now, let us just say that we love this feature and use it when appropriate (which is often).

    If you choose not to enable Siri at this time, you can switch on this feature at any time in the Settings app's General pane.

    The Diagnostics screen appears.

14. **Tap Automatically Send or Don't Send to either send or not send anonymous diagnostic and usage data to Apple.**

    The Welcome to iPad screen appears.

15. **Tap Get Started and let the fun begin.**

    Your iPad's Home screen appears in all its glory.

If you're using a computer-free iPad, that's the end of the story. Instead of using iTunes on your Mac or PC as described in Chapter 3, you have to make do with the available options in specific apps and in the Settings app (covered extensively in Chapter 15).

If you ever need to restore your iPad to factory condition, you'd follow the same steps, as described in Chapter 16.

Locking the iPad

Carrying a naked cellphone in your pocket or a handbag is begging for trouble. Unless the phone has a locking mechanism, you may inadvertently dial a phone number.

You don't have to worry about dialing your boss at 4 a.m. on an iPad — it's not a phone, after all (though apps such as Line2 or Skype can turn it into one). But you still have sound reasons for locking an iPad:

- ✔ You won't inadvertently turn it on.
- ✔ You keep prying eyes at bay.
- ✔ You spare the battery some juice.

Apple makes locking the iPad a cinch.

In fact, you don't need to do anything to lock the iPad; it happens automatically as long as you don't touch the screen for a minute or two. As you find out in Chapter 15, you can also set the amount of time your iPad must be idle before it automatically locks.

Can't wait? To lock the iPad immediately, press the Sleep/Wake button.

If you have an iPad with a Smart Cover or Smart Case (or any of the third-party equivalents), opening and closing the cover locks and unlocks your iPad, but the Smart Cover has the added advantage of awakening your iPad without making you drag the slider (though you may still have to enter a passcode).

Unlocking the iPad is easy, too. Here's how:

1. **Press the Sleep/Wake button or the Home button on the front of the screen.**

   Either way, the onscreen slider appears.

2. **Drag the slider to the right with your finger.**

3. **Enter a passcode if you need to.**

   See Chapter 15 to find out how to password-protect your iPad.

Mastering the Multitouch Interface

With very few exceptions, until the iPhone and iPad came along, people thought of computers as having a physical mouse and a typewriter-style QWERTY keyboard to help you accomplish most of the things you can do on a computer. (The term *QWERTY* is derived from the first six letters on any standard typewriter — you remember those? — or computer keyboard.)

The iPad, like the iPhone, dispenses with a physical mouse and keyboard, which seemed like such a revolutionary step just a few years ago. By now, a virtual keyboard doesn't seem as novel.

Neither does the fact that the designers of the iPad (and iPhone and iPod touch) removed the usual physical buttons in favor of a *multitouch display*. This beautiful and responsive finger-controlled screen is at the heart of the many things you do on the iPad.

In the following sections, you discover how to move around the multitouch interface with ease. Later, we'll home in on how to make the most of the keyboard.

Training your digits

Rice Krispies have *Snap! Crackle! Pop!* Apple's response for the iPad is *Tap! Flick! Pinch!* Oh yeah, and *Drag!*

Fortunately, tapping, flicking, pinching, and dragging are not challenging gestures, so you can master many of the iPad's features in no time:

- **Tap:** Tapping serves multiple purposes. Tap an icon to open an application from the Home screen. Tap to start playing a song or to choose the photo album you want to look through. Sometimes, you *double-tap* (tapping twice in rapid succession), which has the effect of zooming in (or out) of web pages, maps, and e-mails.

- **Flick:** Flicking is just what it sounds like. A flick of the finger on the screen lets you quickly scroll through lists of songs, e-mails, and picture thumbnails. Tap the screen to stop scrolling, or merely wait for the scrolling list to stop.

- **Pinch/spread:** Place two fingers on the edges of a web page, map, or picture and then spread your fingers apart to enlarge the images. Or pinch your fingers together to make the map or picture smaller. Pinching and spreading (or what we call *unpinching*) are cool gestures that are easy to master and sure to wow an audience.

- **Drag:** Here's where you slowly press your finger against the touchscreen without lifting it. You might drag to move around a web page or map that's too large for the iPad's display area.

- **Drag downward from the top of the screen:** This special gesture displays the Notification Center (which you find out about in Chapter 13). Press your finger at the very top of the screen and drag downward.

- **Drag downward from any Home screen without starting at the very top of the screen:** This action summons Spotlight search, a discussion for later in this chapter.

- **Drag upward from the bottom of the screen:** This time, you are calling up Control Center, a handy repository for music controls, Airplane mode (see Chapter 15), Wi-Fi, Bluetooth, Do Not Disturb, Mute/Volume, Timer (Clocks app), Camera, AirPlay, and Brightness controls. Check out Figure 2-1 for one view of Control Center.

Figure 2-1: We think you'll call on Control Center a lot.

✔ **Four- or five-finger swipes and pinches:** To quickly multitask or switch among or view running apps (see the later section, "Multitasking"), use four or five fingers to swipe upward. Swipe left or right (only one finger required) to switch between recently used apps. Finally, pinch using four or five fingers to jump to your Home screen. Swipe up (one finger will do it again) to quit an app. The four- or five-finger swipes and pinches require you to enable Multitasking Gestures in the Settings app's General pane.

Navigating beyond the Home screen

The Home screen we discuss in Chapter 1 is not the only screen of icons on your tablet. After you start adding apps from the iTunes App Store (which you discover in Chapter 11), you may see a row of two or more tiny dots just above the main apps you have parked at the bottom of the screen. Those dots denote additional screens, each containing up to 20 additional icons, not counting the 4 to 6 separate icons that are docked at the bottom of each of these Home screens. (You can actually have fewer than four docked icons at the bottom, but we can't think of a decent reason why you'd want to ditch any of them. In any case, more on these in a moment.)

Here's what you need to know about navigating among the screens:

✔ To navigate between screens, flick your finger from right to left or left to right across the middle of the screen, or tap directly on the dots. The number of dots you see represents the current number of screens on your iPad. The dot that's all white denotes the screen that you're currently viewing.

You can also drag your finger in either horizontal direction to see a different screen. Unlike flicking — you may prefer the term *swiping* — dragging your finger means keeping it pressed against the screen until you reach your desired page.

✔ Make sure you swipe and not just tap, or you'll probably open one of the application icons instead of switching screens.

✔ Press the Home button to jump back to the Home screen. Doing so the first time takes you back to whatever Home screen you were on last. Tapping Home a second time takes you to the first Home screen.

✔ The Dock — that is, the Safari, Mail, Videos, and Music icons in the bottom row — stays put as you switch screens. In other words, only the first 20 icons on the screen change when you move from one screen to another.

You can add one or two more icons to the Dock if you so choose. Or move one of the four default icons into the main area of the Home screen to make space available for additional app icons you may use more often, as described later in this chapter.

Select, cut, copy, and paste

Being able to select and then copy and paste from one place on a computer to another has seemingly been a divine right since Moses, and that's the case on the Apple tablet as well. You can copy and paste (and cut) with pizzazz.

On the iPad, you might copy text or a URL from the web and paste it into an e-mail or a note. Or you might copy a bunch of pictures or video into an e-mail.

Suppose you're jotting down ideas in the Notes application that you'll eventually copy into an e-mail. Here's how to exploit the copy-and-paste feature, using this scenario as an example:

1. **Double-tap a word to select it.**

2. **Tap Select to select the adjacent word or tap Select All to grab everything.**

   You can also drag the blue *grab points* (handles) to select a larger block of text or to contract the text you've already selected, as shown in Figure 2-2. This may take a little practice.

3. **After you select the text, tap Copy. If you want to delete the text block, tap Cut instead.**

4. **Open the Mail program (see Chapter 5) and start composing a message.**

5. **When you decide where to insert the text you just copied, tap the cursor.**

   Up pop the commands Select, Select All, Paste, Quote Level, and Insert Photo or Video, as shown in Figure 2-3. (We get to the last two options in Chapter 5.)

6. **Tap Paste to paste the text into the message.**

A grab handle

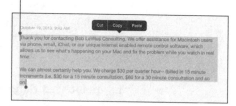

Figure 2-2: Drag the grab handles to select text.

Figure 2-3: Tap Paste to make text appear from nowhere.

Here's the pizzazz part. If you made a mistake when you were cutting, pasting, or typing, shake the iPad. Doing so undoes the last edit (provided that you tap the Undo Paste or Undo options when they appear).

You also see these options:

- *Auto-Correct:* If you happen to select a word with a typo, the iPad may underline that word and (if known) show you the word it thinks you meant to spell. Tap that suggested word to accept it.

- *Replace:* The iPad may show you possible replacement words. For example, replacement words for *test* might be *fest, rest,* or *text.* Tap the word to substitute it for the word you originally typed.

- *Define:* Tap your selected word for a definition, courtesy of the New Oxford American Dictionary, Oxford Dictionary of English, an Apple Dictionary, or a foreign language dictionary if you've downloaded any dictionaries onto your iPad.

Multitasking

Multitasking on the iPad was introduced way back in iOS 4, and it has gotten better ever since, most dramatically with the iOS 7 upgrade. Through multitasking, you run numerous apps in the background simultaneously and easily switch from one app to another. The following examples illustrate what multitasking enables you to do on your iPad:

- ✔ A third-party app, such as Slacker Personal Radio, continues to play music while you surf the web, peek at pictures, or check e-mail. Without multitasking, Slacker would shut down the moment you opened another app.

- ✔ A navigation app can update your position while you're listening to, say, Pandora Internet radio. From time to time, the navigation app will pipe in with turn-by-turn directions, lowering the volume of the music so that you can hear the instructions.

- ✔ If you're uploading images to a photo website and the process is taking longer than you want, you can switch to another app, confident that the images will continue to upload behind the scenes.

- ✔ We've also been able to leave voice notes in the Evernote app while checking out a web page.

Multitasking couldn't be easier — and it's a lot smarter in iOS 7. Now your iPad can anticipate your needs. If it detects, over time, that you tend to turn to your social networking apps around the same time every morning, it will make sure the feeds are ready for you.

Double-press the Home button. You see preview pages with icons just below them for any apps that are already open, as shown in Figure 2-4. Scroll to the right or left to see more apps. Tap the icon or preview screen for the app you want to switch to: The app remembers where you left off. (Scroll all the way to the left, and you'll also see a preview screen for the last Home screen you opened.) If you hold the tablet sideways in landscape mode, the previews for your apps appear sideways, too.

Figure 2-4: Scroll to see the apps you've recently used or are still running.

Apple insists that multitasking will not overly tax the battery or exhaust system resources. The iPad conserves power and resources by putting apps in a state of suspended animation. And as part of iOS7, your iPad will schedule updates only during power-efficient times, such as when your device is connected to Wi-Fi.

Still, we think it's a good idea to shut down apps you're not using because over time, you'll see a battery hit. To remove an app from the multitasking rotation, swipe up the app's preview. Poof — it's gone.

You can use the four- or five-finger gesture to swipe upward to reveal your multitasking options and to swipe left or right to switch between apps, or pinch to return to the Home screen. This is one of our favorite features.

Organizing icons into folders

Finding the single app that you want to use among apps spread out over 15 screens may seem like a daunting task. But Apple felt your pain and added a handy organizational tool: folders. The Folders feature lets you create folder icons, each containing apps that pertain to the name that Apple assigned or you gave to that folder.

To create a folder, follow these steps:

1. **Press your finger against an icon until all the icons on the screen wiggle.**

2. **Decide which apps you want to move to a folder and then drag the icon for the first app on top of the second app.**

   The two apps now share living quarters inside a newly created folder. Apple names the folder according to the category of apps inside the folder.

3. **(Optional) Change the folder name by tapping the X on the bar where the folder name appears and typing a new name.**

To launch an app that's inside a folder, tap that folder's icon and then tap the icon for the app that you want to open.

With iOS 7, you have plenty of room for all your apps. Indeed, you can stash up to 9 apps per page in a folder and have as many as 14 pages. That's a grand total of 126 (more, we suspect, than you'd possibly ever want to tuck away in a folder).

When you drag all the apps from a folder, the folder automatically disappears. You can also drag apps on or off the Dock.

Folders are a great organizational tool. But if you have numerous apps on the iPad, it's a lot easier to create and arrange folders not from the tablet but when syncing your device in iTunes.

Printing

Apple didn't include built-in printer functionality with the original iPad. A variety of third-party apps helped fill the bill to some degree, but still the faithful waited for Apple to come up with a solution. The AirPrint feature that subsequently arrived provided just such a remedy — to a point. You can print wirelessly from the iPad to an AirPrint-capable printer. The first of these compatible features emerged on more than a dozen HP printers. There are now offerings from Epson, Canon, and others.

We hope that Apple will support Bluetooth wireless printing, but that hasn't happened as of this writing. AirPrint works with Mail, Photos, Safari, and iBooks (PDF files). You can also print from apps in Apple's iWork software suite, as well as third-party apps with built-in printing.

Although AirPrint printers don't need any special software, they do have to be connected to the same Wi-Fi network as the iPad.

To print, follow these steps:

1. **Tap the Print command, which appears as an option when you tap the action button in various apps.**

   The button resembles an arrow sticking out of a rectangle.

2. **Tap Select Printer to select a printer, which the iPad locates in short order.**

3. **Depending on the printer, specify the number of copies you want to print, the number of double-sided copies, and a range of pages to print.**

4. **When you're happy with your settings, tap Print.**

If you display the preview pages while a print job is underway, the Print Center app icon appears with all your other recently used apps. A badge indicates how many documents are in the print queue, along with the currently printing document.

Searching for content on your iPad

Using the Safari browser (see Chapter 4), you can search the web via the Google, Yahoo!, Bing, or (with a Chinese keyboard enabled) Baidu search engines.

But you can also search for people and programs across your iPad and within specific applications. We show you how to search within apps in the various chapters dedicated to Mail, Contacts, Calendar, and Music.

Searching across the iPad, meanwhile, is based on the powerful Spotlight feature familiar to Mac owners. Here's how it works:

1. **Swipe down from any Home screen to access Spotlight.**

2. **Tap the bar at the top of the screen that slides into view, and enter your search query using the virtual keyboard.**

The iPad spits out results the moment you type a single character, and the list narrows as you type additional characters.

The results are pretty darn thorough. Say that you entered **Ring** as your search term, as shown in Figure 2-5. Contacts whose last names have Ring in them show up, along with friends who might do a trapeze act in the Ringling Bros. circus. All the songs on your iPad by Ringo Starr show up, too, as do such song titles as Tony Bennett's "When Do the Bells Ring for Me," if that happens to be in your library. The same goes for apps, videos, audiobooks, events, and notes with the word *Ring.*

Figure 2-5: Putting the Spotlight on search.

3. **Tap any listing to jump to the contact, ditty, or application you seek.**

 In Settings (see Chapter 15), you can specify the order of search results so that apps come first, contacts second, songs third, and so on.

 At the very bottom of the Spotlight results list, you can tap to move your search query to the web (using your designated search engine) or to the Wikipedia online encyclopedia.

The Incredible, Intelligent, and Virtual iPad Keyboard

As you know by now, instead of a physical keyboard, several "soft" or "virtual" English-language or (depending upon what you chose during setup) foreign-language keyboard layouts slide up from the bottom of the iPad screen, including variations on the alphabetical keyboard, the numeric and punctuation keyboard, and the more punctuation and symbols keyboard.

Indeed, the beauty of a software keyboard is that you see only the keys that are pertinent to the task at hand. The layout you see depends on the application. The keyboards in Safari differ from the keyboards in Mail. For example, in Mail, you'll see a Return key. In Safari the similarly placed key is labeled Go. Figure 2-6 displays the difference between the Mail (top) and Safari (bottom) keyboards.

Before you consider how to actually *use* the keyboard, we want to share a bit of the philosophy behind its so-called *intelligence*. Knowing what makes this keyboard smart can help you make it even smarter when you use it:

Figure 2-6: The keys on the Mail (top) and Safari (bottom) keyboards.

- ✔ It has a built-in English dictionary that even includes words from today's popular culture. It has dictionaries in other languages, too, automatically activated when you use a given international keyboard, as described in the sidebar "A keyboard for all borders," later in this chapter.

- ✔ It adds your contacts to its dictionary automatically.

- ✔ It uses complex analysis algorithms to predict the word you're trying to type.

- ✔ It suggests corrections as you type. It then offers you the suggested word just below the misspelled word. When you decline a suggestion and the word you typed is *not* in the iPad dictionary, the iPad adds that word to its dictionary and offers it as a suggestion if you mistype a similar word in the future.

Remember to decline incorrect suggestions (by tapping the characters you typed as opposed to the suggested words that appear beneath what you've typed). This helps your intelligent keyboard become even smarter.

- ✔ It reduces the number of mistakes you make as you type by intelligently and dynamically resizing the touch zones for certain keys. You can't see it, but it is increasing the zones for keys it predicts might come next and decreasing the zones for keys that are unlikely or impossible to come next.

Discovering the special-use keys

The iPad keyboard contains several keys that don't actually type a character. Here's the scoop on each of these keys:

✔ **Shift:** If you're using the alphabetical keyboard, the Shift key (arrow pointing up) switches between uppercase and lowercase letters. You can tap the key to change the case, or hold down Shift and slide to the letter you want to be capitalized.

✔ **Caps Lock:** To turn on Caps Lock and type in all caps, you first need to enable Caps Lock (if not already enabled). You do that by tapping Settings➪General➪Keyboard. Tap the Enable Caps Lock item to turn it on. After the Caps Lock setting is enabled, double-tap the Shift key to turn on Caps Lock. (The arrow will be white while the Shift key itself will take on a darker shade of gray.) Tap the Shift key again to turn off Caps Lock. To disable Caps Lock, just reverse the process by turning off the Enable Caps Lock setting (tap Settings➪General➪Keyboard).

✔ **Typewriter:** Enable the Split Keyboard option (tap Settings➪General➪Keyboard), and you can split the keyboard in a most thumb-typist-friendly manner, as shown in Figure 2-7. When you're ready to split your keyboard, press the Typewriter key, and tap Split on the menu.

Figure 2-7: Press and hold the Typewriter key to split the keyboard.

✔ **#+= or 123:** If you're using keyboards that just show numbers and symbols, the traditional Shift key is replaced by a key labeled #+= or 123 (sometimes shown as .?123). Pressing that key toggles between keyboards that just have symbols and numbers.

✔ **International Keyboards:** Only shows up if you've turned on an international keyboard, as explained in the nearby sidebar "A keyboard for all borders."

✔ **Delete:** Tapping this key (otherwise known as Backspace) erases the character immediately to the left of the cursor.

✔ **Return:** Moves the cursor to the beginning of the next line. You might find this key labeled Go or Search, dependent on the app you're using.

✔ **Hide Keyboard:** Tap to hide the keyboard. Tap the screen in the appropriate app to bring back the keyboard.

✔ **Dictation:** Tap the microphone key and start talking. The iPad listens to what you have to say. Tap the key again, and the iPad attempts to convert your words into text. You can use this dictation feature in many of the instances in which you can summon the keyboard, including the built-in Notes and Mail apps, as well as any third-party apps you have on your iPad. See Chapter 14 for more on dictation.

A keyboard for all borders

Apple is expanding the iPad's reach globally with international keyboard layouts on the iPad for dozens of languages. To access a keyboard that isn't customized for Americanized English, tap Settings⇨General⇨Keyboard⇨Keyboards⇨Add New Keyboard. Then flick through the list to select any keyboard you want to use. (Alternatively, tap Settings⇨General⇨International⇨Keyboards.) Up pops the list shown in the figure, with custom keyboards for German, Japanese, Portuguese, and so on. Apple even supplies three versions of French (including keyboards geared to Canadian and Swiss customers) and several keyboards for Chinese. Heck, you can even find UK and Australian versions of English. Within Settings, you can choose software and hardware keyboard layouts.

Have a multilingual household? You can select as many of these international keyboards as you might need by tapping the language in the list. Of course, you can call upon only one language at a time. So when you're in an application that summons a keyboard, tap the International Keyboard button sandwiched between the .?123 key and spacebar (or microphone key if Dictation/Siri is turned on; refer to Figure 2-6) until the keyboard you want to call on for the occasion shows up. Tap again to pick the next keyboard in the corresponding list of international keyboards that you turned on in Settings. If you keep tapping, you come back to your original English keyboard.

To remove a keyboard that you've already added to your list, tap the Edit button in the upper-right corner of the screen showing your enabled keyboards and then tap the red circle with the white horizontal line that appears next to the language to which you want to say *adios.*

One more note about the Chinese keyboards: You can use handwriting character recognition for simplified and traditional Chinese, as shown here. Just drag your finger in the box provided. We make apologies in advance for not knowing what the displayed characters here mean. (We neither speak nor read Chinese.)

When you use dictation, the things you say are recorded and sent to Apple to convert your words into text. Just make sure to proofread what you've said because the process isn't foolproof. Apple also collects other information, including your first name and nickname, names and nicknames of folks in your Contacts list, song names in Music, and more. Apple says this is to help the dictation feature perform its duties. If any of this freaks you out, however, tap Settings⟹General⟹Keyboard and slide the Dictation switch to off. You can also restrict the use of dictations in Settings, as explained in Chapter 15.

If you have an iPhone or iPod touch, it's worth noting that keyboards on the iPad more closely resemble the keyboard layout of a traditional computer rather than those smaller-model devices. That is, the Delete key is on the upper right, the Return (or Go) key is just below it, and the Shift keys are on either side. This similarity to traditional keyboard layouts certainly improves the odds of successful touch-typing.

Finger-typing on the virtual keyboards

The virtual keyboards in Apple's multitouch interface just might be considered a stroke of genius. And (equally) they just might drive you nuts.

If you're patient and trusting, in a week or so, you'll get the hang of finger-typing — which is vital to moving forward, of course, because you rely on a virtual keyboard to tap a text field, enter notes, type the names of new contacts, and so on.

As we note earlier in this chapter, Apple has built intelligence into its virtual keyboard, so it can correct typing mistakes on the fly and take a stab at predicting what you're about to type next. The keyboard isn't exactly Nostradamus, but it does an excellent job of coming up with the words you have in mind.

As you start typing on the virtual keyboard, we think you'll find the following tips extremely helpful:

Figure 2-8: The ABCs of virtual typing.

✔ **See what letter you're typing.** As you press your finger against a letter or number on the screen, the individual key you press darkens until you lift your finger, as shown in Figure 2-8. That way, you know that you struck the correct letter or number.

✔ **Slide to the correct letter if you tap the wrong one.** No need to worry if you touched the wrong key. You can slide your finger to the correct key because the letter isn't recorded until you release your finger.

✔ **Tap and hold to access special accent marks, alternative punctuation, or URL endings.** Sending a message to an overseas pal? Keep your finger pressed against a letter, and a row of keys showing variations on the character for foreign alphabets pops up, as shown in Figure 2-9. This row lets you add the appropriate accent mark. Just slide your finger until you're pressing the key with the relevant accent mark and then lift your finger.

Figure 2-9: Accenting your letters.

Meanwhile, if you press and hold the ".?" key in Safari, it offers you the choice of .com, .net, .edu, or .org, with additional options if you also use international keyboards. Pretty slick stuff, except we miss the dedicated ".com" key that used to be on the keyboard prior to iOS7.

✔ **Tap the spacebar to accept a suggested word, or tap the suggested word to decline the suggestion.** Alas, mistakes are common at first. Say that you meant to type a sentence in the Notes application that reads, "I am typing an important…" But because of the way your fingers struck the virtual keys, you actually entered "I am typing an *importsnt…*" Fortunately, Apple knows that the *a* you meant to press is next to the *s* that showed up on the keyboard, just as *t* and *y* and *e* and *r* are side by side. So the software determines that *important* was indeed the word you had in mind and places it in a little capsule (see Figure 2-10) under the suspect word. To accept the suggested word, merely tap the spacebar. And if for some reason you actually did mean to type *importsnt* instead, tap the suggested word (*important* in this example) to decline it.

Figure 2-10: Fixing an *important* mistake.

If you don't appreciate this feature, you can turn off Auto-Correction in Settings. See Chapter 15 for details. See Chapter 20 for Auto-Correction tricks.

Because Apple knows what you're up to, the virtual keyboard is fine-tuned for the task at hand. This is especially true when you need to enter numbers, punctuation, or symbols. The following tips help you find common special characters or special keys that we know you'll want to use:

- **Putting the @ in an e-mail address:** If you're composing an e-mail message (see Chapter 5), a dedicated @ key pops up on the main Mail keyboard when you're in the To: field choosing who to send a message to. That key disappears from the first view when you tap the body of the message to compose your words. You can still get to the @ by tapping the .?123 key.

- **Switching from letters to numbers:** When you're typing notes or sending e-mail and want to type a number, symbol, or punctuation mark, tap the .?123 key to bring up an alternative virtual keyboard. Tap the ABC key to return to the first keyboard. This toggle isn't hard to get used to, but some may find it irritating.

- **Adding apostrophes:** If you press and hold the Exclamation Mark/Comma key, a pop-up offers the apostrophe.

We already mentioned that the iPad, unlike some tablets from the past (and a few in the present), eschews a pen or stylus. But there are occasions when you might want to call upon a digital pen, and third-party companies such as Wacom fill the bill. Wacom sells the Bamboo Stylus for around $20 to $30, a potentially useful tool for those with too broad, oily, or greasy fingers, or those who sketch, draw, or jot notes. You can find lower-priced styluses as well.

Editing mistakes

We think typing with abandon, without getting hung up over mistyped characters, is a good idea. The self-correcting keyboard can fix many errors (and occasionally introduce errors of its own). That said, plenty of typos are likely to turn up, especially in the beginning, and you have to correct them manually.

A neat trick for doing so is to hold your finger against the screen to bring up the magnifying glass. Use the magnifying glass to position the pointer on the spot where you need to make the correction. Then use the Delete key (also called the Backspace key) to delete the error and press whatever keys you need to type the correct text.

And with that, you are hereby notified that you've survived basic training. The real fun is about to begin.

3

The Kitchen Sync: Getting Stuff to and from Your iPad

· ·

In This Chapter

▶ Starting your first sync

▶ Disconnecting during a sync

▶ Synchronizing contacts, calendars, e-mail accounts, and bookmarks

▶ Synchronizing music, podcasts, videos, photos, books, and applications

▶ Getting your head around iCloud

· ·

*W*e have good news and . . . more good news. The good news is that you can easily set up your iPad so that your contacts, appointments, events, mail settings, bookmarks, books, music, movies, TV shows, podcasts, photos, and applications are synchronized between your computer and your iPad (or other iDevices). And the more good news is that after you set it up, your contacts, appointments, and events can be kept up to date automatically in multiple places — on your computer(s), iPad(s), iPhone(s), and iPod touch(es).

Here's more good news: Whenever you make a change in one place, it's reflected almost immediately in all the other places it occurs. So if you add or change an appointment, event, or contact on your iPad while you're out and about, the information automatically updates on your computers and iDevices. If no Wi-Fi or cellular network is available at the time, the update syncs the next time your iPad encounters a wireless network, all with no further effort on your part.

This communication between your iPad and computer is called *syncing* (short for *synchronizing*). Don't worry: It's easy, and we walk you through the entire process in this chapter.

But wait. We have even more good news. Items that you choose to manage on your computer, such as movies, TV shows, podcasts, and e-mail account settings, are synchronized only one way — from your computer to your iPad, which is the way it should be.

The information in this chapter is based on iTunes version 11.1 (126) and iOS version 7.0.2, the latest and greatest when these words were written. If your screens don't look exactly like ours, you probably need to upgrade to iTunes 11.1 or higher (choose iTunes⇨Check for Updates) or to iOS 7 or higher (on a computer, click the Check for Update button in the Summary tab for your iPad in iTunes; on your iPad, tap Settings⇨General⇨Software Update), or both. By the way, both upgrades — iTunes and iOS — are free, and both offer useful new features and have significant advantages over their predecessors.

Because Apple updates iTunes and iOS often, having the latest and greatest version is a double-edged sword. So sometimes you'll see something in the book that looks different on your iPad because you're using a *newer* version of iOS than we had when we wrote this. If you discover one of these and you're certain you're using the latest and greatest versions of both iTunes and iOS, drop us a note so we can fix it; our e-mail addresses appear at the end of this book's introduction.

In this chapter, you find out how to sync all the digital data your iPad can handle.

iOS 7 does let you set up your iPad computer-free (and as such, you're not *required* to sync your iPad with a computer running iTunes). Turn to Chapter 2 if you really want to set up your iPad computer-free. But some things are easier with a computer than without.

Syncing with iTunes

Synchronizing your iPad with iTunes on a Mac or PC provides three main benefits over computer-free iPad use:

- iTunes makes it easier to manage your media — your music, movies, apps, and so on — than managing it directly on your iPad.
- Managing your iPad's contents with iTunes provides numerous options that you won't find anywhere on your iPad.
- Managing your iPad's apps and Home screen layouts is much easier in iTunes than on your iPad.

Synchronizing your iPad with your computer is a lot like syncing an iPod or iPhone with your computer. If you're an iPod or iPhone user, the process will be a piece of cake. But it's not too difficult, even if you've never used an iPod, an iPhone, or iTunes. Follow these steps:

1. **Start by connecting your iPad to your computer with the USB cable that came with your iPad.**

   When you connect your iPad to your computer, iTunes should launch automatically. If it doesn't, chances are that you plugged the cable into a USB port on your keyboard, monitor, or hub. Try plugging it into one of the USB ports on your computer instead. Why? Because USB ports on your computer supply more power to a connected device than USB ports on a keyboard, monitor, or most hubs, and the iPad requires a lot of that power — even more than an iPod or an iPhone.

You may see an alert asking whether you want iTunes to open automatically when you connect this iPad. Click Yes or No, depending on your preference. You have the opportunity to change this setting later if you like, so don't give it too much thought.

If iTunes still doesn't launch automatically, try launching it manually.

If you prefer to sync wirelessly (although it can be noticeably slower), just launch iTunes manually.

2. **Click the iPad button just below the Search field.**

   If you use more than one iDevice with this computer, the button will say the number of devices (for example, *5 Devices*) rather than *iPad*. Click the button to display a drop-down list and select the device you want.

   You won't see the button if you've made the iTunes sidebar visible (View⇨Show Sidebar/Hide Sidebar or press ⌘+Option+S on a Mac or Alt+Ctrl+S on a PC). You can select your iPad in the sidebar and follow along, but your screens will look slightly different from the ones shown in this chapter.

   If you don't see the iPad button below the Search field or don't see your iPad in the sidebar, and you're positive that it's connected to a USB port *on your computer* (not the keyboard, monitor, or hub), try restarting your computer.

   The Welcome to Your New iPad screen appears.

3. **Click Set Up as New iPad or select a backup from the Restore from This Backup drop-down menu and then click Continue.**

   See Chapter 16 for the scoop on restoring from iCloud or iTunes backups. For this example, we'll tap Set Up as New.

   The Sync with iTunes screen appears.

4. **Click the Get Started button.**

   The iPad screen appears, as shown in Figure 3-1.

5. **Click the Summary tab near the top of the window, as shown in Figure 3-1.**

   If you don't see a Summary tab, make sure your iPad is still connected. If you don't see its name near the top-left corner of the iTunes window, as shown in Figure 3-1, go back to Step 3 and try again.

6. **(Optional) If you want to rename your iPad, click its name and type a new one.**

   We renamed the one in Figure 3-1 *Bob L's iPad 64.*

From the Summary pane, you can set any options that you want from the Options area:

Figure 3-1: The Summary pane is pretty painless.

✔ **Open iTunes When This iPad Is Connected check box:** Select this option if you want iTunes to launch automatically whenever you connect your iPad to your computer.

Why might you choose not to enable this option? If you intend to connect your iPad to your computer to charge it, for example, you might not want iTunes to launch every time you connect it.

If you do choose to enable it, iTunes launches and synchronizes automatically every time you connect your iPad.

Don't worry about this too much right now. As usual, if you change your mind, you can always come back to the Summary pane and deselect the Open iTunes When This iPad Is Connected check box.

If you do select the Open iTunes When This iPad Is Connected check box but don't want your iPad to sync automatically every time it's connected, launch iTunes and choose iTunes⇨Preferences (Mac) or Edit⇨Preferences (PC). Click the Devices tab at the top of the window and select the Prevent iPods, iPhones, and iPads from Syncing Automatically check box. This method prevents your iPad from syncing automatically, even if the Open iTunes When This iPad Is Connected option is selected. If you choose this option, you can sync your iPad by clicking the Sync or Apply button that appears in the lower-right corner of the iTunes window when your iPad is selected in the sidebar. (It says Sync in Figure 3-1.)

✔ **Sync with This iPad Over Wi-Fi:** If you want to sync automatically over your Wi-Fi connection, select this check box.

If you choose to sync wirelessly, your iPad and computer must be on the same Wi-Fi network and your iPad must be plugged into a power source for syncing to occur.

🡒 **Sync Only Checked Songs and Video:** If you want to sync only items that have check marks to the left of their names in your iTunes library, select this check box.

🡒 **Prefer Standard Definition Videos:** If you want high-definition videos you import to be automatically converted into smaller standard-definition video files when you transfer them to your iPad, select this check box.

Standard-definition video files are significantly smaller than high-definition video files. You'll hardly notice the difference when you watch the video on your iPad (unless it's an iPad with a Retina display, in which case you'll almost certainly notice), but you can have more video files on your iPad because they take up less space.

The conversion from HD to standard definition takes a *long* time, so be prepared for very long sync times when you sync new HD video and have this option selected.

If you plan to use Apple's Digital AV Adapter (choose the dock version or Lightning version, as appropriate), or Apple TV ($99) to display movies on an HDTV, consider going with high definition. Although the files will be bigger and your iPad will hold fewer videos, the HD versions look spectacular on a big-screen TV. There's more info on these accessories in Chapter 17.

🡒 **Convert Higher Bit Rate Songs to 128 Kbps AAC:** If you want songs with bit rates higher than 128 Kbps converted into smaller 128-Kbps AAC files when you transfer them to your iPad, select this check box.

A *higher* bit rate means that the song will have better sound quality but use a lot of storage space. Songs that you buy at the iTunes Store or on Amazon, for example, have bit rates of around 256 Kbps. So a 4-minute song with a 256-Kbps bit rate is around 8MB; convert it to 128-Kbps AAC, and it's roughly half that size (that is, around 4MB) while sounding almost as good.

Most people don't notice much (if any) difference in audio quality when listening to music on most consumer audio gear. So unless you have your iPad hooked up to a great amplifier and superb speakers or head-phones, you probably won't hear much difference, but your iPad can hold roughly twice as much music if you choose this option. Put another way, we're very picky about our audio, and we both select this option to allow us to carry more music around with us on our iPads. And neither of us has noticed much impact on sound quality with the headphones or speakers we use with our iPads.

🡒 **Manually Manage Music and Videos:** To turn off automatic syncing in the Music and Video panes, select this check box.

One more thing: If you decide to select the Prevent iPods, iPhones, and iPads from Syncing Automatically check box on the Devices tab in iTunes Preferences (that's iTunes⇨Preferences on a Mac and Edit⇨Preferences on a PC), you can still synchronize manually by clicking the Sync or Apply button in the lower-right corner of the window.

Why the Sync *or* Apply button? Glad you asked. If you've changed *any* sync settings since the last time you synchronized, the Sync button instead says Apply. When you click that button — regardless of its name — your iPad will start to sync.

Backing Up Your iPad

Whether you know it or not, your iPad backs up your settings, app data, photos and videos you shoot, and other information on your iPad whenever you connect to a computer and use iTunes to

   ✔ Sync with your iPad

   ✔ Update your iPad

   ✔ Restore your iPad

Every time you sync your iPad and computer, most (but not all) of your iPad content, including (but not limited to) photos in the Camera Roll, text messages, notes, contact favorites, sound settings, and more, is backed up to either your computer's hard drive or to iCloud before the sync begins. Most of your media, including songs, TV shows, and movies, *isn't* backed up in this process. This shouldn't be a problem; these files are usually restored when you sync with iTunes again.

Backups are saved automatically and stored on your computer by default, or you can choose to back up to iCloud by clicking the appropriate button in the iTunes Summary pane.

To switch to backing up to iCloud using iTunes on your computer, follow these steps:

1. **Connect the iPad to the computer.**

   If iTunes doesn't launch automatically when you connect the iPad, launch it now.

2. **Click the iPad button just below the Search field.**

   If you use more than one iDevice with this computer, the button will say the number of devices (for example, *5 Devices*) rather than *iPad.* Click the button to display a drop-down list and select the device you want. Note that you won't see the button if the iTunes sidebar is visible.

3. **Click the Summary tab.**

4. **In the Automatically Back Up section, click iCloud.**

If you choose to back up to your computer, you can encrypt your backups with a password by selecting the Encrypt iPad Backup check box.

If anything goes wonky, or you get a new iPad, you can restore most (if not all) of your settings and files that aren't synced with iCloud or iTunes on your computer. Or, if you've backed up an iPhone, iPod touch, or another iPad, you can restore the new iPad from the older device's backup.

If you're using an iPad computer-free, here's how to enable backing up to iCloud from your iPad, which we strongly suggest computer-free iPad users do without further delay:

1. **Tap Settings⇨iCloud⇨Storage & Backup.**

2. **Tap iCloud Backup to switch it on (green).**

Choosing this option means your iPad no longer backs up automatically if you connect it to a computer.

If you are a computer-free iPad user, you don't care because you never connect your iPad to a computer. But if you sync your iPad with your computer like many folks do, give some thought to which option suits your needs. Restoring from a computer backup requires physical or Wi-Fi access to that computer, but you don't need Internet access. Restoring from iCloud requires Internet access — and can happen anywhere on Earth that has it.

One last thing to look at on the Backup section: If you want to password-protect your iPad backups (your iPad creates a backup of its contents automatically every time you sync), be sure to also select the Encrypt iPad Backup check box from the Backup area.

Backups are good; pick one or the other and move on.

Disconnecting the iPad

When a connected iPad is syncing with your computer, you see the eject icon to the right of its name in the Devices drop-down menu (and in the sidebar, if it's visible) turn into a sync icon, as shown in Figure 3-2, and spin around.

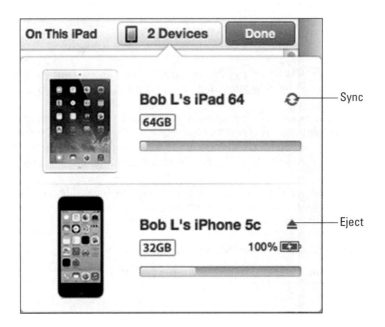

Figure 3-2: The eject icon (Bob L's iPhone 5c) turns into a sync icon (Bob L's iPad 64) during a sync.

At the same time, a message appears at the top of the iTunes window to inform you that your iPad is syncing, as shown in Figure 3-3.

When the sync is finished, the wheel in Figure 3-2 stops spinning and morphs back into an eject icon, and the message in Figure 3-3 disappears.

If you disconnect your iPad before the sync finishes, all or part of the sync may fail. While it isn't usually a problem, it's safer to cancel the sync and let it finish gracefully than to yank the cable out while a sync is in progress. So just don't do that, okay?

To cancel a sync properly and *safely* disconnect your iPad from your Mac or PC, click the little *x* to the right of the sync message in iTunes, as shown in Figure 3-3.

Cancel sync.

Figure 3-3: Click the *x* to cancel a sync.

Synchronizing Your Data

Your next order of business is to tell iTunes what data you want to synchronize between your iPad and your computer.

To get started, first select your iPad by clicking the iPad button (or the Devices drop-down menu, if you have more than one iDevice) just below the Search field.

You can also select your iPad in the sidebar on the left side of the iTunes screen (if the sidebar is visible), but if you do, your screen may not look like the figures in this chapter.

Click the Info tab, which is to the right of the Summary tab.

If you're using iCloud to sync contacts, calendars, bookmarks, or notes, you won't be able to enable these items in iTunes, as we're about to describe. Turn off iCloud syncing on your iPad (Settings⇨iCloud) for items you want to sync with your Mac.

If you're using Mac OS X 10.9 Mavericks, you'll discover that iTunes has no Info pane, so you can't sync contacts, calendars, reminders, and mail accounts using iTunes. Instead, you must use iCloud. If that describes you, feel free to skip the rest of this section and go directly to the next section.

On some displays you may see only one or two sections at any time and have to scroll up or down to see the others.

The Info pane has five sections: Sync Contacts, Sync Calendars, Sync Mail Accounts, Other, and Advanced. The following sections look at them one by one. One last thing: To use your iPad with your Google or Yahoo! account, you must first create an account on your iPad, as described in Chapter 5. After you've created a Yahoo! or Google account on your iPad, you can enable contact or calendar syncing with it in the Settings app's Mail, Contacts, Calendars section.

Contacts

In Figure 3-4, note that the section is named Sync Contacts because this image was captured on a Mac. Contacts (formerly known as Address Book) is the Mac application that syncs with your iPad's Contacts app.

If you use a PC, you see a drop-down list that gives you the choices of Outlook, Google Contacts, Windows Address Book, or Yahoo! Address Book. Don't worry — the process works the same on either platform.

The iPad syncs with the following address book programs:

- **Mac:** Address Book and other address books that sync with Address Book, such as Microsoft Outlook 2011 or the discontinued Microsoft Entourage
- **PC:** Windows Contacts (Vista, Windows 7, Windows 8), Windows Address Book (XP), Microsoft Outlook, and Microsoft Outlook Express
- **Mac and PC:** Yahoo! Address Book and Google Contacts

You can sync contacts with multiple applications.

Here's what each option does:

- ✔ **All Contacts:** One method is to synchronize all your contacts, as shown in Figure 3-4. This will synchronize every contact in your Mac or PC address book with your iPad's Contacts app.
- ✔ **Selected Groups:** You can synchronize any or all groups of contacts you've created in your computer's address book program. Just select the appropriate check boxes in the Selected Groups list, and only those groups will be synchronized.

Figure 3-4: Want to synchronize your contacts? This is where you set up things.

If you sync with your employer's Microsoft Exchange calendar and contacts, any personal contacts or calendars already on your iPad will be wiped out.

Calendars

The Calendars section of the Info pane determines how synchronization is handled for your appointments, events, and reminders. You can synchronize all your calendars, as shown in Figure 3-5. Or you can synchronize any or all individual calendars you've created in your computer's calendar program. Just select the appropriate check boxes.

The iPad syncs with the following calendar programs:

- ✔ **Mac:** iCal or Calendar
- ✔ **PC:** Microsoft Exchange and Outlook 2003, 2007, and 2010
- ✔ **Mac and PC:** Google and Yahoo! Calendars

You can sync calendars with multiple applications.

Figure 3-5: Set up sync for your calendar events here.

Mail Accounts

You can sync account settings for your e-mail accounts in the Mail Accounts section of the Info pane. You can synchronize all your e-mail accounts (if you have more than one), or you can synchronize individual accounts, as shown in Figure 3-6. Just select the appropriate check boxes.

Figure 3-6: Transfer e-mail account settings to your iPad here.

The iPad syncs with the following mail programs:

- ✔ **Mac:** Mail
- ✔ **PC:** Microsoft Outlook 2003, 2007, and 2010
- ✔ **Mac and PC:** Gmail, Yahoo! Mail, iCloud, AOL, Hotmail, other POP and IMAP accounts

E-mail account settings are synchronized only one way: from your computer to your iPad. If you make changes to any e-mail account settings on your iPad, the changes aren't synchronized back to the e-mail account on your computer. Trust us, this is a very good feature, and we're glad Apple did it this way.

By the way, the password for your e-mail account may or may not be saved on your computer. If you sync an e-mail account and the iPad asks for a password when you send or receive mail, do this: Tap Settings on the Home screen, tap Mail, tap your e-mail account's name, and then type your password in the appropriate field.

Other

The Other section has a single item: Sync Safari Bookmarks.

Select the check box for Sync Safari Bookmarks if you want to sync your Safari bookmarks; don't select it if you don't.

Just so you know, the iPad syncs bookmarks with the following web browsers:

- **Mac:** Safari
- **PC:** Microsoft Internet Explorer and Safari

Advanced

Every so often, the contacts, calendars, mail accounts, or bookmarks on your iPad get so screwed up that the easiest way to fix things is to erase that information from your iPad and replace it with information from your computer.

If that's the case, go to the Advanced section of the Info pane and click to select the appropriate check boxes, as shown in Figure 3-7. Then, the next time you sync, that information on your iPad will be replaced with information from your computer.

Figure 3-7: Replace the information on your iPad with the information on your computer.

Because the Advanced section is at the bottom of the Info pane and you have to scroll down to see it, you can easily forget that the Advanced section is there. Although you probably won't need to use this feature very often (if ever), you'll be happy you remembered that it's there if you do need it.

One last thing: Check boxes in the Advanced section are disabled for items not selected, as described in the previous sections (Contacts, Calendars, Mail Accounts, and Bookmarks in Figure 3-5). If you're using iCloud and you want to replace any of these items on your iPad, you must first enable that item as discussed in the previous sections of this chapter. In other words, to replace contacts, calendars, mail accounts, or bookmarks in Figure 3-7, we first had to disable iCloud syncing. Only then could we enable the check boxes for Sync Contacts, Sync Calendars, Sync Mail Accounts, and Sync Bookmarks.

Synchronizing Your Media

If you chose to let iTunes manage synchronizing your data automatically, welcome. This section looks at how you get your media — your music, podcasts, videos, and photos — from your computer to your iPad.

Podcasts and videos (but not photos) from your computer are synced only one way: from your computer to your iPad. If you delete a podcast or a video that got onto your iPad via syncing, the podcast or video will not be deleted from your computer when you sync.

That said, if you buy or download any of the following items from the Apple iTunes, iBook, or App Store on your iPad, the item *will* be copied back to your computer automatically when you sync:

- Songs
- Ringtones
- Podcasts
- Videos
- iBooks, e-books, and audiobooks
- Apps
- Playlists that you create on your iPad

And if you save pictures from e-mail messages, the iPad camera, web pages (by pressing and holding on an image and then tapping the Save Image button), or screen shots (which can be created by pressing the Home and Sleep/Wake buttons simultaneously), these too can be synced with your photo application (such as iPhoto, Aperture, or Adobe Photoshop Elements).

You use the Apps, Tones, Music, Movies, TV Shows, Podcasts, iTunes U, Books, and Photos panes to specify the media that you want to copy from your computer to your iPad. The following sections explain the options you find in each pane.

To view any of these panes, make sure that your iPad is still selected and then click the appropriate button near the top of the window.

The following sections focus only on syncing. If you need help acquiring apps, music, movies, podcasts, or anything else for your iPad, this book contains chapters dedicated to each of these topics. Just flip to the most applicable chapter for help.

The last step in each section is "Click the Sync or Apply button in the lower-right corner of the window." You have to do this only when selecting that item for the first time and if you make any changes to the item after that.

Sharp-eyed readers may notice that we aren't covering syncing iPad apps in this chapter. Apps are so darn cool that we've given them an entire chapter, namely Chapter 11. In that chapter, you discover how to find, sync, rearrange, review, and delete apps, and much, much more.

Tones

If you have custom ringtones in your iTunes library, select the Sync Ringtones check box in the Tones pane. Then you can choose either all ringtones or individual ringtones by selecting their check boxes. Ringtones can be used also as text tones and alarms.

Music, music videos, and voice memos

To transfer music to your iPad, select the Sync Music check box in the Music pane. You can then select the option for Entire Music Library or Selected Playlists, Artists, and Genres. If you choose the latter, click the check boxes next to particular playlists, artists, and genres you want to transfer. You also can choose to include music videos or voice memos or both by selecting the appropriate check boxes at the top of the pane (see Figure 3-8).

If none of the options just mentioned sounds just right (pun intended), you may prefer using the On This iPad tab, which is covered in some detail later in this chapter.

If you choose Entire Music Library and have more songs in your iTunes library than storage space on your iPad, you'll see an error message when you try to sync. You'll also see a yellow alert on the right side of the Capacity chart at the bottom of the screen, along with how much over your iPad's capacity adding the entire music library would make you. To avoid such

Figure 3-8: Use the Music pane to copy music, music videos, and voice memos from your computer to your iPad.

errors, select playlists, artists, and genres that total less than the free space on your iPad, which is also displayed in the Capacity chart at the bottom of the iTunes screen.

Music, podcasts, and video are notorious for using massive amounts of storage space on your iPad. If you try to sync too much media content, you see lots of error messages. Forewarned is forearmed.

Finally, if you select the Automatically Fill Free Space with Songs check box, iTunes fills any free space on your iPad with music. Think long and hard about enabling this option. We recommend against it because when it's enabled, you can easily run out of space for pictures and videos you shoot or documents you save (to name just a few of the possible consequences of filling your iPad with songs).

How much space did I use?

If you're interested in knowing how much free space is available on your iPad, look near the bottom of the iTunes window while your iPad is connected. You'll see a chart that shows the contents of your iPad, color-coded for your convenience. As you can see in the figure, this iPad has 49.66GB of free space. Hover your cursor over any color to see a bubble with info on that category, as shown for Photos in the figure.

You can find similar information about space used and space remaining on your iPad by tapping Settings⇨General⇨Usage. The iPad's display isn't as pretty as the one pictured here, but it is useful when you need that info and you're not near your computer.

Movies

To transfer movies to your iPad, select the Sync Movies check box and then choose an option for movies you want to include automatically from the pop-up menu, as shown in Figure 3-9. If you choose an option other than All, you can optionally select individual movies and playlists by selecting the boxes in appropriate sections.

TV shows

The procedure for syncing TV shows is slightly different from the procedure for syncing movies. First, select the Sync TV Shows check box to enable TV show syncing. Then choose how many episodes to include and whether you want all shows or only selected shows from the two pop-up menus, as shown in Figure 3-10. If you want to also include individual episodes or episodes on playlists, select the appropriate check boxes in the Shows, Episodes, and Include Episodes from Playlists (not visible in Figure 3-10) sections of the TV Shows pane.

Regardless of the choices you make in the pop-up menus, you can always select individual episodes by selecting their check boxes.

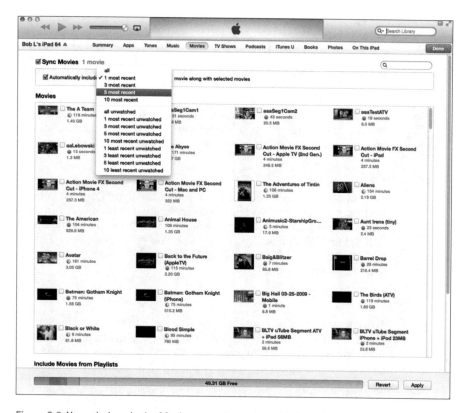

Figure 3-9: Your choices in the Movies pane determine which movies are copied to your iPad.

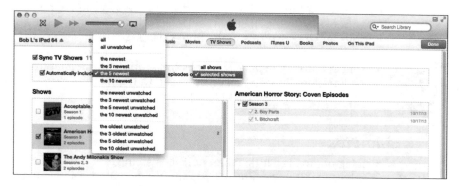

Figure 3-10: These menus determine how TV shows are synced with your iPad.

Podcasts, iTunes U, and books

You can also sync podcasts, educational content from iTunes U, two types of books — e-books for reading and audiobooks for listening — and photos.

If you like to read e-books or watch or listen to podcasts or iTunes U courses, visit the App Store (see Chapter 11) and grab copies of Apple's free Podcasts, iBooks, and iTunes U apps. Audiobooks, on the other hand, don't require a special app; you can listen to them using the Music app (see Chapter 7).

Podcasts

To transfer podcasts to your iPad, select the Sync Podcasts check box in the Podcasts pane. Then you can automatically include however many podcasts you want by making selections from the two pop-up menus, the same way you did for TV Shows. If you have podcast episodes on playlists, you can include them by selecting the appropriate check box in the Include Episodes from Playlists section.

iTunes U

To sync educational content from iTunes U, first select the Sync iTunes U check box to enable iTunes U syncing. Then choose how many episodes to include and whether you want all collections or only selected collections from the two pop-up menus. If you want to also include individual items or items on playlists, select the appropriate check boxes in the Items section and Include Items from Playlists section of the iTunes U pane.

Books

By now we're sure you know the drill: You can sync all your e-books and audiobooks as well as just sync selected titles by choosing the appropriate buttons and check boxes in the Books pane.

To sync e-books, you need the free iBooks app; download it from the App Store. For more information on apps and the App Store, read Chapter 11, or see Chapter 10 to start using iBooks.

Photos

Syncing photos is a little different from syncing other media because your iPad has a built-in camera — two cameras, actually — and you may want to copy pictures or videos you take with the iPad to your computer, as well as copy pictures stored on your computer to your iPad.

The iPad syncs photos and videos with the following programs:

- **Mac:** Aperture version 3.2 or later or iPhoto version 9.2 or later
- **PC:** Adobe Photoshop Elements or Adobe Photoshop Album

You can also sync photos with any folder on your computer that contains images.

In the Photos pane, select the Sync Photos From check box, and then choose an application or folder from the pop-up menu (which says Aperture in Figure 3-11).

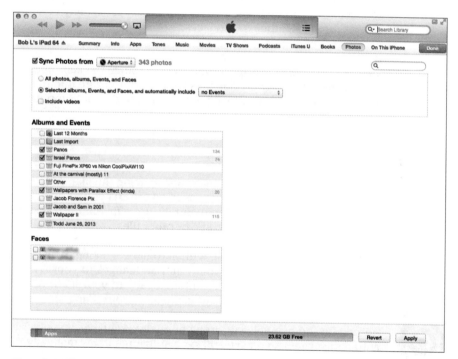

Figure 3-11: The Photos pane determines which photos will be synchronized with your iPad.

If you choose an application that supports photo albums (such as Photoshop Elements, Aperture, or iPhoto), projects (Aperture), events (iPhoto), facial recognition and Places (Aperture or iPhoto), or any combination thereof, you can automatically include recent projects (Aperture), events (iPhoto), or faces (Aperture and iPhoto) by making a selection from the same pop-up menu.

Note that although Photoshop Elements includes features called Places and Faces, those features are not supported by your iPad.

You can also type a word or phrase in the search field (an oval with a magnifying glass) to search for a specific event or events.

If you choose a folder full of images, you can create subfolders inside it that will appear as albums on your iPad. But if you choose an application that doesn't support albums or events, or a single folder full of images with no subfolders, you have to transfer all or nothing.

Because we selected Aperture in the Sync Photos From menu, and Aperture 3 (the version installed on our Mac) supports projects and faces in addition to albums and photos, we have the option of syncing any combination of photos, projects, albums, and faces.

If you've taken any photos with your iPad or saved images from a web page, an e-mail, an MMS message, or an iMessage since the last time you synced, the appropriate program launches (or the appropriate folder is selected), and you have the option of uploading the pictures to your computer.

Manual Syncing

This chapter has focused on automatic syncing thus far. Automatic syncing is great; it selects items to sync based on criteria you've specified, such as genre, artist, playlist, and album. But it's not efficient for transferring a few items — songs, movies, podcasts, or other files — to your iPad.

The solution? Manual syncing. With automatic syncing, iTunes updates your iPad automatically to match your criteria. Changes to your iTunes library since your last sync are synced automatically to your iPad. With manual syncing, you merely drag individual items to your iPad.

Automatic and manual sync aren't mutually exclusive. If you've set up automatic syncing, you can still sync individual items manually.

You can manually sync music, movies, TV shows, podcasts, and iTunes U lessons but not photos and info such as contacts, calendars, and bookmarks.

To configure your iPad for manual syncing, follow these steps:

1. **Connect your iPad to your computer via USB or Wi-Fi.**

   If iTunes doesn't open automatically, open it manually.

2. **Click the iPad button just below the Search field.**

   Remember, if iTunes' sidebar is visible, you won't see the button. (Choose View⇨Show Sidebar/Hide Sidebar to hide it.)

   Also, as mentioned previously, the button won't say *iPad* if you have more than one iDevice. Instead, it will display the number of devices you have, such as *5 Devices*. Click the button to display a list of your devices, and select the device you want.

3. **(Optional) Click the Summary tab and select Manually Manage Music and Videos in the Options section.**

   This step disables automatic syncing for music and videos.

   If you're happy with automatic syncing and just want to get some audio or video from your computer to your iPad, feel free to skip this step.

To add items from iTunes to your iPad without using the syncing controls or performing an actual sync, follow these steps:

1. **Click the On This iPad tab.**

2. **Click the Add To button (near the top-right corner of the iTunes window).**

   A new pane appears on the right side of the iTunes window.

3. **Drag your chosen media from the left side of the iTunes window to the pane on the right, as shown in Figure 3-12.**

Figure 3-12: Drag and drop to copy media to your iPad.

In Figure 3-12, we dragged The Beatles from the Artists tab, but don't forget that you can drag media from all those other tabs — Songs, Albums, Genres, and so on. And you can add other types of content, such as movies, TV shows, podcasts, and books. Just choose a category from the Library pop-up menu (which displays Music in Figure 3-12).

You can add a media file to your iPad without syncing in two other ways. Both methods require your iPad to be connected to your computer via Wi-Fi or USB, so they work only if you see the iPad (or *# of Devices*) button below the search field:

- ✔ Click the little angle bracket in a circle (shown in the margin) next to any song, album, movie, TV show, book, or other media. Choose Add To from the pop-up menu. A list of possible destinations will appear; click your iPad in the list and the file will be added to your iPad.

- ✔ Click any eligible item (or items) in your iTunes library and start dragging the item or items to the right. A pane with a list of connected devices appears on the right; drag the item to your iPad in the list, as shown in Figure 3-13.

And that's pretty much all you need to know to sync files automatically or manually, so you can view or listen to whatever you like on your iPad. And if you haven't figured out how watch movies or listen to audio on your iPad yet, it's only because you haven't read Part III on multimedia, where watching and listening to your iPad are made crystal-clear.

Figure 3-13: Drag a song or other media content to the right in the iTunes window, and this pane appears like magic.

iCloud: Apple's Free and Easy Wireless Service

Apple's iCloud service is more than just a wireless hard drive in the sky. Rather, iCloud is a complete wireless storage and data synchronization solution. In a nutshell, iCloud stores and manages your digital stuff — your music, photos, contacts, events, and more — keeping everything updated on all your computers and iDevices automatically with no physical (wired) connection or action on your part. Like so many things Apple makes, iCloud just works.

iCloud "pushes" information such as e-mail, calendars, contacts, reminders, and bookmarks to and from your computer — and to and from your iPad and other iDevices sporting iOS 5 or later — and then keeps those items updated on all devices wirelessly, without human intervention. It also includes non-synchronizing options, such as Photo Stream (Chapter 9), e-mail (Chapter 5), Find My iPad, Find My Friends, and 5GB of online storage.

Your free iCloud account includes 5GB of free storage, which is all many (if not most) users will need. If you find yourself needing more storage, 10-, 20-, and 50-gigabyte upgrades are available for $20, $40, and $100 a year, respectively.

A nice touch is that music, apps, books, periodicals, movies, and TV shows purchased from the iTunes Store, as well as photos in your Photo Stream, don't count against your 5GB of free storage. (If you don't know what your iPad's delicious Photo Stream and Shared Photo Streams are all about, find out more in Chapter 9.) And if you subscribe to iTunes Match, even tracks you've ripped yourself or acquired from other sources don't count against your 5GB of free storage.

You'll find that the things that do count against your storage space — such as mail, documents, photos taken with your iPad camera, account information, settings, and other app data — don't use much space. So that free 5GB is all many users require.

If you want to have your e-mail, calendars, contacts, and bookmarks synchronized automatically and wirelessly (and believe us, you do), here's how to enable iCloud syncing on your iPad:

1. **Tap Settings on your Home screen.**

2. **Tap iCloud in the list of settings on the left.**

3. **Provide your Apple ID and password.**

4. **Sign in.**

Now you can tap any of the individual On/Off switches to enable or disable iCloud sync for the following:

- ✔ Mail
- ✔ Contacts
- ✔ Calendars
- ✔ Reminders
- ✔ Bookmarks
- ✔ Notes
- ✔ Passbook
- ✔ Photos
- ✔ Documents & Data
- ✔ Find My iPad

Note that even though iCloud lets you stream or download movies, TV shows, songs, podcasts, or other media files from the iTunes Store, if you don't have a speedy Internet connection, you may not be able to enjoy them because they will stutter or stall.

Tap Storage & Backup near the bottom of the screen to manage your iCloud storage, enable or disable iCloud backups, upgrade your storage plan, or initiate a backup to iCloud right now.

Part II
The Internet iPad

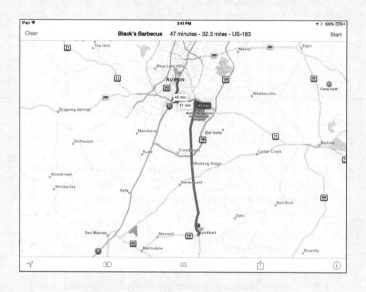

Check out your options for getting online (whether with Wi-Fi, 3G, or 4G) at www. dummies.com/extras/ipad.

In this part...

- Explore Safari, the best web browser to ever to grace a hand-held device. Take advantage of links and bookmarks and find out how to open multiple web pages at the same time. And run a web search wirelessly with your iPad.

- See how easy it is to set up e-mail accounts and send and receive real honest-to-goodness e-mail messages and attachments.

- Marvel at the Maps app's unerring ability to show you where you are on a map. Discover the joys of step-by-step driving directions and real-time traffic info.

4

Going on a Mobile Safari

" *Y* ou feel like you're actually holding the web right in the palm of your hand."

Marketers use lines like that because, well, that's what marketers do. But when an Apple marketer says such a thing to describe surfing the web on the iPad, a lot of truth is behind it. The spectacular Retina display that was introduced with the third-generation iPad, in combination with the snappy Apple-designed, A5X chip (third generation) or A6X chip (fourth generation) with quad-core graphics inside the machine, makes browsing on Apple's tablets an absolute delight. The iPad mini with the Retina display and the iPad Air got ever-more-powerful A7 chips. Not that the robust processors in earlier iPads were anything to sneeze at.

In this chapter, you discover the pleasures — and the few roadblocks — in navigating cyberspace on your iPad.

Surfin' Dude

A version of the Apple Safari web browser is a major reason that the 'Net on the iPad is very much like the 'Net you've come to expect on a more traditional computer. Come to think of it, the Internet often looks a lot better on iPads with the striking Retina display. And the screens on iPad models without the Retina display aren't too shabby either. Safari for the Mac and for Windows is one of the very best web browsers in the business. In our view, Safari on the iPhone has no rival as a cellphone browser. As you might imagine, Safari on the iPad is even more appealing.

Through older iterations of iOS, Apple revved up Safari's performance with what the company refers to as a *Nitro JavaScript engine*. Even a consumer-friendly company like Apple can't help but rely on geeky terms every now and then.

Exploring the browser

We start our cyber-expedition with a quick tour of the Safari browser. Take a gander at Figure 4-1: Not all browser controls found on a Mac or PC are present. Still, Safari on the iPad has a familiar look and feel. We describe these controls and others throughout this chapter.

Figure 4-1: The iPad's Safari browser.

Before plunging in, we recommend a little detour. Find out more about the wireless networks that enable you to surf the web on the iPad in our web extras at www.dummies.com/extras/ipad.

Blasting off into cyberspace

Surfing the web begins with a web address, of course.

Here are a few tips for using the keyboard in Safari (and see Chapter 2 for more help with using the virtual keyboard):

- Because so many web addresses end with the suffix .com (pronounced *dot com*), the virtual keyboard has a few shortcuts worth noting. Press and hold your finger against the ".?" key, and you'll see that .com option. You'll see other common web suffixes as well — .edu, .net, .org, .us, .ro, .eu. Some of the options appear only if you've selected an international keyboard (as discussed in Chapter 2).

- The moment you tap a letter, you see a list of web addresses that match those letters. For example, if you tap the letter *E* (as we did in the example shown in Figure 4-2), you see web listings for eBay, ESPN, and others. Tapping *U* or *H* instead may display listings for *USA TODAY* or the *Houston Chronicle* (shameless plugs for the newspapers where we're columnists).

Models with Siri can lend a hand, um, voice, as you surf. If you call upon Siri and ask the voice genie inside the iPad to open the Safari app, Siri obliges. If you mention a specific website to Siri — "ESPN.com," say — Siri opens your designated search engine (Google, Bing, or Yahoo!), as discussed later in this chapter. And if Siri heard you right, the site you mentioned appears at the top of the search results.

The iPad has two ways to determine websites to suggest when you tap certain letters:

- **Bookmarks:** One method is the websites you already bookmarked from the Safari or Internet Explorer browsers on your computer (and synchronized, as we describe in Chapter 3). More on bookmarks later in this chapter.

- **History:** The second method iPad uses when suggesting websites when you tap a particular letter is to suggest sites from the History list — those cyberdestinations where you recently hung your hat. Because history repeats itself, we also tackle that topic later in this chapter.

✓ **Smart search field:** When you type an address into the search field, you also see icons for sites you frequent most often, and you can tap any of those icons to jump immediately to that site.

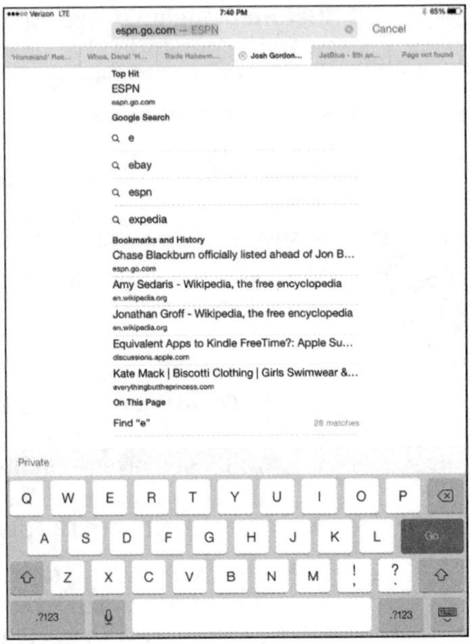

You might as well open your first web page now — and it's a full *HTML* page, to borrow from techie lingo:

1. **Tap the Safari icon docked at the bottom of the Home screen.**

   If you haven't moved it, it's a member of the Fantastic Four on the Dock (along with Mail, Videos, and Music). Chapter 1 introduces the Home screen.

2. **Tap the smart search field (refer to Figure 4-1).**

3. **Begin typing the web address, or *URL*, on the virtual keyboard that slides up from the bottom of the screen.**

4. **Do one of the following:**

   • *To accept one of the bookmarked (or other) sites that show up in the list, merely tap the name.*

   Safari automatically fills in the URL in the address field and takes you where you want to go.

   • *Keep tapping the proper keyboard characters until you enter the complete web address for the site you have in mind and then tap the Go key on the right side of the keyboard.*

   You don't need to type **www** at the beginning of a URL. So if you want to visit www.theonion.com (for example), typing **theonion.com** is sufficient to transport you to the humor site. For that matter, Safari can take you to this site even if you type **theonion** without the .com.

Because Safari on the iPad runs a variation of the iPhone mobile operating system, every so often you may run into a site that serves up the light, or mobile, version of a website, sometimes known as a *WAP site*. Graphics may be stripped down on these sites. Alas, the producers of these sites may be unwittingly discriminating against you for dropping in on them using an iPad. In fact, you may be provided a choice of which site you want — the light or

Figure 4-2: Web pages that match your search letter.

the full version. Bravo! If not, you have our permission to berate these site producers with letters, e-mails, and phone calls until they get with the program.

Zoom, zoom, zoom

If you know how to open a web page (if you don't, read the preceding section in this chapter), we can show you how radically simple it is to zoom in on pages so that you can read what you want to read and see what you want to see, without enlisting a magnifying glass.

Try these neat tricks for starters:

✔ **Double-tap the screen so that the area of the display that you make contact with fills the entire screen.** It takes just a second before the screen comes into focus. By way of example, check out Figure 4-3, which shows two views of the same *Sports Illustrated* web page. In the first view, you see what the page looks like when you first open it. In the second one, you see how the Top Stories box takes over much more of the screen after you double-tap it. The area of the screen you double-tapped is the area that swells up. To return to the first view, double-tap the screen again.

Figure 4-3: Doing a double-tap dance zooms in and out.

- ✔ **Pinch the page.** Sliding your thumb and index finger together and then spreading them apart (or, as we like to say, *unpinching*) also zooms in and out of a page. Again, wait just a moment for the screen to come into focus.

- ✔ **Press down on a page and drag it in all directions, or flick through a page from top to bottom.** You're panning and scrolling, baby.

- ✔ **Rotate the iPad to its side.** This reorients from portrait to a widescreen landscape view. The keyboard is also wider in this mode, making it a little easier to enter a new URL.

  However, this little bit of rotation magic won't happen if you set and enabled the Screen Orientation Lock feature that we describe in Chapter 1.

Reading clutter-free web pages

It's all too easy to get distracted reading web pages nowadays, what with ads, videos, and other clutter surrounding the stuff you actually want to take in. So pay attention to the horizontal lines that often appear in the smart search field, as shown in Figure 4-4 (left). Tap those lines to view the same article without the needless diversions, as shown in Figure 4-4 (right). Tap the lines again to return the standard web view.

Tap for clutter-
free reading.

Figure 4-4: Reducing clutter when reading a web story.

Finding Your Way Around Cyberspace

In this section, we discuss ways to navigate the Internet on your iPad with links and tabs.

Looking at lovable links

Because Safari functions on the iPad the same way that browsers work on your Mac or PC, links on the device behave in much the same way.

Text links that transport you from one site to another are typically underlined or shown in blue, red, or bold type, or merely as items in a list. Tap the link to go directly to that site or page.

Tapping other links leads to different outcomes:

- **Open a map:** Tapping a map launches the Maps application that is, um, addressed in Chapter 6.

- **Prepare an e-mail:** Tap an e-mail address, and the iPad opens the Mail program (see Chapter 5) and prepopulates the To field with that address. The virtual keyboard is also summoned so that you can add other e-mail addresses and compose a subject line and message. This shortcut doesn't always work when an e-mail address appears on a web page.

To see the URL for a link, press your finger on the link and hold it there until a list of options appears, as shown in Figure 4-5.

Use this method also to determine whether a picture has a link. Just hold your finger down on the picture; if it's linked, you see the web address that the link points to.

As for the other link options shown in Figure 4-5, here's what two of them do:

- **Open:** Opens the page in this tab.

- **Copy:** Copies the link's URL to your iPad's Clipboard so that you can paste it elsewhere.

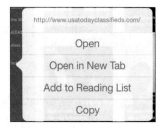

Figure 4-5: Press and hold on a link (Classifieds), and a list of options appears.

You hear more about the other two options — Open in New Tab and Add to Reading List — a little later in this chapter.

Not every web link cooperates with the iPad. As this book goes to press, the iPad doesn't support some common web standards — most notably, Adobe Flash video. If you see an incompatible link, nothing may happen — or a message may appear, asking you to install a plug-in. For more about getting Flash to work on your iPad, see the nearby sidebar, "Support for the Flash-deprived."

Support for the Flash-deprived

The iPad's lack of support for Adobe Flash video is a void that (frankly) is unlikely to ever get addressed: Even Adobe is no longer embracing Flash for mobile devices. But because Flash has been a backbone for video and animations across cyberspace, you may still come across web destinations that rely on it. All is not lost, even with the absence of Flash. Apple does support emerging standards for audio and video — *HTML5,* among others. And Adobe, too, is now backing HTML5.

In the meantime, you may be able to open Flash videos on the iPad through a couple of workarounds. Skyfire Labs sells a $4.99 iPad app that can support Flash on many sites. But Skyfire's alternative browser is limited to videos; it doesn't support Flash games, apps, or animations. Meanwhile, the free iSwifter app from YouWeb promises to (partially) address this shortcoming. So along with video, iSwifter's browser can deliver Flash games on Facebook and Google.

Another workaround for some: Tap into your virtual private network (VPN) connection to control your desktop computer from the iPad. If such a connection is available, you can access the browser on that computer. For another potential solution from Parallels, check out Chapter 19.

Tabbed browsing

When we surf the web on a Mac or PC, we rarely go to a single web page and call it a day. In fact, we often have multiple web pages open at the same time. Sometimes we choose to hop around the web without closing the pages we visit. Sometimes a link automatically opens a new page without shuttering the old one. (If these additional pages are advertisements, this isn't always welcome.)

Safari on the iPad lets you open multiple pages simultaneously, via a brilliant rendition of tabbed browsing similar to the desktop version of browsers like Safari.

After you have one page open, here are two ways to open additional web pages in Safari so that they appear on the tab bar at the top of the screen (rather than replace the page you're currently viewing):

✔ **Tap the + button (see Figure 4-6) on the top-right corner of the browser.** A new tab named Favorites will appear, as shown in Figure 4-6. Now type a URL, tap a bookmark or icon for a favorite or frequently visited site, or initiate a search, and it will appear in this tab.

✔ **Hold your finger on a link until a list of options appears (refer to Figure 4-5), and then tap Open in New Tab.**

A new tab

Figure 4-6: A new tab, ready to display any page you choose.

To switch tabs, just tap the tab. To close a tab, tap the gray X that appears on the left edge of the active tab.

iCloud Tabs

Though the iPad is your likely traveling companion just about everywhere you go, we know that you also browse the web from your smartphone or personal computer. If that smartphone happens to be an iPhone and the computer is a Macintosh (or Windows PC running Safari), you can take advantage of iCloud Tabs, a feature that lets you resume reading web pages that you started looking at on those other devices. It works with the iPod touch, too. To access iCloud Tabs, tap the icon that resembles a cloud near the upper-right corner of Safari (refer to Figure 4-1).

A window like the one in Figure 4-7 appears, revealing the tabs still open on your other devices. Tap the tab you want to return to on the list.

Revisiting Web Pages Time and Again

Surfing the web would be a real drag if you had to enter a URL every time you want to navigate from one page to another. That's why bookmarks, Web Clips, Reading lists, and History lists are so useful. All so you can find those favorite websites in the future.

Book (mark) 'em, Dano

You already know how useful bookmarks are and how you can synchronize bookmarks from the browsers on your computer. It's equally simple to book-mark a web page directly on the iPad. Follow these steps:

1. **Make sure that the page you want to book-mark is open, and then tap the Action button at the top of the screen.**

   The Action button looks like an arrow trying to escape a rectangle. You have many options beyond bookmarking when you tap the action button (refer to Figure 4-1, though not all the options are visible in the figure). You can tap Message, Mail, Twitter, or Facebook. Sina Weibo and Tencent Weibo (Chinese variations of Twitter) are also available, provided you added a Chinese keyboard in Settings (see Chapter 2). Or you can tap Bookmark, Add to Reading List, Add to Home Screen, Copy, and Print, as we show you here. You can also use the wireless feature called AirDrop to share the page with people nearby via Wi-Fi or Bluetooth, provided you have a fourth-generation iPad or later, or the iPad mini. See Chapter 13 to find out how to use AirDrop.

2. **Tap Bookmark.**

   A new Add Bookmark window opens with a default name for the bookmark, its web address, and its folder location.

3. **Give it a name and folder location:**

   - *Accept the default bookmark name and default bookmark folder:* Tap Save.

   - *Change the default bookmark name:* Tap the X in the circle next to the name, enter the new title (using the virtual keyboard), and then tap Save.

Figure 4-7: iCloud Tabs can return you to a site you've been reading on other iCloud-capable devices.

   - *Change the location where the bookmark is saved:* Tap the > symbol to the right of the suggested location (likely Favorites), tap the folder where you want the bookmark to be kept so that a check mark appears, and then tap Save.

To open a bookmarked page after you set it up, tap the Bookmarks icon to the right of the smart search field. (Refer to Figure 4-1.)

If you don't see bookmarks right away, make sure that the leftmost of the three tabs at the top of the screen is highlighted in blue. The other tabs are for the Reading list and for shared links — those that are shared by your contacts from selected social networks.

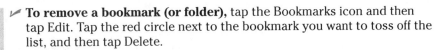

If the bookmark you have in mind is buried inside a folder, tap the folder name first and then tap the bookmark you want.

Altering bookmarks

If a bookmarked site is no longer meaningful, you can change it or get rid of it:

- ✔ **To remove a bookmark (or folder),** tap the Bookmarks icon and then tap Edit. Tap the red circle next to the bookmark you want to toss off the list, and then tap Delete.

  To remove a single bookmark or folder, swipe its name from left to right and then tap the red Delete button.

- ✔ **To change a bookmark name or location,** tap Edit at the bottom-right corner of the Bookmarks window. Tap a given bookmark, and an Edit Bookmark window appears, showing the name, URL, and location of the bookmark already filled in. Tap the fields you want to change. In the Name field, tap the X in the gray circle and then use the keyboard to enter a new title. In the Location field, tap the > symbol and scroll up or down the list until you find a new home for your bookmark.

- ✔ **To create a new folder for your bookmarks,** tap Edit and then tap New Folder. Enter the name of the new folder, and choose where to put it.

- ✔ **To move a bookmark up or down in a list,** tap Edit and then drag the three bars to the right of the bookmark's name to its new resting place.

If you take advantage of iCloud, the web pages you've bookmarked on your Mac and on your other iOS devices will be available on the iPad, and vice versa.

Saving it for later with the Reading List

When you visit a web page you'd like to read, but just not now, the Reading List feature is sure to come in handy, including when you're offline. Here's how it works:

- ✔ **Saving a page for later:** Tap the Action button and then tap Add to Reading List. Or, if you see a link to a page you'd like to read later, press on the link until a list of options appears (refer to Figure 4-5) and then tap Add to Reading List.

- ✔ **Reading a page on your Reading List:** Tap the Bookmarks icon and tap the page in the Reading List, as shown in Figure 4-8.

- ✔ **Keeping track of what you've read:** Tap Show Unread to display only those items that you haven't gotten to yet.

✏ **Removing items from the Reading List:** Swipe the item from right to left, and then tap its red Delete button.

The Reading List feature used to require an active Internet connection, which is why we always admired Marco Arment's superb Instapaper app — and still do. It's just $4.99 in the App Store.

In Settings, you can choose to use your cellular network (if available) to save Reading List items from iCloud so you can read them offline.

Finally, don't forget that you can share your Reading List (and Bookmarks) among your computers and iOS devices with iCloud, as described in Chapter 3.

Clipping a web page

You frequent lots of websites, but some way more than others. You're constantly online to consult your daily train schedule, for example. In their infinite wisdom, the folks at Apple let you bestow special privileges on frequently visited sites, not just by bookmarking pages but also by affording them their unique Home screen icons. Apple used to call these *Web Clips,* and we still like the term. Creating one is dead simple. Follow these steps:

1. **Open the web page in question, and tap the Action button.**

2. **Tap Add to Home Screen.**

   Apple creates an icon out of the area of the page that was displayed when you saved the clip, unless the page has its own custom icon.

3. **Type a new name for your Web Clip or leave the one that Apple suggests.**

4. **Tap Add.**

   The icon appears on your Home screen.

Figure 4-8: Tap a page in the Reading List to read it.

As with any icon, you can remove a Web Clip by pressing and holding its icon until it starts to wiggle. Then tap the X in the corner of the icon, and tap Delete. Of course, you can also move the Web Clip to a more preferred location on one of your Home screens or on your Dock.

Letting history repeat itself

Sometimes you want to revisit a site that you failed to bookmark, but you can't remember the darn destination or what led you there in the first place. Good thing you can study the history books.

Safari records the pages you visit and keeps the logs on hand for several days. Here's how to access your history:

1. **Tap the Bookmarks icon and then tap History.**

   The History option is at the top of the Bookmarks list.

2. **Tap the day you think you hung out at the site.**

   Sites are listed under such headings as "This Morning," "Thursday Evening," "Thursday Morning," or segregated by a specific date.

3. **When you find it, tap the listing.**

   You're about to make your triumphant return.

To clear your history so that nobody else can trace your steps — and just what is it you're hiding? — tap Clear at the bottom-right corner of the History list. Alternatively, starting on the Home screen, tap Settings⇨Safari⇨Clear History. In both instances, per usual, you have a chance to back out without wiping the slate clean.

Saving web pictures

You can capture most pictures you come across on a website — but be mindful of any potential copyright violations, depending on what you plan to do with the images. To copy an image from a website, follow these steps:

Figure 4-9: Hold your finger against a picture in Safari to save it to the iPad.

1. **Press your finger against the image.**

2. **Tap the Save Image button that appears, as shown in Figure 4-9.**

   Saved images end up in your Photos library in the Camera Roll, from which they can be synced back to a computer.

   Tap Copy instead, and you can paste the image into an e-mail or as a link in a program, such as Notes.

   In some cases, typically advertisements, you also see an Open button or an Open in New Tab button, which takes you to the ad image.

Sharing Your Web Experiences

When you find a great website that you just must share, Safari lets you tweet it, post it to Facebook, or — go old-school — and print it.

To make Twitter and Facebook work, of course, the iPad must know your username and password, which you can fill in inside Settings (see Chapter 15).

Tap the Action button, and you find these sharing options:

- **AirDrop:** Share the page with other people who have compatible devices and AirDrop. You'll need to turn on AirDrop in Control Center (just drag upward from the bottom of the screen). Then you can choose whether to make your iPad discoverable to everyone or only people in your contacts. AirDrop works only with fourth-generation iPads or later and the iPad mini.

- **Message:** Send a link to the web page in a text or an iMessage.

- **Mail:** The Mail program opens with a link for the page in the message and the name of the site or page in the Subject line.

- **Twitter:** The iPad adds a link to the web page to an outgoing tweet. Of course, you must fill in the rest of the actual post.

- **Facebook:** Post the page — and whatever comments you choose to add — to the popular social network.

- **Sina Weibo** and **Tencent Weibo:** If available, you post via these Chinese blogging services. You need to activate a Chinese keyboard or language to see these options.

- **Print:** The iPad searches for an AirPrint printer. If you have one, you can choose the number of copies you want. Tap Print to complete the job.

Launching a Mobile Search Mission

Most of us spend a lot of time using search engines on the Internet. And the search engines we summon most often are Google, Yahoo!, and Microsoft Bing, at least in the United States. If you're in China, chances are you search Baidu. In any event, all these search options are available on the iPad.

With iOS 7, Apple brought the previously separate address bar and search fields together into a single convenient, unified strip called the *smart search field,* following the path taken on most popular web browsers for PCs and Macs. Although you can certainly use the virtual keyboard to type *google.com, yahoo. com,* or *bing.com* into this field, Apple doesn't require that tedious effort. Instead, just type your search query directly in the box. The big American-known search engines are available on the iPad, and you can switch from one to another in

Settings. If you've turned on a Chinese keyboard in Settings (see Chapter 2), you also see an option for a popular search engine in China called Baidu.

To conduct a web search on the iPad, tap the smart search field. You immediately see icons for your favorite web destinations, with Apple betting on your frequent return visits. But when you start typing in the smart search field, a Google (or other) search mission commences, with Top Hits — an educated guess, really — shown at the top.

You see other search suggestions as you start tapping additional letters. In Figure 4-10, for example, typing the letters *le* yields such suggestions as Lexmark, LeBron James, and league of legends. Tap any search results that look promising, or tap Go on the keyboard to immediately land on the Top Hit. Or keep tapping out letters to generate more search results.

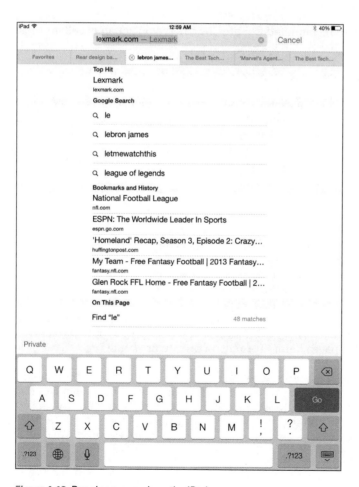

Figure 4-10: Running a search on the iPad.

You can also find a search word or phrase on the very web page you have onscreen. Initially you entered a search term in the search field and scrolled to the bottom of the resulting list to tap On This Page. Because that was unknown to many users, Apple has added a section labeled Find on Page. You're informed of the number of matches; if it's more than one, you can move back and forth through them with the right- and left-pointing arrows at the bottom of the screen.

To switch the search box from Google to Yahoo! to Bing or (if available) Baidu, check out the "Smart Safari Settings" section, later in this chapter.

As mentioned earlier in this chapter, Siri can open Safari — all you have to do is ask. We also mentioned that Siri can (in some cases, anyway) take you to your favorite search engine, just by you uttering the name of a website.

Of course, much of what Siri can do is web-centric. So now is as good a time as any to recommend Chapter 14. There you get an excellent sense of all that she can do.

You also conduct a web search by initiating a Spotlight search. As a reminder, you can summon the Spotlight search field by swiping down from any Home screen. Type (or dictate) your search term and then scroll down to the bottom of the list below any search results that point to the use of the term on the iPad itself (meaning inside messages, notes, apps, and so on). Tap Search Web to search the web with the term you entered, or tap Search Wikipedia to run that search inside the Wikipedia online encyclopedia.

Private Browsing

Don't want to leave any tracks while you surf? Don't worry, we won't ask and we won't tell. Turn on private browsing for a "what happens in Safari stays in Safari" tool. Those truly bent on staying private will also want to tap Clear History, as we mention earlier in this chapter.

To go incognito, tap Bookmarks, and then tap the Private button at the bottom-left corner of the screen. You're given the option to close your existing pages before turning on private browsing.

After private browsing is on, any traces of your visit to nonono.com (or wherever) are nowhere to be found. Your history is wiped clean, open tabs don't appear in iCloud Tabs, and your AutoFill information is not stored anywhere. To remind you that you're browsing privately, the Safari interface takes on a darker shade — a not-so-subtle message here, we suppose, that you might be engaging in a shady or naughty activity. We don't pass judgment. Besides, we assume that you're just a private soul, and we certainly respect that.

To come out of hiding, tap the bookmarks icon and then tap Private again.

The history of pages you've visited can be useful and a huge timesaver, so don't forget to disable this option again when you're done doing whatever it is you don't want people to know you're doing.

You can separately turn on a Do Not Track setting in Settings. Speaking of which, kindly move on to the next section.

Smart Safari Settings

Along with the riches galore found on the Internet are places in cyberspace where you're hassled. You might want to take action to protect your privacy and maintain your security.

To get started, tap the Settings icon on the Home screen and then tap Safari.

The following settings enable you to tell your iPad what you want to be private and how you want to set your security options:

- **Search Engine:** Tap the search engine you desire (just as long as that search engine happens to be Google, Yahoo!, Bing, or Baidu).

- **AutoFill:** Safari can automatically fill out web forms by using your personal contact information, usernames and passwords, or information from your other contacts. Tap AutoFill and then tap the On/Off switch to enable or disable AutoFill.

  - Tap *Use Contact Info* if you're comfortable using the information found about your Contacts.

  - Tap *My Info* to select yourself in your contacts so that Safari knows which address, phone numbers, e-mail addresses, and other information to use when it fills in a form.

  - Tap the *Names & Passwords* On/Off switch to enable or disable Safari's capability to remember usernames and passwords for websites. You also get to decide whether credit card information can be used and saved.

  - Tap *Clear All* to permanently delete all saved AutoFill names and passwords.

Turning on AutoFill can compromise your security if someone gets hold of your iPad.

- **Open New Tabs in Background:** Enable this, and when you open new tabs in Safari, they'll load, even if you're reading a different page in another tab.

- **Favorites/Show Favorites Bar:** Apple lets you quickly access Favorite bookmarks when you enter an address, search, or create a new tab. If you're cool with this, leave the default setting as Favorites. If you enable the Show Favorites Bar option, you'll be able to see Safari's Bookmarks bar between the smart search field and Tab bar.

- **Block Pop-ups:** *Pop-ups* are those web pages that appear whether or not you want them to. Often, they're annoying advertisements. But on some sites, you welcome the appearance of pop-ups, so remember to turn off blocking under such circumstances.

- **Smart Search Field:** We've been talking about the smart search field throughout this chapter. Here you get to pick whether the iPad can provide search engine suggestions, and/or preload the "Top Hit."

- **Cookies:** We're not talking about crumbs you may have accidentally dropped on the iPad. *Cookies* are tiny bits of information that a website places on the iPad when you visit so that the site recognizes you when you return. You need not assume the worst; most cookies are benign.

  If this concept wigs you out, you can take action and block cookies from third parties and advertisers: If you tap the Never option, you will theoretically never again receive cookies on the iPad. Of course, you can always receive cookies too. You can also tap Always to accept cookies from all sites.

  If you set the iPad so that it doesn't accept cookies, certain web pages won't load properly, and other sites such as Amazon won't recognize you or make any of your preferred settings or recommendations available.

  Tap Safari to return to the main Safari Settings page.

- **Clear History:** Tap this button to erase everything in Safari's history, leaving nary a trace of the pages you've visited.

- **Clear Cookies and Data:** Tap this button to clear all your stored cookies (see the earlier bullet on cookies for more details).

- **Fraudulent Website Warning:** Safari can warn you when you land on a site whose producers have sinister intentions. The protection is better than nothing, but don't let down your guard. The Fraud Warning feature isn't foolproof. The setting is on by default.

✔ **JavaScript:** Programmers use JavaScript to add various kinds of functionality to web pages, from displaying the date and time to changing images when you mouse over them. However, some security risks have also been associated with JavaScript. If you do turn it off, though, some things might not work as you expect. But this setting is found under the Advanced topic for a reason, meaning that Apple doesn't think too many of you should mess with this setting. We generally leave things as they are, but go with whatever makes you comfortable.

✔ **Advanced:** Although the Advanced settings are indeed advanced, you can drop by if you're curious about how much data you're consuming at different sites. Those statistics are found here. Developers may also drop in on Advanced settings to turn on a Web Inspector feature that most readers of this book need not — in most instances, anyway — concern themselves with.

5

The E-Mail Must Get Through

....

....

*O*n any computing device, e-mails come and go with a variety of emotions. Messages may be amusing or sad, frivolous, or serious. Electronic missives on the iPad are almost always touching.

The reason, of course, is that you're touching the display to compose and read messages. Okay, so we're having a little fun with the language. But the truth is, the bundled Mail application on the iPad is a modern program designed not only to send and receive text e-mail messages, but also to handle rich HTML e-mail messages — formatted with font and type styles and embedded graphics. If someone sends you mail with a picture, it's quite likely that the picture is visible right in the body of the message. (That's the default behavior, but your results may vary depending on the sender's e-mail capabilities and your iPad's mail settings.)

Furthermore, your iPad can read several types of file attachments, including (but not limited to) PDFs, JPG images, Microsoft Word documents, PowerPoint slides, and Excel spreadsheets, as well as stuff produced through Apple's own iWork software. Better still, all this sending and receiving of text, graphics, and documents can happen in the background so that you can surf the web or play a game while your iPad quietly and efficiently handles your e-mail behind the scenes.

Apple even lets you grant VIP status to important senders so that there's almost no chance you'll miss mail from the people who matter most. Let's see, there's your spouse, your kids, your boss . . . are we missing anybody?

Prep Work: Setting Up Your Accounts

First things first. To use Mail, you need an e-mail address. If you have broadband Internet access (that is, a cable modem, FiOS, or DSL), you probably received one or more e-mail addresses when you signed up. If you're one of the handful of readers who doesn't already have an e-mail account, you can get one for free from Yahoo! (`http://mail.yahoo.com`), Google (`http://mail.google.com`), AOL (`www.aol.com`), or numerous other service providers.

Or you can get a free premium e-mail account (for example, `Your_Name@iCloud.com`) from Apple as part of iCloud. From your Home screen, just tap Settings➪Mail, Contacts, Calendars➪iCloud.

Many free e-mail providers add a small bit of advertising at the end of your outgoing messages. If you'd rather not be a billboard for your e-mail provider, either use the address(es) that came with your broadband Internet access (`yourname@comcast.net` or `yourname@att.net`, for example) or pay a few dollars a month for a premium e-mail account that doesn't tack advertising (or anything else) onto your messages.

Finally, while the rest of the chapter focuses on the Mail app, you can also use Safari to access most e-mail systems, if that's your preference.

Setting up your account the easy way

Chapter 3 explains the option of automatically syncing the e-mail accounts on your Mac or Windows PC with your iPad. If you chose that option, your e-mail accounts should be configured on your iPad already. You may proceed directly to the later section "See Me, Read Me, File Me, Delete Me: Working with Messages."

If you haven't yet chosen that option but want to set up your account the easy way now, go to Chapter 3, read about syncing e-mail accounts, and then sync your iPad with your Mac or PC. Then you, too, can proceed directly to the section "See Me, Read Me, File Me, Delete Me: Working with Messages," later in this chapter.

Remember that syncing e-mail accounts doesn't have any effect on your e-mail messages; it merely synchronizes the *settings* for e-mail accounts so you don't have to set them up manually on your iPad.

Setting up your account the less-easy way

If you don't want to sync the e-mail accounts on your Mac or PC, you can set up an e-mail account on your iPad manually. It's not quite as easy as clicking a box and syncing your iPad, but it's not rocket science either. Here's how you get started:

✔ **If you have no e-mail accounts on your iPad,** the first time you launch Mail, you see the Welcome to Mail screen. Your choices are iCloud, Microsoft Exchange (business e-mail), Google (Gmail), Yahoo!, AOL, Microsoft Outlook.com, and Other.

Merely tap the account type you want to add to the iPad and follow the steps in the next section, the section "Setting up an account with another provider," or the section "Setting up corporate e-mail," later in this chapter.

✔ **If you have one or more e-mail accounts on your iPad already and want to add a new account manually,** tap Settings on the Home screen and then tap Mail, Contacts, Calendars➪Add Account.

You see an Add Account screen shown in Figure 5-1, with the same account options that are shown on the Welcome to Mail screen. Proceed to one of the next three sections, depending on the type of e-mail account you selected.

Setting up an e-mail account with iCloud, Gmail, Yahoo!, AOL, or Microsoft Outlook

If your account is with iCloud, Gmail, Yahoo!, AOL, or Outlook, follow these steps:

1. **Tap the appropriate button on the Welcome to Mail screen. (See Figure 5-1.)**

2. **Enter your name, e-mail address, password, and optional description, as shown in Figure 5-2.**

   You can describe this account (such as Work or Personal), but the field tends to fill in automatically with the same contents in the Address field unless you tell it differently.

3. **Tap the Next button in the upper-right corner of the screen.**

   You're finished. That's all there is to setting up your account. You can now proceed to "See Me, Read Me, File Me, Delete Me: Working with Messages."

Figure 5-1: Tap a button to set up an account.

REMEMBER

On June 30, 2012, Apple completed the transition from MobileMe to iCloud. Apple says that if you had an active MobileMe account when you signed up for iCloud, you can keep your me.com or mac.com e-mail address and any e-mail aliases you have created.

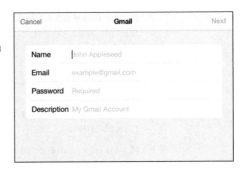

Figure 5-2: Just fill 'em in and tap Next, and you're ready to rock.

Setting up an account with another provider

If your e-mail account is with a provider other than iCloud, Gmail (Google), Yahoo!, AOL, or Microsoft, you have a bit more work ahead of you. You need a bunch of information about your e-mail account that you may not know or have handy.

We suggest that you scan the following instructions, note the items you don't know, and go find the answers before you continue. To find the answers, look at the documentation you received when you signed up for your e-mail account or visit the account provider's website and search there.

Here's how you set up an account:

1. **Starting at the Home screen, tap Settings⇨Mail, Contacts, Calendars⇨Add Account⇨Other.**

2. **Under Mail, tap Add Mail Account.**

3. **Fill in the name, address, password, and description in the appropriate fields, and then tap Next.**

   With any luck, that's all you'll have to do. The iPad will look up and hopefully be able to retrieve your account credentials. If that doesn't happen, continue with Step 4.

4. **Tap the button at the top of the screen that denotes the type of e-mail server this account uses, IMAP or POP, as shown in Figure 5-3.**

Figure 5-3: If you set up an IMAP or POP e-mail account, you may have a few more fields to fill in before you can rock.

5. **Fill in the Internet hostname for your incoming mail server, which looks something like** `mail.`*`providername`*`.com`**.**

6. **Fill in your username and password.**

7. **Enter the Internet hostname for your outgoing mail server, which looks something like** `smtp.`*`providername`*`.com`**.**

8. **Enter your username and password in the appropriate fields.**

9. **Tap the Next (sometimes Save) button in the upper-right corner to create the account.**

   You're now ready to begin using your account. See the section "See Me, Read Me, File Me, Delete Me: Working with Messages."

Some outgoing mail servers don't need your username and password. The fields for these items on your iPad note that they're optional. Still, we suggest that you fill them in anyway. It saves you from having to add them later if your outgoing mail server does require an account name and password, which almost all do these days.

Setting up corporate e-mail

The iPad makes nice with the Microsoft Exchange servers that are a staple in large enterprises, as well as many smaller businesses.

What's more, if your company supports Microsoft Exchange ActiveSync, you can exploit push e-mail so that messages arrive pronto on the iPad, just as they do on your other computers. (To keep everything up to date, the iPad also supports push calendars and push contacts.) For push to work with an Exchange Server — at press time, anyway — your company must be simpatico with one of the last several iterations of Microsoft Exchange ActiveSync. Ask your company's IT or tech department if you run into an issue.

Setting up Exchange e-mail isn't particularly taxing, and the iPad connects to Exchange right out of the box. You still might have to consult your employer's techie-types for certain settings.

Start setting up your corporate e-mail on your iPad by following these steps:

1. **Tap the Exchange listing on the Welcome to Mail or Add Account screen. (Refer to Figure 5-1.)**

2. **Fill in what you can: your e-mail address, domain, username (sometimes** *`domain\user`***), and password. Or call on your IT staff for assistance. Tap Next when you're done.**

3. **On the next screen, as shown in Figure 5-4, enter the Server e-mail address, assuming that the Microsoft Autodiscover service didn't already find it. Tap Next when you're done.**

   That server address may begin with exchange.*company*.com.

4. **Choose which information you want to synchronize through Exchange by tapping each item you want.**

   You can choose Mail, Contacts, Calendars and Reminders. When one of these switches is turned on, a green button is visible, as in Figure 5-5; otherwise, what you see appears dimmed.

5. **Tap Save.**

Figure 5-4: You're on your way to a corporate e-mail account.

The company you work for doesn't want just anybody having access to your e-mail — heaven forbid if your iPad is lost or stolen. So your bosses may insist that you change the passcode lock inside Settings on your iPad. (This is different from the password for your e-mail account.) Skip over to Chapter 15 to find instructions for adding or changing a passcode. (We'll wait for you.) And if your iPad ends up in the wrong hands, your company can remotely wipe the contents clean.

You can choose how long you want the iPad to keep e-mail synchronized. Head to Settings; tap Mail, Contacts, Calendars; and then tap the e-mail account using ActiveSync. Tap Mail Days to Sync, and tap No Limit or pick another time frame (1 day, 3 days, 1 week, 2 weeks, or 1 month).

If you're moonlighting at a second job, you can configure more than one Exchange ActiveSync account on your iPad; prior to iOS 5, there was a limit of just one such account per device.

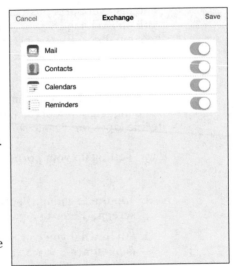

Figure 5-5: Keeping your mail, contacts, and calendars in sync.

See Me, Read Me, File Me, Delete Me: Working with Messages

Now that your e-mail accounts are all set up, it's time to figure out how to receive and read the stuff. Fortunately, you've already done most of the heavy lifting when you set up your e-mail accounts. Getting and reading your mail are a piece of cake.

You can tell when you have unread mail by looking at the Mail icon at the bottom of your Home screen. The cumulative number of unread messages across all your e-mail inboxes appears in a little red capsule in the upper-right area of the icon. If you have many unread messages, you may see the number appear as 4..6 (signifying, in this case, 46,376 messages — yes, we get lots of mail).

This "badge" is the default behavior. If you don't care for it, you can turn it off in the Settings app's Notification Center pane.

In the following sections, you find out how to read messages and attached files and send messages to the Trash or maybe a folder when you're done reading them. Or, if you can't find a message, check out the section on searching your e-mail messages. You can read your e-mail just like you can on a desktop or notebook computer; the way you do so just works a little differently on the iPad's touchscreen.

Reading messages

To read your mail, tap the Mail icon on the Home screen. Remember that what appears onscreen depends on whether you're holding the iPad in landscape or portrait mode, and what was on the screen the last time you opened the Mail app:

- **Landscape:** With the iPad in landscape mode, you see All Inboxes at the top of the Mailboxes section (see Figure 5-6), which, as its name suggests, is a repository for all the messages across all your accounts. The number to the right of All Inboxes (46,922 in Figure 5-6) matches the number (or abbreviated shortcut) on the Mail icon on your Home page. Again, it's the cumulative tally of unread messages across all your accounts.

  Below the All Inboxes listing are the inboxes for your individual accounts. The number to the right of them, as you'd expect, is the number of unread messages in those accounts (39,415 in Gmail and 6,291 in AOL in the example shown in Figure 5-6).

  If you tap an account, you see the available subfolders for that account (Drafts, Sent Mail, Trash, and so on).

Move message

Tap to see all records.　Flag message　Trash

Action

Compose new
message.

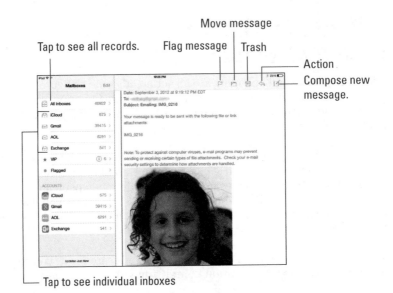

Tap to see individual inboxes

Figure 5-6: When you're holding the iPad sideways, Mail looks something like this.

One of these accounts is the VIP Mailbox. The VIP Mailbox lists all the messages from senders you deem the most important. We tell you how to give someone VIP status in the later section "More things you can do with messages."

Depending on the last time the Mail app was open, you may alternatively see previews of the actual messages in your inbox in the left panel. Previews show the name of the sender, the time a message arrived, the subject header, and the first two lines of the message. (In Settings, you can change the number of lines shown in the preview from one line to five. Or you can show no preview lines.)

✔ **Portrait:** When you hold the iPad in portrait mode, the last incoming message fills the entire screen. Figure 5-7 shows this view. You have to tap an Inbox button (in the upper-left corner of the screen)

Figure 5-7: When you're holding the iPad in portrait mode, the message fills the screen.

to summon a panel that shows other accounts or message previews. You can also summon the panel by swiping from the left edge of the screen to the right. These overlay the message that otherwise fills the screen.

Messages display in *threads,* or conversations, making them easy to follow. Of course, you can still view accounts individually. Follow these steps to read your e-mail:

1. **If the e-mail mailbox you want to see isn't front and center, tap the Mailboxes button in the upper-left corner of the screen to summon the appropriate one.**

   Again, this button may say All Inboxes or some other folder name, and it may say the name of the e-mail account that is currently open. Within an e-mail account, you can see the number of unread messages in each mailbox.

2. **(Optional) Swipe down and release the left panel listing your accounts to summon new messages.**

   You know the iPad is searching for new mail when you see a spinning gear.

3. **Swipe down one of the inboxes or accounts to refresh those specific mailboxes. To summon the unified inbox, tap All Inboxes instead.**

   If a blue dot appears next to a message, the message hasn't been read.

4. **Tap a message to read it.**

5. **When you're done reading, tap the Mailboxes button in the upper-left corner of the message.**

   The button carries different names depending on which account you have open. For example, it may say Exchange, Inbox, or something else.

6. **Read additional messages.**

   When a message is onscreen, the buttons for managing incoming messages appear at the top, most of which you're already familiar with.

   • *In portrait mode:* Tap the up/down arrows that correspond to the next or previous message. (Refer to Figure 5-7.)

   • *In landscape mode (and from within an account):* Tap a preview listing to the left of a message to read the next or previous message or any other visible message on the list. Scroll up or down to find other messages you may want to read.

Threading messages

Apple lets you *thread* messages, or have Mail automatically group related missives. The beauty of this arrangement is that you can easily trace an e-mail conversation. When you organize messages by thread, the related messages appear as a single entry in the mailbox, with a double right-pointing arrow cluing you in that the message is indeed part of a larger ongoing exchange. If a message is not part of a thread, you just see the time, day, or date that that single message arrived. Figure 5-8 (left) shows that Bob and Rebecca are hanging together by a thread — tapping the listing reveals underlying messages that make up the conversation. When you tap the message preview, you see previews of those underlying messages, as shown in Figure 5-8 (right).

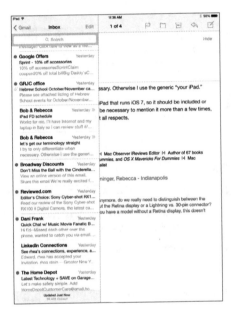
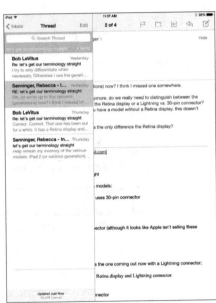

Figure 5-8: Your e-mails are hanging together by a thread.

When you look at a message that's part of a thread, the numbers at the top of the screen (visible in portrait mode) tell you the message's location in the conversation. For example, in Figure 5-8 (right), the message we chose to read is number 2 of 4 in this thread.

To turn on threading, go to the Home screen and tap Settings➪Mail, Contacts, Calendars➪Organize By Thread. Finally, tap the button so that green is visible, as shown in Figure 5-9. You may have to scroll down to see the Organize by Thread setting.

Figure 5-9: Organize by Thread keeps related messages together.

You can search for an item in the thread by scrolling to the top of the thread's Mail listing and typing your query in the Search Thread box. Consider this a prelude to the upcoming section on searching e-mail messages.

Managing messages

Managing messages typically involves either moving the messages to a folder or deleting them. To herd your messages into folders, you have the following options:

- **To create a folder to organize messages you want to keep,** tap an account under the Accounts listings on the left side of the screen, and tap Edit. Tap New Mailbox, and type a name for the mailbox and location for it.

- **To file a message in another folder,** tap the Move Message icon (refer to Figure 5-6). When the list of mailboxes appears, tap the folder where you want to file the message. It's kind of cool watching the entire message fly and land in the new folder that you've designated.

- **To read a message that you've filed away,** tap the folder where the message now resides and then tap the header or preview for the message in question.

- **To delete, move, or mark multiple messages,** tap Edit. In both portrait and landscape, Edit appears at the top of your inbox or another mailbox when those mail folders are selected. Tap Edit, and it becomes a Cancel button, and Delete, Move, and Mark buttons appear at the bottom of the list, as shown in Figure 5-10. Tap each message you want to select so that a check mark appears.

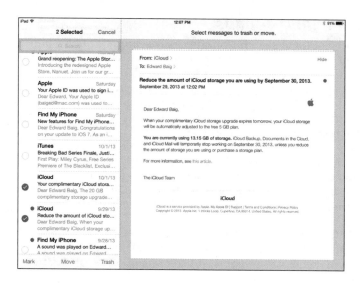

Figure 5-10: Wiping out, moving, or marking messages, *en masse*.

• *Tap Trash* to delete all selected messages.

• *Tap Move* to move all selected messages to another folder, and then tap the new mailbox in which you want those messages to hang out.

• *Tap Mark* to mark all selected messages as Read (and Unread) and Flagged (and Unflagged).

✏ **To delete a single message,** tap the Delete Message icon that resembles a trash can. You have a chance to cancel in case you tap the Delete Message icon by mistake, provided the Ask Before Deleting switch is turned on in Settings.

✏ **To delete a single message without opening it,** swipe one finger in a leftward direction across the message in the mailbox list and then tap the red Delete button that appears to the right of the message. You will also see a More button when you swipe left. Tapping More gives you, well, several more options: From here, you can reply, forward, flag, mark as unread, move to Junk, or move a message elsewhere.

In certain Mail accounts, Gmail being one, the Delete option may be replaced by an Archive option, depending on your preference. That means you're not so much getting rid of a message as stashing it aside, or to be precise, saving the deleted message in your All Mail folder. If the Archive message option does present itself, you can turn the feature on or off in Settings.

Searching e-mails

With Spotlight search, you can easily search through a bunch of messages to find the one you want to read fast — such as that can't-miss stock tip from your broker. You can type **stock** or whichever search term seems relevant in the search box at the top of a mailbox preview pane. All matching e-mails that have already been downloaded appear. And you can run a search to find words within the body of an e-mail message from the Mail app. (For more on Spotlight search, see Chapter 2.)

Search within Mail is really quite powerful. For example, you can search by time-frame by typing something along the lines of "March meetings." That will find all the appropriate messages having to do with meetings that month. You can also search to find just flagged messages from your VIPs ("Flag unread VIP").

Via the iPad, you can also search just the current mailbox or across all your mailboxes. Just scroll to the top of the mailbox previews pane and tap either the All Mailboxes tab or the Current Mailbox tab after you enter your search query.

If you're using Exchange, iCloud, or certain IMAP-type e-mail accounts, you may even be able to search messages that are stored on the server.

Don't grow too attached to attachments

Your iPad can even receive e-mail messages with attachments in a wide variety of popular file formats. (See the nearby sidebar "Keeping files in order" if you're not sure what file formats are.) Which file formats does the iPad support? Glad you asked:

- **Images:** `.jpg`, `.tiff`, `.gif`, `.png`
- **Microsoft Word:** `.doc`, `.docx`
- **Microsoft PowerPoint:** `.ppt`, `.pptx`
- **Microsoft Excel:** `.xls`, `.xlsx`
- **Web pages:** `.htm`, `.html`
- **Apple Keynote:** `.key`
- **Apple Numbers:** `.numbers`
- **Apple Pages:** `.pages`
- **Preview and Adobe Acrobat:** `.pdf`
- **Rich Text:** `.rtf`
- **Text:** `.txt`
- **Contact information:** `.vcf`

If the attachment is a file format that the iPad doesn't support (for example, an Adobe Photoshop `.psd` file), you see the name of the file, but you can't open it on your iPad, at least without an assist from third-party apps that you may have installed.

Keeping files in order

In very simple terms, computers of any type, including tablets like the iPad — and the software that runs on them — must have some way to recognize the files that run on the system and to act appropriately upon them. Long ago, the bright minds in technology cooked up standard ways to organize the layout of data so files that serve a particular purpose adhere to a similar structure. You recognize such files by *filename extension,* the suffix that is separated by a dot or period after its name. Of course, many more file formats exist than most folks will ever need to become familiar with. But you — or, more precisely, the hardware and software you're working with — will encounter some popular file types repeatedly. Such formats include `.doc` for Microsoft Word documents and `.jpg` for images. If any computer you're using ever encounters files that don't seem to open or respond, it's likely because the machine doesn't have the software to recognize such files. The good news is that the iPad supports most of the common file types it encounters, though not quite every file type.

Here's how to read a supported attachment:

1. **Open the e-mail that contains the attachment, which you can identify by a little paper clip icon.**

2. **Tap the attachment.**

   It typically appears at the bottom of the message, so you probably need to scroll down to see it.

   In some cases, the attachment downloads to your iPad and opens automatically. In other instances, you may have to tap the Tap to Download button that represents the attachment.

3. **Read or (in the case of a picture) eyeball the attachment.**

4. **Tap the attachment you're reading (in the case of a document), and tap Done to return to the message text.**

   Or you can (again, for a document) open the Pages word processor if you've purchased that application or downloaded it free if you bought a device with iOS 7. You can also open the doc in certain other apps you may have. Incidentally, the documents you create in the Pages app are automatically saved to your iPad. With the latest version of Pages, you can also save a document to iCloud, where it can be made available automatically to the version of Pages for Mac computers. If you have a Windows PC, you can work with an iCloud version of Pages.

You can open an attachment from a different app than may have otherwise been summoned to duty. Just touch and hold the attachment in the e-mail, and then tap the app from the options that present themselves. For example, you might open a Word document with Apple's Pages word processor if that optional app resides on your iPad (or in an online storage locker such as Dropbox).

More things you can do with messages

Wait! You can do even more with your incoming e-mail messages:

- ✔ **To see all recipients of a message,** tap the right-pointing arrow to the right of the sender's name.

  If all recipients are displayed, you will see the word; tap it to hide all names except the sender's.

- ✔ **To add an e-mail recipient or sender to your contacts,** tap the name or e-mail address at the top of the message and then tap Create New Contact or Add to Existing Contact.

- ✔ **To make a sender a VIP,** tap the name or e-mail address at the top of the message and then tap Add to VIP. You may want to give VIP status to the important people in your life, such as your significant other, family members, boss, or doctor. A star appears next to any incoming messages from a VIP. You can summon mail from all your VIPs by tapping the VIP folder in the list of Mailboxes. To demote a VIP to what we jokingly refer to as an NVIP (translation: not very important person), tap the name or e-mail at the top of the message and then tap Remove from VIP.

✔ **To mark a message as unread or to flag it,** tap the Flag icon at the top of a message. These options appear:

- *Mark as Unread:* Choose Mark as Unread for messages that you may want to revisit at some point but which don't necessarily have some special significance. The message is again included in the unread message count on the Mail icon on your Home screen, and its mailbox again has a blue dot next to it in the message list for that mailbox. You can tap Mark as Read if the message loses its significance.

- *Flag:* Choose Flag for those messages that deserve special status or that you want to find again in a hurry.

- *Move to Junk:* We all get crap e-mail. This option moves those messages to your junk pile.

✔ **To zoom in and out of a message,** use the pinch and unpinch gestures, at which we suspect you now excel. See Chapter 2 if you need help with your touchscreen moves.

✔ **To follow a link in a message,** tap the link. Links typically display in blue, but sometimes in other colors and sometimes underlined. If the link is a URL, Safari opens and displays the web page. If the link is a phone number, the iPad gives you the chance to add it to your contacts (or copy it). If the link is a map, Maps opens and displays the location. If you tap a date, you can create an event on that date or show it in Calendar. And, last but not least, if the link is an e-mail address, a new preaddressed blank e-mail message is created.

If the link opens Safari, Contacts, or Maps, and you want to return to your e-mail, press the Home button on the front of your iPad and then tap the Mail icon. Or double-press the Home button and select the Mail icon from the gallery of running apps.

Darling, You Send Me (E-Mail)

Sending e-mail on your iPad is a breeze. You'll encounter several subspecies of messages: pure text, text with a photo, a partially finished message (a *draft*) that you want to save and complete later, or a reply to an incoming message. You can also forward an incoming message to someone else — and in some instances print messages. The following sections examine these message types one at a time.

Sending an all-text message

To compose a new e-mail message, tap Mail on the Home screen. Once again, what you see next depends on how you're holding your iPad. In landscape mode, your e-mail accounts or e-mail folders are listed in a panel along the left side of the screen, with the actual message filling the larger window on the right.

Now, to create a new message, follow these steps:

1. **Tap the Compose New Message button. (Refer to Figure 5-6.)**

   The New Message screen, like the one shown in Figure 5-11, appears (except your new message won't have text typed in the message body yet).

2. **Type the names or e-mail addresses of the recipients in the To field, or tap the + button to the right of the To field to choose a contact(s) from your iPad's contacts list.**

   If you start typing an e-mail address, e-mail addresses that match what you typed appear in a list below the To or Cc field. If the correct one is in the list, tap it to use it.

3. **(Optional) Tap the field labeled Cc/Bcc, From.**

   Doing so breaks the field into separate Cc, Bcc, and From fields, as shown in Figure 5-11.

   The Cc/Bcc label stands for *carbon copy/blind carbon copy. Carbon copy* (a throwback term from another era) is kind of an FYI to a recipient. It's like saying, "We figure you'd appreciate knowing this, but you don't need to respond."

   When using Bcc, you can include a recipient on the message, but other recipients can't

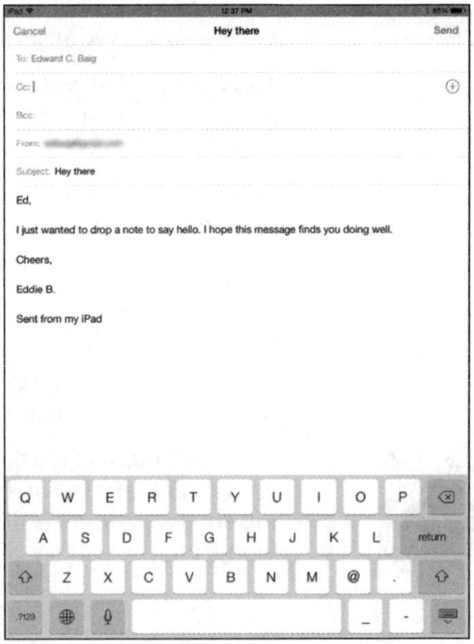

Figure 5-11: The New Message screen appears, ready for you to start typing the recipient's name.

see that this recipient has been included. It's great for those secret agent e-mails! Tap the respective Cc or Bcc field to type names. Or tap the + symbol that appears in those fields to add a contact.

4. **(Optional) If you tap From, you can choose to send the message from any of your e-mail accounts on the fly, assuming, of course, that you have more than one account set up on the iPad.**

5. **Type a subject in the Subject field.**

   The subject is optional, but it's considered poor form to send an e-mail message without one.

6. **Type your message in the message area.**

   The message area is immediately below the Subject field. You have ample space to get your message across.

   Apple includes a bunch of landscape-orientation keyboards in various applications, including Mail. When you rotate the iPad to its side, you can compose a new message using a wider-format virtual keyboard.

7. **Tap the Send button in the upper-right corner of the screen.**

   Your message wings its way to its recipients almost immediately. If you aren't in range of a Wi-Fi network or a cellular network when you tap Send, the message is sent the next time you're in range of one of these networks.

Formatting text in an e-mail

One of the goodies in Mail is the capability to format e-mail text by underlining, bolding, or italicizing it. First you select the text by pressing your finger against the screen until you see the options to select some or all of the text. After making your selection, you see various other options: Cut, Copy, Paste, BIU, Quote Level, or Insert Photos or Video. To format text, tap the BIU button. Then apply whichever style (Bold, Italics, Underline) suits your fancy.

If you tap Quote Level — another option that appears when you tap the right-pointing arrow after selecting a word — you can quote a portion of a message you're responding to. *Note:* Increase Quote Level must be turned on in Settings. You can also increase or decrease the indentation in your outgoing message.

Sending a photo with an e-mail message

Sometimes a picture is worth a thousand words. When that's the case, here's how to send an e-mail message with a photo attached:

1. **Tap the Photos icon on the Home screen.**

2. **Find the photo you want to send.**

3. **Tap the Action button (the little rectangle with the arrow springing out of it) in the bottom-left corner of the screen.**

4. **Tap the Mail button.**

   An e-mail message appears onscreen with the photo already attached. In fact, the image may appear to be embedded in the body of the message, but the recipient receives it as a regular e-mail attachment.

   On the Cc/Bcc line of your outgoing message, you see the size of the attached image. If you tap the size of the image shown, a new line appears, giving you the option to choose an alternative size among Small, Medium, Large, or Actual Size (in other words, keeping what you have). Your choice affects both the visible dimensions and file size of the photo (with the actual sizes of the file as measured in kilobytes or megabytes reported for each possible choice).

5. **Choose what size you want to send your photo.**

6. **Address the message and type whatever text you like, as you did for an all-text message in the preceding section, and then tap the Send button.**

You actually have an alternative way of inserting pictures (or videos) into your outgoing mail messages. In the preceding "Formatting text in an e-mail" section, we mention an Insert Photos or Video option that appears after you press your finger against the body of a message that you are composing. Tap Insert Photos or Video, tap the album in which the photo (or video) you want to send exists, and then tap that photo or video. Tap Use to embed the image and proceed with addressing (if not already addressed), composing, and sending the message.

Saving an e-mail to send later

Sometimes you start an e-mail message but don't have time to finish it. When that happens, you can save it as a draft and finish it some other time. Here's how:

1. **Start an e-mail message, as described in one of the two previous sections.**

2. **When you're ready to save the message as a draft, tap the Cancel button in the upper-left corner of the screen.**

3. **Tap the Save Draft button if you want to save this message as a draft and complete it another time.**

If you tap the Delete Draft button, the message disappears immediately without a second chance. Don't tap Delete Draft unless you mean it.

To work on the message again, tap the Drafts mailbox. A list of all messages you saved as drafts appears. Tap the draft you want to work on, and it reappears on the screen. When you're finished, you can tap Send to send it or tap Cancel to save it as a draft again.

The number of drafts appears to the right of the Drafts folder, the same way that the number of unread messages appears to the right of other mail folders, such as your inbox.

Replying to, forwarding, or printing an e-mail message

When you receive a message and want to reply to it, open the message and then tap the Action button (the curved arrow at the upper-right corner of the screen, as shown in Figure 5-12). Then tap the Reply, Reply All, Forward, or Print button, described as follows:

Figure 5-12: Reading and managing an e-mail message.

- ✔ **Reply and Reply All:** The Reply button creates an e-mail message addressed to the sender of the original message, with the content of that original message embedded in your reply. The Reply All button creates an e-mail message addressed to the sender and all other recipients of the original message, plus Ccs. (The Reply All option appears only if more than one recipient was on the original e-mail.) In both cases, the subject is retained with a *Re:* prefix added. So if the original subject were *iPad Tips,* the reply's subject would be *Re: iPad Tips.*

- ✔ **Forward:** Tapping the Forward button creates an unaddressed e-mail message that contains the text of the original message. Add the e-mail address(es) of the person or people you want to forward the message to, and then tap Send. In this case, rather than a *Re:* prefix, the subject is preceded by *Fwd:.* So this time, the subject would be *Fwd: iPad Tips.*

- ✔ **Print:** Of course, you'd tap Print if you wanted to print using an AirPrint-capable printer.

If you want to add a level of indentation when you forward or reply to a message, tap Settings➪Mail, Contacts, Calendars➪Increase Quote Level. Tap to turn the switch On (if it's not On already).

You can edit the subject line of a reply or a forwarded message or edit the body text of a forwarded message the same way you'd edit any other text. It's usually considered good form to leave the subject lines alone (with the *Re:* or *Fwd:* prefix intact), but you may want to change them sometimes. Now you know that you can.

To send your reply or forwarded message, tap the Send button as usual.

Settings for sending e-mail

You can customize the mail you send and receive in lots of ways. In this section, we explore settings for sending e-mail. Later in this chapter, we show you settings that impact the way you receive and read messages. In each instance, start by tapping Settings on the Home screen.

You can customize your mail in the following ways:

- **To hear an alert when you successfully send a message:** From the main Settings screen, tap Sounds. Make sure that the Sent Mail setting is turned on. You'll know because you'll see a sound type listed (among alert sounds and ring tones), "Swoosh" by default. If you tap Sent Mail in settings, you can select another sound besides Swoosh or choose None if going silent is your preference.

  If you want to change other settings, tap the Sounds button at the top of the screen. If you're finished setting the settings, tap the Home button on the front of your iPad.

  No matter what setting you've just accessed, if you want to continue using Settings, tap whichever left-pointing button appears at the top of the screen — sometimes it's General, sometimes Mail, sometimes Contacts, or sometimes something else. After you return to the previous screen, you can change other settings. Similarly, you can tap the Home button on the front of your iPad when you're finished setting any setting. That action always saves the changes you just made and returns you to the Home screen.

- **To add a signature line, phrase, or block of text to every e-mail message you send:** Tap Settings⇨Mail, Contacts, Calendars⇨Signature on the right. The default signature is *Sent from my iPad.* You can add text before or after it, or delete it and type something else. Your signature is affixed to the end of all your outgoing e-mail. You can choose a signature that is the same across all your accounts or select different signatures for each account.

- **To have your iPad send you a copy of every message you send:** Tap Settings⇨Mail, Contacts, Calendars and then turn on the Always Bcc Myself setting.

✓ **To set the default e-mail account for initiating e-mail from outside the Mail application:** Tap the Settings icon on the Home screen and then tap Mail, Contacts, Calendars⇨Default Account. Tap the account you want to use as the default. For example, when you want to e-mail a picture directly from the Photos application, this designated e-mail account is the one that's used. Note that this setting applies only if you have more than one e-mail account on your iPad.

Setting Your Message and Account Settings

This final discussion of Mail involves more settings that deal with your various e-mail accounts.

Checking and viewing e-mail settings

Several settings affect the way you can check and view e-mail. You might want to modify one or more, so we describe what they do and where to find them:

✓ **To specify how often the iPad checks for new messages:** Tap the Settings icon on the Home screen; tap Mail, Contacts, Calendars⇨Fetch New Data. You're entering the world of *fetching* or *pushing*. Check out Figure 5-13 to glance at your options. If your e-mail program (or, more precisely, the e-mail server behind it) supports push and the Push setting is enabled on your iPad, fresh messages are sent to your iPad automatically as soon as they hit the server. If you turned off push or your e-mail program doesn't support it in the first place, the iPad fetches data instead. Choices for fetching are Every 15 Minutes, Every 30 Minutes, Hourly, and Manually. Tap the one you prefer. With push e-mail, messages can show up on the Lock screen and in the Notification Center.

✓ **To hear an alert sound when you receive a new message:** Tap Sounds on the main Settings screen and then tap the New Mail setting. The Ding sound is

Figure 5-13: Fetch or push? It's your call.

there by default. Do nothing if you're satisfied with the Ding you hear each time a new message arrives. If you aren't satisfied, tap New Mail and select an alternative sound from the list, or tap None if you don't want to hear any such alert.

✔ **To set the number of lines of each message to be displayed in the message list:** From the main Settings screen, tap Mail, Contacts, Calendars⇨Preview; then choose a number. Your choices are None, 1, 2, 3, 4, and 5 lines of text. The more lines of text you display in the list, the fewer messages you can see at a time without scrolling. Think before you choose 4 or 5.

✔ **To specify whether the iPad shows the To and Cc labels in message lists:** From the main Settings screen, tap Mail, Contacts, Calendars and turn the Show To/Cc Label setting on or off.

✔ **To turn the Ask before Deleting warning on or off:** From the main Settings screen, tap Mail, Contacts, Calendars; then turn the Ask Before Deleting setting on or off. If this setting is turned on, you need to tap the Trash icon at the bottom of the screen and then tap the red Delete button to confirm the deletion. When the setting is turned off, tapping the Trash icon deletes the message, and you never see a red Delete button.

✔ **To specify whether the iPad will automatically display images that are embedded in an e-mail:** Tap Load Remote Images so that the On button displays. If it's off, you can still manually load remote images. Certain security risks have been associated with loading remote images, and they can also hog bandwidth.

✔ **To organize your mail by thread:** Tap Organize By Threads so that the setting is on.

Altering account settings

The last group of settings we explore in this chapter deals with your e-mail accounts. You most likely will never need most of these settings, but we'd be remiss if we didn't at least mention them briefly. So here they are, whether you need 'em or not:

✔ **To stop using an e-mail account:** Tap the Settings icon on the Home screen; tap Mail, Contacts, Calendars⇨*Account Name* and flip the switch so that Mail is turned off. As a reminder, when Mail is on, you see green by the Mail switch. Otherwise, the switch is gray.

This setting doesn't delete the account; it only hides it from view and stops it from sending or checking e-mail until you turn it on again. (You can repeat this step to turn off Calendars, Contacts, Reminders, and Notes within a given account.)

✏ **To delete an e-mail account:** Tap the Settings icon on the Home screen; tap Mail, Contacts, Calendars⇨*Account Name*⇨Delete Account⇨Delete. Tap Cancel if you change your mind and don't want your account blown away.

You can find still more advanced Mail settings, reached the same way: Tap the Settings icon on the Home screen; tap Mail, Contacts, Calendars; and then tap the name of the account you want to work with.

The settings you see under Advanced (sometimes shown as Advanced Settings) and how they appear vary by account. This list describes some of the settings you might see:

✏ **To specify how long until deleted messages are removed permanently from your iPad:** Tap Advanced⇨Remove. Your choices are Never, After One Day, After One Week, and After One Month. Tap the choice you prefer.

✏ **To choose whether drafts, sent messages, and deleted messages are stored on your iPad or on your mail server:** Tap Advanced and then choose the setting under Mailbox Behaviors stored On My iPad or stored On the Server. You can decide for Drafts, Sent Messages, and Trash. If you choose to store any or all of them on the server, you can't see them unless you have an Internet connection (Wi-Fi or cellular). If you choose to store them on your iPad, they're always available, even if you don't have Internet access. Under Mailbox behaviors, in certain circumstances, you also get to determine whether to delete or archive discarded messages.

We strongly recommend that you don't change these next two items unless you know exactly what you're doing and why. If you're having problems with sending or receiving mail, start by contacting your ISP (Internet service provider), e-mail provider, or corporate IT person or tech department. Then change these settings only if they tell you to. Again, these settings and exactly where and how they appear vary by account.

✏ **To reconfigure mail server settings:** Tap Host Name, User Name, or Password in the Incoming Mail Server or Outgoing Mail Server section of the account settings screen and make your changes.

✏ **To adjust Use SSL, Authentication, IMAP Path Settings, or Server Port:** Tap Advanced and then tap the appropriate item and make the necessary changes.

And that, as they say in baseball, retires the side. You're now fully qualified to set up e-mail accounts and send and receive e-mail on your iPad. But, as the late Apple cofounder Steve Jobs was wont to say, there is one more thing. . . .

Getting the iMessage

The Messages app lets you exchange iMessages, pictures, contacts, videos, audio recordings, and locations with anyone using an Apple i-device with iOS 5 or higher or with a Mac running OS X Mountain Lion or OS X Mavericks.

In the following sections, find out how each of the iMessages features works.

Sending iMessages

Tap the Messages icon on the Home screen to launch the Messages app and then tap the Compose New Message button, the little pencil-and-paper icon in the upper-left corner of the screen (on the Messages list) to start a new text message.

At this point, with the To field active and awaiting your input, you can do three things:

- ✐ **If the recipient *is* in your Contacts list, type the first few letters of the name.** A list of matching contacts appears. Scroll through it if necessary and tap the name of the contact.

  The more letters you type, the shorter the list becomes. And after you've tapped the name of a contact, you can begin typing another name so that you can send this message to multiple recipients at once.

- ✐ **Tap the blue circled + icon on the right side of the To field to select a name from your Contacts list.**

- ✐ **If the recipient *isn't* in your Contacts list, type his or her phone number or e-mail address.**

You have a fourth option if you want to compose the message first and address it later. Tap inside the text-entry field (the narrow rectangular area just above the keyboard and to the left of the Send button) to activate it and then type (or dictate) your message. When you've finished typing, tap the To field and use one of the preceding techniques to address your message.

You aren't limited to sending an iMessage to a single person. To initiate a group message, type the names or phones numbers of everyone you want to include in the To field.

When you've finished addressing and composing, tap the Send button to send your message on its merry way. And that's all there is to it.

Being a golden receiver: Receiving iMessages

First things first. Decide whether you want to hear an alert when you receive a message:

- ✔ **If you want to hear an alert sound when you receive a message,** tap the Settings icon on your Home screen, tap Sounds⇨Text Tone, and then tap one of the available sounds. You can audition the sounds by tapping them. (Ed, as a film buff, prefers the "Noir" sound.) If you have a Mac, you can create your own text tones in GarageBand.

  You hear the sounds when you audition them in the Settings app, even if you have the ring/silent switch set to Silent. After you exit the Settings app, however, you *won't* hear a sound when a message arrives if the ring/silent switch is set to Silent.

- ✔ **If you *don't* want to hear an alert when a message arrives,** (instead of tapping one of the listed sounds) tap the first item in the list of alert tones: None.

- ✔ **If you don't want any messages, you can turn iMessages off.** The Do Not Disturb feature that arrived with iOS 6 lives up to its name. Flip the switch in Settings so the setting is turned on, and you see a moon icon in the status bar. Even easier, turn Do Not Disturb on via Control Center, and you won't be inundated with messages. For more about this feature and other settings, head to Chapter 15.

The following pointers explain what you can do with iMessages that you receive:

- ✔ **Receiving a message when your iPad is asleep:** All or part of the text and the name of the sender appear on the Unlock screen, as shown in Figure 5-14. Slide to the right to reply to a specific message, as we're doing to the first message in Figure 5-14 (you still will have to get past any passcodes first).

Figure 5-14: This is what message notifications look like when your iPad is slumbering.

✔ **Receiving a message when your iPad is awake and unlocked:** All or part of the message and the name of the sender appear at the top of the screen in front of whatever's already there. If what's already there is your Home screen, as shown in Figure 5-15, you'll notice that the Messages icon displays the number of unread messages.

Figure 5-15: This is what a notification looks like when your iPad is awake.

All these notifications are on by default; turn them off in the Settings app's Notification Center pane if you don't care for them. And you'll also see any notifications for messages you've received in Notification Center.

✔ **Reading or replying to a message:** Tap the Messages icon on your Home screen, swipe downward from the top of the screen to display the Notification Center, or tap the notification if you can be quick about it (it fades away in a few seconds).

✔ **Following the conversation:** Each conversation you have is saved as a series of text bubbles. Your messages appear on the right side of the screen in blue bubbles; the other person's messages appear on the left in gray ones, as shown in Figure 5-16. When your message has been delivered, that fact will be noted just below the last bubble in your exchange, as you'll also see in

Figure 5-16: This is what an iMessage conversation looks like.

Figure 5-16. If there was a problem delivering the message, you will see Not Delivered instead. If at first you don't succeed, try again.

✔ **Forwarding a conversation:** If you want to forward all or part of a conversation to another iMessage user, press against a text bubble and tap the More button. This brings up a Forward button at the bottom-right hand corner of the screen (it appears as a curved arrow). Tap any additional text, photo, or video bubbles you want to forward (the one you pressed to summon the More button is already selected) so a check mark appears in a circle to the left of all bubbles you want to forward. Then tap the Forward button at the lower right of the screen. The contents of the text bubbles with check marks are copied to a new text message; specify a recipient and then tap Send.

✔ **Deleting part of a single conversation thread:** Press against a text bubble and tap More. A circle appears to the left of each text bubble. Tap a text bubble and a check mark appears in the circle. When you've added a check mark to all the text bubbles you want to delete, tap the Delete button (it resembles a trash can) at the bottom of the screen, and then tap Delete Message(s). Or, to delete the entire conversation in one fell swoop, tap the Delete All button at the top of the screen and then tap Delete Conversation.

✔ **Deleting an entire conversation thread:** Tap the Edit button at the upper left of the Messages list, tap the red – (minus) icon that appears to the left of the person's name, and then tap the Delete button that appears to the right of the name.

Sending pix and vids in a message

To send a picture or video in a message, follow the instructions for sending a text message and then tap the Camera icon to the left of the text-entry field at the bottom of the screen. You'll then have the option of using an existing picture or video or taking a new one. You can also add text to photos or videos. When you're finished, tap the Send button.

If you *receive* a picture or video in a message, it appears in a bubble just like text, as shown in Figure 5-16. Tap it to see it full-screen.

Tap the Action button in the upper-right corner for additional options, such as sharing the image on Facebook or Twitter, assigning it to a contact, or more. If you don't see the icon, tap the picture or video once, and the icon will magically appear.

Smart messaging tricks

Here are some more things you can do with messages:

✔ **Search your messages for a word or phrase.** Type the word or phrase in the Search field at the top of the Messages screen.

✏ **Send Read Receipts to allow others to be notified when you have read their missives.** Tap Settings⇨Messages, and slide the switch so that Send Read Receipts is on.

You can see within iMessages when your own message has been delivered and read, and when the other person is readying a response.

✏ **Use a Bluetooth keyboard for typing instead of the onscreen keyboard.** Follow the instructions in Chapter 15 to pair your Bluetooth keyboard with your iPad.

The Apple Wireless Keyboard ($69) works with the iPad and iPhones. Find out more in Chapter 17.

✏ **Dictate a message (third-generation iPads or later).** Tap the microphone key on your keyboard and start talking. Tap the microphone key again when you're done.

✏ **Open a URL included in an iMessage.** Tap it to open that web page in Safari.

✏ **Send an e-mail to an address included in an iMessage.** Tap it to open a preaddressed e-mail message in Mail.

✏ **See an included street message in an iMessage.** Tap it to see it on a map in Maps.

✏ **Choose how you can be reached via iMessage.** Tap Settings⇨ Messages⇨Send & Receive. From there, you can add another e-mail address or remove any addresses that are already present. You can also pick the e-mail address (or phone number) to from where to start new conversations.

✏ **Show the Subject field.** Flip the switch to show a Subject field with your messages.

✏ **Block a sender.** If someone is harassing you or has left your good graces, you can block him or her. Choose Settings⇨Messages⇨Blocked and pick a name from your Contacts. You will no longer receive messages or FaceTime calls from this person.

And that's all there is to it. You are now an official iMessage maven.

6

Maps Are Where It Is

*I*n our other book, *iPhone For Dummies,* we say that the Maps feature was one of the sleeper hits of our iPhone experience and an application we both use more than we expected because it's so darn handy. Since we first discovered the Maps app via our iPhones, the app has become better and more capable. With Maps on the iPad or iPhone, you can quickly and easily discover exactly where you are, find nearby restaurants and businesses, get turn-by-turn driving instructions from any address to any other address, and see real-time traffic information and a photographic street view of many locations as well.

The Maps app has improved a lot since Apple took it over (from Google) in iOS 6. And as much as we loved the Google-based Maps app in iOS 1 through 5, we're starting to love the new one even more.

Apple says it's "beautifully designed from the ground up (and the sky down)", and we have to agree — it's more beautiful than ever. But beyond its good looks, zooming in and out is faster than ever, and the spoken turn-by-turn navigation with real-time traffic updates actually works in most places. Plus it has a cool 3D flyover view.

You can't use the Maps app unless you're connected to the Internet via Wi-Fi, 3G, or 4G. See Chapter 1 to find out how to connect.

Finding Your Current Location with Maps

We start with something supremely simple yet extremely useful — determining your current location. At the risk of sounding like self-help gurus, here's how to find yourself:

1. **Make sure Location Services is enabled by tapping Settings⇨Privacy⇨Location Services.**

   Tap the Location Services and Maps switches to On (green) if necessary.

2. **Tap the Home button to return to the Home screen.**

3. **Tap the Maps icon on your Home screen.**

4. **Tap the little arrow icon in the lower-left corner of the screen.**

   The arrow icon turns blue, as shown in the margin, which assures you that Location Services is doing its thing and you'll soon see a blue circle (see Figure 6-1), which indicates your approximate location.

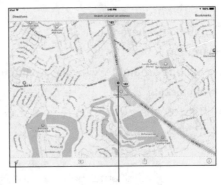

Just so you know, if you tap, drag the map, or zoom in and/or out, your iPad continues to update your location, but it doesn't continue to center the marker. That's a good thing, but it also means that the location indicator can move off the screen. If that happens, or you move around and the

Tap to find your location.

Your current location

Figure 6-1: A blue marker shows your GPS location.

location indicator moves away from the middle of the screen, just tap the arrow icon. Your iPad updates your location and adjusts the map so your location indicator is in the middle of the screen.

Searching

The Maps app wouldn't be very useful if you couldn't use it to find things. In the following sections, we show you how to search for places you want to go and people you want to see — including people you have stored as contacts.

Finding a person, place, or thing

To find a person, place, or thing with Maps, follow these steps:

1. **Tap the Search field at the top of the screen to make the keyboard appear, and then type what you're looking for.**

   You can search for addresses, zip codes, intersections, towns, landmarks, and businesses by category and by name, or in combinations such as *New York, NY 10022; pizza 60645;* or even *BBQ Lockhart TX.*

2. **(Optional) If the letters you type match names in your contacts list, the matching contacts appear in a list below the Search field; tap a name to see a map of that contact's location.**

   Maps is smart about it, too; it displays only the names of contacts that have a street address. See the section "Connecting maps and contacts," later in this chapter, for more details.

3. **When you finish typing, tap Search.**

   After a few seconds, a map appears. If you searched for a single location, it's marked with a pushpin. If you searched for a category (*BBQ Lockhart TX,* for example), you see multiple pushpins, one for each matching location, as shown in Figure 6-2.

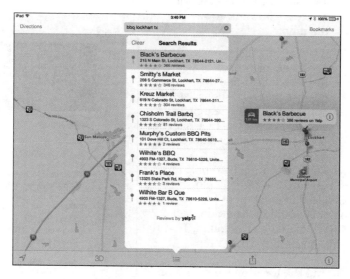

Figure 6-2: If you search for *BBQ Lockhart TX,* you see pushpins for all BBQ joints near Lockhart, TX.

How does Maps do that?

Maps uses iPad's Location Services to determine your approximate location using available information from your wireless data network. Wi-Fi–only models use local Wi-Fi networks; iPad Wi-Fi + 3G and 4G models use assisted GPS plus cellular data. If you're not using Location Services, turning it off conserves your battery.

(To turn it off, tap Settings⇨General⇨Location Services.) Don't worry if Location Services is turned off when you tap the Arrow icon — you're prompted to turn it on. Keep in mind that Location Services may not be available in all areas at all times.

When you tap the Search field, a handy drop-down list shows the search terms you've used recently. Tap any item in the list to search for it again.

Connecting maps and contacts

Maps and contacts go together like peanut butter and jelly. For example, here are two helpful tasks that illustrate maps and contacts at work.

To see a map of a contact's street address, follow these steps:

1. **Tap the Bookmarks button near the top-right corner of the screen.**

2. **Tap the Contacts button at the bottom of the overlay.**

3. **Tap the contact's name whose address you want to see on the map.**

   Alternatively, just type the first few letters of a contact's name in the Search field, and then tap the name in the Suggestions list that appears below the Search field whenever what you type matches one or more contact names.

If you find a location by typing an address into the Search field, you can add that location to one of your contacts or create a new contact with a location you've found. To do either one, follow these steps:

1. **Tap the location's pushpin on the map.**

2. **Tap the little *i* in a circle to the right of the location's name (as shown to the right of Black's Barbecue in Figure 6-2).**

   That contact's Info screen opens. (See Figure 6-3.)

3. **Tap Create New Contact or Add to Existing Contact, whichever is applicable.**

4. **Fill in the new contact information and tap Done. Or, select an existing contact from the list that appears.**

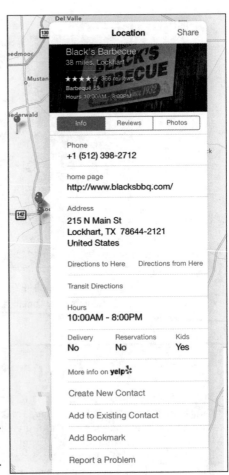

Figure 6-3: The Info screen for Black's Barbecue appears as an overlay.

You work with your contacts by tapping the Contacts icon on your Home screen. Go to Chapter 12 to find out more about the Contacts app.

Don't forget that you can swipe across your iPad screen with four or five fingers to switch apps. So if you're in Contacts, a four- or five-finger swipe from right to left should bring you back to the Maps app. If you have a lot of open apps, you might need more than one swipe to find the Maps app.

And don't forget you could also use a four-finger swipe upward to reveal the multitasking screen.

If nothing happens when you swipe with four or five fingers, tap Settings⇨General, scroll down to the Multitasking Gestures On/Off switch, and make sure it's set to On.

You can also get driving or walking directions from most locations, including a contact's address — to any other location including another contact's address. You see how to do that in the "Smart Map Tricks" section, later in this chapter.

Viewing, Zooming, and Panning

The preceding section talks about how to find just about anything with Maps. Now here's a look at some ways that you can use what you find. First, find out how to work with what you see on the screen. Three views are available at any time: Standard, Hybrid, and Satellite. Select a view by tapping the little *i*-in-a-circle in the lower-right corner of the screen; an overlay appears with the view buttons and several other options, as shown in Figure 6-4.

In Standard, Hybrid, or Satellite view, you can zoom to see either more or less of the map — or scroll (pan) to see what's above, below, or to the left or right of what's on the screen:

✔ **Zoom out:** Pinch the map or tap using *two* fingers. To zoom out even more, pinch or tap using two fingers again.

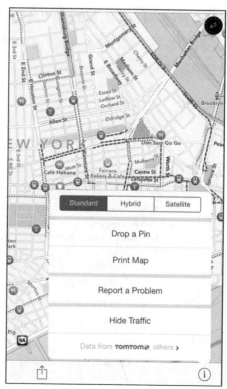

Figure 6-4: Tap the little *i*-in-a-circle to see these options.

This may be a new concept to you. To tap with two fingers, merely tap with two fingers touching the screen simultaneously (rather than the usual one finger).

✔ **Zoom in:** Unpinch the map (some people refer to this gesture as a *spread*) or double-tap (the usual way — with just one finger) the spot you want to zoom in on. Unpinch or double-tap with one finger again to zoom in even more.

An *unpinch* is the opposite of a pinch. Start with your thumb and a finger together and then spread them apart.

You can also unpinch with two fingers or two thumbs, one from each hand, but you'll probably find that a single-handed pinch and unpinch are handier.

✔ **Scroll:** Flick or drag up, down, left, or right to pan your view of the map.

Tap the 3D button at the bottom of the screen to see the map from a three-dimensional bird's-eye view.

Saving Time with Bookmarks, Recents, and Contacts

In Maps, three tools can save you from typing the same locations repeatedly. You see these options on the overlay displayed when you tap the word *Bookmarks* near the upper-left corner of the screen.

At the bottom of this overlay, you see three buttons: Bookmarks, Recents, and Contacts. The following sections give you the lowdown on these buttons.

Bookmarks

Bookmarks in the Maps application work like bookmarks in Safari. When you have a location you want to save as a bookmark so that you can reuse it later without typing a single character, follow these steps:

1. **Tap the little *i* in a blue circle to the right of the location's name or description.**

   The Info screen for that location appears. (Refer to Figure 6-3.)

2. **Tap the Add to Bookmarks button.**

   You may have to scroll down the Info screen to see the Add to Bookmarks button.

After you add a bookmark, you can recall it at any time. To do so, tap the Bookmarks icon, tap the Bookmarks button at the bottom of the overlay, and then tap the bookmark name to see it on a map.

The first things you should bookmark are your home and work addresses and your zip codes. These are things you use all the time with Maps, so you might as well bookmark them now to avoid typing them over and over.

Use zip code bookmarks to find nearby businesses. Choose the zip code bookmark, and then type what you're looking for, such as *78729 pizza, 60645 gas station,* or *90201 Starbucks.*

You can also drop a pin anywhere on the map. A *pin* is similar to a bookmark but is often handier than a bookmark because you can drop it by hand. Why? If you don't know the exact address or zip code for a location but can point it out on a map, you can drop a pin (but you couldn't create a bookmark). You drop a pin as follows:

1. **Tap the little *i* -in-a-circle in the lower-right corner.**

2. **Tap the Drop a Pin button. (Refer to Figure 6-4.)**

   A pin drops onscreen, and you see the words `Dropped Pin` with a little *i* in a blue circle on the right.

3. **Tap and hold the location you want to mark with a pin.**

4. **Tap the little *i*.**

   The Dropped Pin overlay appears. You can fill in some details about the pin and take similar actions to those that appear in the Info screen (refer to Figure 6-3).

To manage your bookmarks, tap the Edit button in the upper-left corner of the Bookmarks overlay. Then:

✔ **To move a bookmark up or down in the Bookmarks list:** Drag the little icon with three gray bars that appears to the right of the bookmark upward to move the bookmark higher in the list or downward to move the bookmark lower in the list.

✔ **To delete a bookmark from the Bookmarks list:** Tap the – sign in a red circle to the left of the bookmark's name and then tap the red Delete button.

When you're finished using bookmarks, tap anywhere outside the overlay to return to the map.

Recents

The Maps app automatically remembers locations you've searched for and directions you've viewed in its Recents list. To see this list, tap the Bookmarks icon, and then tap the Recents button at the bottom of the overlay. To see a recent item on the map, tap the item's name.

To clear the Recents list, tap the Clear button in the upper-left corner of the overlay, and then tap the big red Clear All Recents button at the bottom of the overlay, or tap Cancel if you change your mind.

When you're finished using the Recents list, tap anywhere outside the overlay to return to the map.

Contacts

To see a list of your contacts, tap the Bookmarks icon and then tap the Contacts button at the bottom of the overlay. To see a map of a contact's location, tap the contact's name in the list.

To limit the contacts list to specific groups (assuming that you have some groups in your contacts list), tap the Groups button in the upper-left corner of the overlay and then tap the name of the group. Now only contacts in this group display in the list.

When you're finished using the contacts list, tap the Done button in the upper-right corner of the overlay to return to the map.

Smart Map Tricks

The Maps application has more tricks up its sleeve. Here are a few nifty features you may find useful.

Getting route maps and driving directions

You can get route maps and driving directions to any location from any location (within reason; our tech editor tried to get driving directions from 1600 Pennsylvania Ave. in Washington, DC, to 10 Downing Street in London, but that didn't work) as follows:

1. **Tell your iPad to get directions for you.**

   You can do so in a couple of ways:

   - *When you're looking at a map screen:* Tap the Directions button in the upper-left corner of the screen. The Search field transforms into Start and End fields.

   - *If a pushpin is already on the screen:* Tap the pushpin and then tap the little *i* in a blue circle to the right of the name or description. This action displays the item's Info screen. Tap the Directions to Here or Directions from Here button to get directions to or from that location, respectively.

- *Ask Siri for directions:* Press and hold the Home button, and ask her, "How do I get to ____?" (This, of course, works only if your iPad includes Siri. See Chapter 14 for more on Siri.)

2. **Tap in the Start or End field to designate the starting and ending points of your trip.**

   You can either type them or choose them from a list of your bookmarks, recent maps, or contacts.

3. **(Optional) If you need to swap the starting and ending locations, tap the little swirly arrow button between the Start and End fields.**

4. **(Optional) Tap the car, walking-person, or bus icon above the Start and End fields to choose driving, walking, or public transportation directions.**

   Public transportation directions require a third-party app assist. If you haven't installed one, Maps so informs you and offers to whisk you to the App Store with an automated search for public transit apps.

5. **When the start and end locations are correct, tap the Route button in the upper-right corner of the Directions overlay.**

   Suggested routes appear on the map, as shown in Figure 6-5.

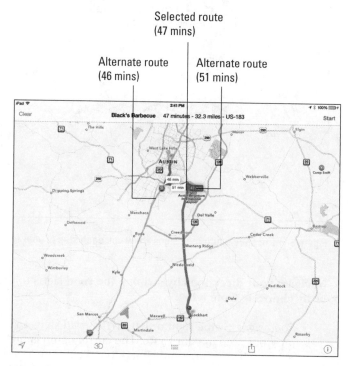

Figure 6-5: Three routing options for travel from the State Capitol in Austin, Texas, to Black's Barbecue in Lockhart, Texas.

If multiple possible routes exist, Maps shows you up to three, as in Figure 6-5. To switch routes, just tap the route you want to switch to. Notice that the text at the top of the screen updates to tell you the time and distance of the selected route (47 minutes; 32.3 miles via US 183 in Figure 6-5).

6. **If Maps suggests several routes, select one by tapping its light blue line or balloon.**

   In Figure 6-5, the 47-minute route is selected.

Tap the little *i*-in-a-circle in the lower-right corner of the map you're viewing and then tap the Show Traffic button to help you decide which route will be most expedient.

7. **Tap the Start button in the upper-right corner of the screen to begin your directions.**

   When you tap the Start button, a series of stark white "road signs" appear across the top of the map, one for each step in the directions, as shown in Figure 6-6.

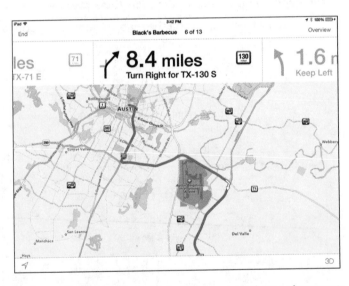

Figure 6-6: The stark white road signs show you each step of your route.

8. **Navigate your directions by swiping the road signs to the left or right or by choosing from a list:**

   • *Road signs:* Swipe right or left on the road signs to see the next or previous step in your route. The current step is highlighted and a blue circle appears on the map to indicate the location of that step. The other (next or previous) steps are dimmed slightly (refer to Figure 6-6).

• *List:* If you prefer to see your driving directions displayed as a list with all the steps at once, tap the Overview button near the top-right corner of the screen and then tap the List button at the bottom of the screen, dead center; the steps appear in an overlay, as shown in Figure 6-7.

The List button appears on the Route screen (refer to Figure 6-5) but disappears when you tap Start (refer to Figure 6-6). Remember to tap the Overview button to make it reappear.

Tap any step in the list to see that leg of the trip displayed on the map.

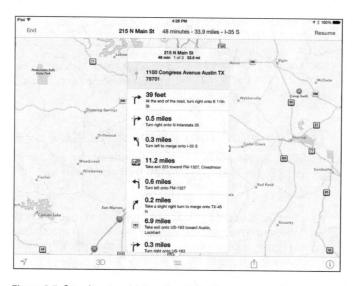

Figure 6-7: Step-by-step driving directions displayed as a list.

If you want to return to the step-by-step road sign directions and map again, tap the Resume button in the upper-right corner of the screen or tap any step in the list overlay.

The list disappears, and the road signs and map reappear.

Getting traffic info in real time

You can find out the traffic conditions for the map you're viewing by tapping the little *i*-in-a-circle in the lower-right corner of the map, and then tapping the Traffic switch so that it says On. When you do this, major roadways are color-coded to inform you of the current traffic speed, as shown in Figure 6-8. Here's the key:

✔ **Green:** 50 or more miles per hour

✔ **Yellow:** 25 to 50 miles per hour

✔ **Red:** Under 25 miles per hour

✔ **Gray:** No data available at this time

Traffic info doesn't work in every location, but the only way to find out is to give it a try. If no color codes appear, assume that it doesn't work for that particular location.

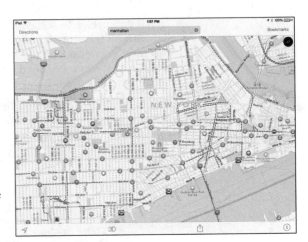

Figure 6-8: Lower Manhattan in midafternoon has more traffic than most other cities at rush hour.

Getting more info about a location

If a location has a little *i* in a blue circle to the right of its name or description (refer to Figure 6-2), you can tap it to see additional information about that location.

As we explain earlier in this chapter, you can get directions to or from that location, add the location to your bookmarks or contacts, or create a new contact from it. You can do two more things with some locations from each location's Info screen:

✔ Tap its e-mail address to launch the Mail application and send an e-mail to it.

✔ Tap its URL to launch Safari and view its website.

Not all locations have these options, but we thought you should know anyway.

Part III
The Multimedia iPad

See www.dummies.com/extras/ipad to find out about the iTunes U and Podcasts apps.

In this part...

- Enjoy listening to music, podcasts, and audiobooks, plus get tips and hints for making your audio even more enjoyable.

- Everyone loves movies; learn how to capture good video with your iPad, watch video on your iPad, and share video with others with (what else?) your iPad.

- Find out how to shoot photos with your iPad, store them, sync them, and do all kinds of other interesting things with them.

- Join the e-book craze: Download and read a good book right on your iPad with the nifty iBooks app.

7

Get in Tune(s): Audio on Your iPad

In This Chapter

▶ Checking out your iPad's inner iPod
▶ Browsing your library
▶ Taking control of your tunes
▶ Customizing your audio experience
▶ Shopping with the iTunes app

*Y*our iPad is perhaps the best iPod ever — especially for working with audio and video. In this chapter, we show you how to use your iPad for audio; in Chapter 8, we cover video.

We start with a quick tour of the iPad's Music application. Then we look at how to use your iPad as an audio player. After you're nice and comfy with using it this way, we show you how to customize the listening experience so that it's just the way you like it. Then we offer a few tips to help you get the most out of using your iPad as an audio player. Finally, we show you how to use the iTunes Store app to buy music, audiobooks, videos, and free content such as podcasts and iTunes U courses.

We assume that your iPad already contains audio content — songs, podcasts, or audiobooks. If you don't have any audio on your iPad yet, we humbly suggest that you get some before you read the rest of this chapter (or Chapter 8, for that matter). You can get audio by syncing (flip to Chapter 3 and follow the instructions) or buying it from the iTunes Store (see the last section in this chapter) on your iPad.

Okay, now that you have some audio content on your iPad to play with, are you ready to rock?

Introducing the iPod inside Your iPad

To use your iPad as an iPod, tap the Music icon on the right side of the Dock at the bottom of the screen (unless you've moved the app elsewhere).

Figure 7-1 provides a quick overview of the Music app for your enjoyment and edification. Because the Songs tab is selected in Figure 7-1, the middle of the screen displays the songs available on our iPad.

At the top of the screen are the music controls and buttons; at the bottom are eight tabs: Radio, Genius, Playlists, Artists, Songs, Albums, Genres, and More. If you don't see these icons, tap the back button in the upper-left corner of the screen (which looks like a little arrow pointing to the left).

If you don't see every song in your library, chances are you've typed something into the Search field or are looking at a shared Music library instead of the songs on your iPad.

Along the right side of the screen, you see the letters of the alphabet from A to Z. Tap one to jump to that letter instantly when you're browsing Playlists, Songs, Artists, or Albums.

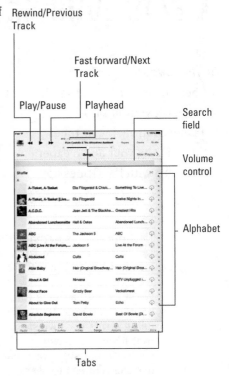

Rewind/Previous Track

Fast forward/Next Track

Play/Pause   Playhead

Search field

Volume control

Alphabet

Tabs

Figure 7-1: These components are what you find on the Music app's main screen.

If you don't see the alphabet on the right side of the screen, you may not have enough items on that tab to warrant it, or you may be looking at a category such as Genres (described in the "Browsing among the tabs" section, later in the chapter), which doesn't have an alphabetical index. Don't worry.

You can find a particular song, artist, album, genre, composer, or audiobook by using the Search field or by browsing the tabs. The following sections show you how.

Note that you no longer use the Music app to enjoy podcasts or iTunes U content on your iPad. These days, you'll need to grab the Podcasts and iTunes U apps, both free in the App Store (see Chapter 11), to play back podcasts or iTunes U courses.

iTunes Radio

If you've ever listened to a streaming radio service such as Pandora, Spotify, or Radical.fm, you will grok Apple's new iTunes Radio immediately.

In a nutshell, iTunes Radio features more than 300 DJ-curated and genre-focused streaming radio stations. You can also create your own stations based on music you love. The more you listen to and fine-tune stations — by tapping the Play More Like This or Never Play This Song button (you'll hear more on these important buttons in just a moment) — the more you'll like what the station plays for you.

Did we mention that iTunes Radio is available on your iPhone, iPad, iPod touch, Mac, PC, and Apple TV for free? You'll hear the occasional ad, but if you subscribe to iTunes Match ($24.99 a year; see the upcoming sidebar for details), you can listen ad-free.

But enough about what it is. Tap the Radio icon at the bottom of the Music app, and to start listening, tap a featured station, as shown in Figure 7-2. A song begins playing immediately.

Tap to listen.

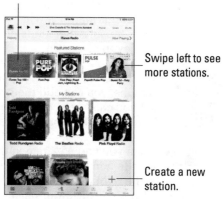

Swipe left to see more stations.

Create a new station.

Figure 7-2: Tap a featured station to listen to it; swipe across stations to see additional ones.

There are basically two kinds of stations:

- **Featured:** These are the stations that iTunes created. You find these stations at the top of the screen; swipe left on the featured stations to see additional choices. At this time, you can't customize these stations. What you see is what you get, but the featured stations are updated frequently with new additions.

- **Custom:** These are the stations you create, and they're listed under the featured stations. While featured stations are nice to try out, custom stations are the heart of iTunes Radio.

  Tap the New Station button to start a station of your own. You can then search for an artist, a genre, or a song. Tap an artist, a song, or a genre (or any combination), and your station is created based on your choice.

If you ever need to edit your custom station, tap the red Edit button to the left of My Stations (refer to Figure 7-2). You can rename the station; add artists, songs, or genres; or delete the station from your iPad.

Deleting a station on your iPad deletes the station everywhere: from your Mac or PC, Apple TV, and other iDevices. If you've put a lot of time and effort into fine-tuning a station, think twice before you delete it because once it's gone, it's gone forever.

Fine-tuning your station

If you want stations you create to play more songs you like, you need to fine-tune the stations. When a song you love or hate is playing, just tap the little star on the left of the play/pause button, as shown in Figure 7-3. Three options slide up from the bottom of the screen.

If you love the song, tap Play More Like This or Add to iTunes Wish List (or both). The star turns red, as shown in Figure 7-3, when you choose Play More Like This. If you hate it, tap Never Play This Song, and you'll never hear it again (at least, not on this station). When you're done, tap anywhere outside of the overlay to dismiss it.

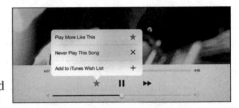

Figure 7-3: Tap the star, and the fine-tuning options appear.

You can't fine-tune songs played on featured stations; you can add them to your wish list, but you can't select Play More Like This or Never Play This Song for them.

 When you find any item in the iTunes Store and want to add it to your Wish List, click the arrow to the right of the Buy button and choose Add to Wish List. To view or change your Wish List, click the iTunes Store, click the Lists button next to the Library button in the upper-right corner of the iTunes window, and then click the Wish List tab (or click My Wish List in the Quick Links section).

Using the Info overlay

What you *can* do — and this works with songs on both featured and custom stations — is tap the little *i*-in-a-circle near the top of the screen to display the song's Info overlay, as shown in Figure 7-4.

The Info overlay lets you start a new station from the artist or song that's playing, allow or disallow explicit content on the station, and share the station with friends via the usual methods.

Figure 7-4: The Info overlay for a custom station based on the music of The Beatles.

The Tune This Station slider shown in Figure 7-4 appears only for custom stations; you can't tune a featured station. Adjust it to hear more hits, get more variety, or discover more new artists and tracks. Clear as mud? You can also tap the song title ("Like a Rolling Stone" in Figure 7-4) to see all the tracks on the album in the iTunes Store, or tap the price ($1.29 in the figure) to purchase the track that's playing.

Even though you can't tune a featured station, you can start your own custom station based on a song or artist you hear on a featured station.

When you're done with the Info screen, tap anywhere outside of the overlay to dismiss it.

Finding music with the Search field

With the Music app open, the easiest way to find music is to type a song, artist, album, or composer name into the Search field in the lower-right corner of the screen.

---

iTunes Match: All your music, all the time, on all your devices

If you own more music than your iPad can hold or if you'd prefer to devote your gigabytes to something other than music — such as photos or videos — you'll like the Apple iTunes Match service. For a mere $24.99 a year, Apple stores your music library (up to 25,000 songs) in the cloud and lets you stream or download any of them any time you like on up to ten devices (which must have a decent Internet connection).

It all happens in iTunes, and it works beautifully. When you enable iTunes Match, the first thing it does is compare your iTunes Library with the 20 million tracks sold in the iTunes Store. If it finds a match, the song is already available from iCloud, and you can listen to it or download it to your device at any time (as long as you have an Internet connection, of course).

After it matches all the songs it can, iTunes uploads all songs it couldn't match (up to a maximum of 25,000). In a few hours (or days), those songs are available from iCloud on all your devices on demand as well.

Four more cool things you should know about iTunes Match:

- Songs purchased from the iTunes Store don't count against your total of 25,000 songs.

- Your iTunes Match content doesn't count against your free 5GB of iCloud storage.

- All the songs iTunes matches (with its 20 million tracks) are 256 Kbps AAC DRM-free files, even if your original was of lower quality. That means the songs you stream or download from iCloud are likely to sound better than the originals in your iTunes Library.

- iTunes Radio will play commercial-free.

For just $25 a year, you can ignore the whole syncing thing between your Mac or PC and your iPad (Chapter 3 covers syncing), at least for music. As long as Internet access is available, your entire music library is available on your iPad (and up to nine other devices), and you'll be able to listen to radio stations without commercials.

You can also find songs (or artists, for that matter) without opening the Music app by typing their names in a Spotlight search, as we mention in Chapter 2. An even cooler way to hear music without opening the Music app is to ask Siri to play a song, album, or artist. (Chapter 14 gives you the scoop on Siri.)

Browsing among the tabs

If you'd rather browse your music library, tap the appropriate tab at the bottom of the screen — Playlists, Artists, Songs, Albums, Genres, and More— and all items of that type appear. Or you can tap the More button to browse Compilations or Composers, or to connect to a shared library, as described later in this chapter.

After tapping one of these tabs, you can find a playlist, song, artist, album, or genre by

- **Flicking upward or downward** to scroll up and down the list until you find what you're looking for.

- **Tapping one of the little letters on the right side of the screen** to jump to that letter in the list (all categories except Genres).

Then, when you find what you're looking for, here's what happens (depending on which tab is selected):

- **Playlists:** A list of playlists available on this iPad appears. Tap a playlist and the songs it contains appear in a list. Tap a song to play it.

- **Songs:** The song plays.

  If you're not sure which song you want to listen to, try this: Tap the Shuffle button at the top of the screen (shown earlier in Figure 7-1). Your iPad then plays songs from your music collection at random.

- **Artists:** A list of artists' names appears. Tap an artist, and all the albums and songs by that artist appear; tap a song, and it plays.

  To see the list of artists again, you can either tap the Artists button near the upper-left corner of the screen or tap the Artists tab at the bottom of the screen.

  Figure 7-5 shows the scrolling list of albums you'll see after you tap an artist's name. (In this case, that artist is Bleu, one of Bob's favorite singer/songwriters.)

- **Albums:** The Albums option works pretty much the same way as Artists, except you see a list of album covers instead of a list of artists. Tap an album, and its contents appear.

To play one of the songs on the album, tap it. To return to the list of albums, tap the Albums button near the upper-left corner of the screen or tap the Albums tab at the bottom.

✔ **Genres:** When you tap Genres, a list of genres — Comedy, Rock, Pop, Hip Hop/Rap, and so on — appears. Tap a genre, and a list of the songs in that genre appears.

✔ **More:** Tap More to see Compilations and Composers, which work the same as the Playlist, Songs, and other tabs.

TIP
If you're looking for other iTunes content such as movies or TV shows, you find them in the Videos app, which we cover in Chapter 8. Podcasts are found in the Podcasts app, and iTunes U courses are found in the iTunes U app — both of these apps are free, but you must get them from the App Store.

Figure 7-5: Bob tapped Bleu in the list of artists, and this appeared.

What's the difference between artists and composers?

If you're wondering about the difference between an artist and a composer, imagine this if you will: You have a recording in your iTunes Library of a track entitled *Symphony No. 5 in C Minor.* The composer will always be Ludwig van Beethoven, but the artist could be the London Symphony Orchestra, the Los Angeles Philharmonic, the Austin Klezmer Ensemble, or many other performers. Here's another example: The ballad "Yesterday" was composed by John Lennon and Paul McCartney but has been performed by artists that include The Beatles, Ray Charles, Boyz II Men, Dave Grusin, Marianne Faithfull, and many others.

Now you may be wondering where your iPad gets this kind of info because you know you didn't supply it. Check this out: Click a track in iTunes on your computer, choose File⇨Get Info, and then click the Info tab at the top of the window.

That's just some of the information that can be embedded in an audio track. This embedded information, sometimes referred to as the track's *tags,* is what your iPad uses to distinguish between artists and composers. If a track doesn't have a composer tag, you won't find it on the Composers tab on your iPad.

Taking Control of Your Tunes

If you've read along so far, you have the basics down and can find and play songs. Here we take a look at some of the things you can do with your iPad when it's in Music mode.

Playing with the audio controls

First things first: We look at the controls you use after you tap a song. Take a peek at Figure 7-1 to see exactly where all these controls are located on the screen:

- **Volume control:** Drag the little dot to the left or right to reduce or increase the volume level.

- **Previous Track/Rewind button:** When a track is playing, tap once to go to the beginning of the track or tap twice to go to the start of the preceding track in the list. Touch and hold this button to rewind the track at double speed.

- **Play/Pause button:** Tap to play or pause the track.

- **Next Track/Fast Forward button:** Tap to skip to the next track in the list. Touch and hold this button to fast-forward at double speed.

You can display playback controls any time a track is playing. Better still, this trick works even when you're using another app or your Home screen(s): Just swipe upward from the bottom of the iPad screen to bring up the Control Center, which includes musical controls as shown in Figure 7-6.

Figure 7-6: These controls appear — even if you're using another app — when you swipe upward from the bottom of the screen.

The playback controls *may or may not override the audio from* apps that have their own audio, such as many games, any app that records audio, and VoIP (Voice over Internet Protocol) apps such as Skype.

You can even control music from the Control Center when your iPad screen is locked.

- **Scrubber bar and Playhead:** Drag the little dot (the *Playhead*) along the Scrubber bar to skip to any point within the track.

You can adjust the scrub rate by sliding your finger downward on the screen as you drag the Playhead along the Scrubber bar. Check out the section on the hidden iTunes scrub speed tip in Chapter 20 for additional details. By the way, this slick trick also works in many other apps that use a Scrubber bar, most notably the Videos app.

✔ **Repeat:** Tap Repeat and an overlay offers three options:

- Repeat the current song.
- Repeat the current playlist, album, artist, genre, etc.
- Repeat off.

✔ **Create:** Tap Create and an overlay offers four options:

- Create a new radio station (from scratch).
- Create a new radio station from the current song.
- Create a new radio station from the artist performing the current song.
- Create a new Genius Playlist based on the current song.

✔ **Shuffle:** Tap this button to play songs at random; tap again to play songs in the order they appear onscreen. When Shuffle is enabled, it turns kind of pinkish and says, "Shuffle All."

But wait, there's more. If you tap the Now Playing button (upper left), the album art fills the screen. Tap anywhere to see the controls and tabs at the top and bottom of the screen.

Notice that when album art is onscreen, the Store button and Search field at the top of the screen disappear, and the Back and Track List buttons take their places, as shown in Figure 7-7.

Earlier in this section, we explain how to use the volume control, Rewind/Previous Track button, Play/Pause button, Fast Forward/Next Track button, and Scrubber bar/Playhead. They may look slightly different on this screen, but they work in exactly the same way.

The new buttons at the top of the screen are as follows:

✔ **Back:** Tap this button to return to the preceding screen.

✔ **Track List:** Tap this button to see all the tracks on the album that's currently playing, as shown in Figure 7-8; tap any song to play it.

Back button   Track List button

Figure 7-7: You see these additional buttons after you tap the Now Playing button.

If you tap the song title (*Accidents Will Happen* in Figure 7-7), five dots appear in its place. Swipe or tap the dots and they turn to stars; use the stars to rate the song from zero to five stars. In Figure 7-8, we've rated the song that's playing four stars. Tap anywhere but on the stars and the song title returns in place of the dots or stars.

Why would you want to assign star ratings to songs? One reason is that you can use star ratings to filter songs in iTunes on your Mac or PC. Another is that you can use them when you create Smart Playlists in iTunes. And last but not least, they look cool.

Creating playlists

Playlists let you organize songs around a particular theme or mood: operatic arias, romantic ballads, British invasion — whatever. Younger folks sometimes call them *mixes.*

Although it may be easier to create playlists in iTunes on your computer, your iPad makes it relatively easy to create (and listen to) playlists:

  ✔ **To create a playlist on your iPad,** tap the Playlists tab at the bottom of the screen and then tap the New Playlist button at the top of the list of playlists on the left. You're asked to name your playlist. Do so and then tap Save. A list of all the songs on your iPad will appear in alphabetical order. Tap the ones you want to include; they'll change to gray after you add them, as shown in Figure 7-9.

  After you've tapped every song you want in the list, tap the Done button in the upper right.

Figure 7-8: We've given this tune a four-out-of-five-star rating.

Figure 7-9: This is how to create a playlist on your iPad.

You can select tracks for your playlist from the Songs, Artists, Albums, or Composers tabs that appear at the bottom of the screen while you're creating your playlist.

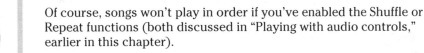 **To listen to a playlist,** tap the Playlists tab and then tap its name to see a list of the songs it contains. If the list is longer than one screen, flick upward to scroll down. Tap a song in the list, and the song plays. When that song is over or you tap the Next Song button, the next song in the playlist plays. This continues until the last song in the playlist has played, at which point your iPad shuts up.

Of course, songs won't play in order if you've enabled the Shuffle or Repeat functions (both discussed in "Playing with audio controls," earlier in this chapter).

Although you can't create Smart Playlists on your iPad, they totally rock. What is a Smart Playlist? Glad you asked. A *Smart Playlist* is a special playlist that selects tracks based on criteria you specify, such as Artist Name, Date Added, Rating, Genre, Year, and many others. Fire up iTunes on your computer and choose File➪New Smart Playlist to get started.

And that's all there is to selecting, creating, and playing songs in a playlist.

It doesn't take a Genius

Genius selects songs from your music library that go great together. To use it, either tap the Genius tab at the bottom of the screen or tap the Create button and choose Genius Playlist. What happens next depends on which way you started.

If you tapped the Genius tab at the bottom of the screen your iPad will display a collection of pre-made Genius mixes with names like Hip Hop, Classic Rock, New Wave, Punk, and so on, which are based on the songs in your library. Tap one and your iPad selects 25 songs of that type that it thinks will go well together.

If you tap the Create button on the main screen (refer to Figure 7-1) and choose Genius Playlist, your iPad selects 25 songs it thinks will go well with the current song. If no song is currently playing when you choose Genius Playlist, an alphabetical list of songs appears and you'll need to select a song for the Genius playlist to be generated.

The less popular the song, artist, or genre, the more likely Genius will choke on it. When that happens, you see an alert that asks you to try again because this song doesn't have enough related songs to create a Genius playlist.

When you create a Genius playlist, you find it at the top of your Playlists list; tap it and you see the 25 songs that Genius selected. You see three new buttons near the top of the screen:

- ✔ **New:** Select a different song to use as the basis for a Genius playlist.

- ✔ **Refresh:** See a list of 25 songs that "go great with" the song you're listening to (or the song you selected). If you don't like the selection, tap Refresh again and different tracks will appear. Keep tapping until you're satisfied with the Genius's choices.

- ✔ **Save:** Save this Genius playlist so that you can listen to it whenever you like.

When you save a Genius playlist, it inherits the name of the song it's based upon and appears in your library with a Genius icon that looks like the Genius button. And the next time you sync your iPad, the Genius playlist magically appears in iTunes.

If you like the Genius feature, you can also create a new Genius playlist in iTunes and then sync it with your iPad.

A brief AirPlay interlude

You may or may not see another icon that's useful for listening to music. This one appears in your Control Center and is called AirPlay. The Airplay icon and its overlay look like this:

AirPlay is a wicked-cool technology baked into every copy of iOS version 4.2 or higher. AirPlay lets you wirelessly stream music, photos, and video to AirPlay-enabled devices such as Apple's AirPort Extreme, AirPort Express Wi-Fi base stations, and Apple TV, as well as third-party AirPlay-enabled devices, including (but not limited to) speakers and HDTVs.

The AirPlay icon and selector overlay appear only if your iPad detects an AirPlay-enabled device on the same Wi-Fi network. Bob has two Apple TVs at his house, so he sees those options when he taps the AirPlay icon. Tapping Great Room Apple TV sends whatever is playing on the Music app to the Apple TV in the den. The Apple TV is, in turn, connected to his home theater sound system and high-def TV via HDMI.

If you use an Apple TV as your AirPlay-enabled device, you can also stream music, video, and photos from your iPad to your HDTV.

Finally, iPads also offer a cool "video mirroring" option when used with a second- or third-generation Apple TV. To use this awesome feature, swipe up from the bottom of the screen to bring up Control Center, and then tap the AirPlay icon. When you select an Apple TV, a switch appears for the Mirroring option. Enable it and whatever appears on your iPad's screen also appears on your big screen TV.

If you have an HDMI-equipped TV and/or a decent sound system and have decent Wi-Fi bandwidth, you'll love Apple TV and AirPlay.

Customizing Volume and Equalizer Settings

You can tweak volume and equalizer settings to customize your iPad-as-an-iPod experience. If you've noticed and been bothered that the volume of some songs is higher than others, check out the iTunes Sound Check feature. If you want to adjust certain frequencies, the equalizer enables you to do so. And if you want to set a maximum volume limit, tell your iPad to make it so. The following sections explain how.

Play all songs at the same volume level

The iTunes Sound Check option automatically adjusts the level of songs so that they play at the same volume relative to each other. That way, one song never blasts out your ears even if the recording level is much louder than that of the song before or after it. To tell the iPad to use these volume settings, you first have to turn on the feature in iTunes on your computer. Here's how to do that:

1. **Choose iTunes⇨Preferences (Mac) or Edit⇨Preferences (PC).**

2. **Click the Playback tab.**

3. **Select the Sound Check check box to enable it.**

Now you need to tell the iPad to use the Sound Check settings from iTunes. Here's how to do *that:*

1. **Tap the Settings icon on the iPad's Home screen.**

2. **Tap Music in the list of settings.**

3. **Tap the Sound Check On/Off switch so that it turns green.**

Choose an equalizer setting

An *equalizer* increases or decreases the relative levels of specific frequencies to enhance the sound you hear. Some equalizer settings emphasize the bass (low-end) notes in a song; other equalizer settings make the higher frequencies more apparent. The iPad has more than a dozen equalizer presets, with names such as Acoustic, Bass Booster, Bass Reducer, Dance, Electronic, Pop, and Rock. Each one is ostensibly tailored to a specific type of music.

The way to find out whether you prefer using equalization is to listen to music while trying different settings. To do that, first start listening to a song you like. Then, while the song is playing, follow these steps:

1. **Tap the Home button on the front of your iPad.**

2. **Tap the Settings icon on the Home screen.**

3. **Tap Music in the list of settings.**

4. **Tap EQ in the list of Music settings.**

5. **Tap different EQ presets (Pop, Rock, R&B, or Dance, for example), and listen carefully to the way they change how the song sounds.**

6. **When you find an equalizer preset that you think sounds good, tap the Home button, and you're finished.**

If you don't like any of the presets, tap Off at the top of the EQ list to turn off the equalizer.

At the risk of giving away one of the tips in Chapter 20, we feel obliged to mention that you may get somewhat longer battery life if you keep EQ turned off.

Set a volume limit for music (and videos)

You can instruct your iPad to limit the loudest listening level for audio or video. To do so, here's the drill:

1. **Tap the Settings icon on the Home screen.**

2. **Tap Music in the list of settings.**

3. **Tap Volume Limit in the list of Music settings.**

4. **Drag the slider to adjust the maximum volume level to your liking.**

The Volume Limit setting limits the volume of only music and videos; it doesn't apply to podcasts or audiobooks. And, although the setting works with any headset, headphones, or speakers plugged into the headset jack on your iPad, it doesn't affect the sound played on your iPad's internal speaker.

By the way, speaking of that lone internal iPad speaker, it's not in stereo although it sounds pretty good just the same. Of course, when you plug in headphones, you hear rich stereo output.

Shopping with the iTunes Store App

Last but certainly not least, the iTunes Store app lets you use your iPad to download, buy, or rent just about any song, album, movie, or TV show. And, if you're fortunate enough to have an iTunes gift card or gift certificate in hand, you can redeem it directly from your iPad.

If you want to do any of that, however, you must first sign in to your iTunes Store account. Follow these steps:

1. **Tap the Settings icon on the Home screen.**

2. **Tap Store in the list of settings.**

3. **Tap Sign In.**

4. **Type your username and password.**

Or, in the unlikely event that you don't have an iTunes Store account already, follow these steps:

1. **Tap the Settings icon on the Home screen.**

2. **Tap Store in the list of settings.**

3. **Tap Create New Account.**

4. **Follow the onscreen instructions.**

After the iTunes Store knows who you are (and, more importantly, knows your credit card number), tap the iTunes Store icon on your Home screen (or the Store button in the Music app) and shop until you drop. It works almost exactly the same as the iTunes App Store, which you read about in Chapter 11.

8

iPad Video: Seeing Is Believing

*P*icture this scene: The smell of popcorn permeates the room as you and your family congregate to watch the latest Hollywood blockbuster. A motion picture soundtrack swells up. The images on the screen are stunning. And all eyes are fixed on the iPad.

Okay, here comes the reality check. The iPad is not going to replace a wall-sized high-definition television as the centerpiece of your home theater (though as you discover, you can watch material that originates on the iPad on the bigger screen). Then again, it's worth pointing out that the gorgeous Retina display on third-generation and later iPads has a higher-resolution screen than even the high-definition television in your living room — and is just about the finest-looking display we've ever seen on a handheld device. But you shouldn't have an inferiority complex if you have one of the near-ten-inch displays on an iPad 2. Those screens look terrific, too, even when you're not viewing them head-on. And now that the top-of-the-line iPad mini has also graduated to a Retina display, even a small-screen iPad is going to grab your attention.

Bottom line: No matter which iPad you own, watching movies and other videos on Apple's prized tablet is a cinematic treat. What's more, you have front and rear cameras that can help turn you, under certain circumstances, into a filmmaker — right from the device.

And video on the iPad ventures into another area: video chat. You can keep in touch with friends and loved ones by gazing into each other's pupils. It's all done through a version of *FaceTime,* a clever video-chat program that comes with your iPad. In the interest of equal time, we'd also like to point out that you can do video chats on your iPad by downloading a popular third-party app such as Skype — and do clever group chats via another app called Spin from Net Power & Light.

We get to FaceTime later in this chapter. For now, and without any further ado, we get on with the show!

Finding Stuff to Watch

You have a few main ways to find and watch videos on your iPad. You can fetch all sorts of fare from the iTunes Store, whose virtual doors you can open directly from the iPad.

Or you can sync content that already resides on your Mac or PC. (If you haven't done so yet, now is as good a time as any to read Chapter 3 for all the details on syncing.)

The videos you can watch on the iPad generally fall into one of the following categories:

- ✔ **Movies, TV shows, and music videos from the iTunes Store:** You can watch these by tapping the Videos icon on the Home screen.

  The iTunes Store features dedicated sections for purchasing or renting episodes of TV shows, as shown in Figure 8-1, and for buying or renting movies, as shown in Figure 8-2.

  Pricing varies, but it's not atypical (as of this writing) to fork over $1.99 to pick up an episode of a popular TV show in standard definition or $2.99 for high-def versions. And a few shows are free. You can also purchase a complete season of a favorite show. The final season of a classic show, such as *Lost,* for example, costs $24.99 in standard-def and $29.99 in high-def.

  A new release feature film typically costs $19.99 in high definition or $14.99 in standard def. But you can find HD movies for

Figure 8-1: Buying and watching TV on the iPad is gleeful.

as little as $9.99 and sometimes even cheaper than that.

You can also rent many movies, typically for $2.99, $3.99, or $4.99, though Apple usually serves up a juicy 99-cent rental as well. Not all movies can be rented, and we're not wild about current rental restrictions — you have 30 days to begin watching a rented flick and a day to finish watching after you've started, though you can watch as often as you want during the 24-hour period. But that's showbiz for you. Such films appear in their own Rented Movies section in the video list, which you get to by tapping Videos. The number of days before your rental expires displays.

In some instances, *World War Z* being one example, purchasing a movie also affords you so-called iTunes Extras for your Mac or PC, featuring the kind of bonus content that is sometimes reserved for DVDs.

Tap a movie listing in iTunes, and you can generally preview a trailer before buying (or renting) and check out additional tidbits: the plot summary, credits, reviews, and customer ratings, as well as other movies that appealed to other buyers of this one. See Figure 8-3. And you can search films by genre or top charts (the ones other people are buying or renting), or rely on the Apple Genius feature for recommendations based on stuff you've already watched. (Genius works for movies and TV much the way it works for music, as we explain in Chapter 7.)

Figure 8-2: You can spend hours watching movies on the iPad.

Figure 8-3: Bone up on a movie before buying or renting it.

Apple also groups movies by various themes, Date Night Movies and Indie New Releases being two examples.

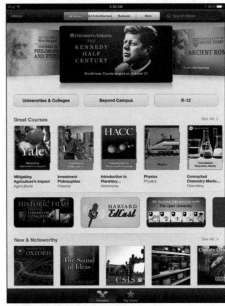

Figure 8-4: Get smart. iTunes U offers a slew of lectures on diverse topics.

- **The boatload of video podcasts and courseware, featured in the free Podcasts and iTunes U apps, both from Apple:** Podcasts started out as another form of Internet radio, although instead of listening to live streams, you downloaded files onto your computer or iPod to take in at your leisure. Lots of audio podcasts are still available, but the focus here is on video. You can watch free episodes that cover *Sesame Street* videos, sports, investing, political shows, and much more. And you can take a seminar at Harvard, Stanford, and other prestigious institutions. Indeed, iTunes U boasts more than 600,000 free lectures and other educational resources from around the world, many of them videos. Better still: no homework, no grades, and no tuition. Check out Figure 8-4.

- **Videos that play via entertainment apps:** For example, Netflix offers an app that enables you to use your Netflix subscription, if you have one, to stream video on your iPad. Amazon's appealing Amazon Instant Video streaming app for members of its service is also available. Various TV networks offer their own apps so that you can catch up on favorite shows on your iPad. The Hulu Plus subscription app also lets you tap into current and past shows. And if you're an HBO subscriber, go for the HBO Go app.

- **The movies you've created in iMovie software or other software on the Mac or, for that matter, other programs on the PC:** Plus you can view all the other videos you may have downloaded from the Internet, though sometimes you must convert these to a format that the iPad recognizes.

- **Videos you've given birth to using the rear- or front-facing camera:** A version of iMovie is made for iPads (and iPhones) too. The optional app costs $4.99 but is free for anyone running a new iOS 7 device, and a free upgrade is available if you had an earlier version. Check out the "Shooting Your Own Videos" section, later in this chapter, for direction on creating movies with the iPad.

You may have to prepare some videos so that they'll play on your iPad. To do so, highlight the video in question after it resides in your iTunes library. In iTunes, choose File⇨Create Version⇨Create iPad or Apple TV Version. Alas, creating an iPad version of a video doesn't work for all the video content you download off the Internet, including video files in the AVI, DivX, MKV, Flash, WMV, and Xvid formats.

For a somewhat technical workaround without potential conversion hassles, try the $2.99 Air Video app from InMethod s.r.o. The utility app can deliver AVI, DivX, MKV, and other videos that wouldn't ordinarily play on your iPad. You can also check out a limited free version. You have to download the free Air Video Server software to your Mac or PC to stream content to your iPad, even across the Internet. Or, for converting from a broader range of formats, try the excellent (and free) HandBrake application from `http://handbrake.fr/`.

For more on compatibility, check out the nearby "Are we compatible?" sidebar (but read it at your own risk).

Are we compatible?

The iPad works with a whole bunch of video, although not everything you'll want to watch will make it through. Several Internet video standards — notably Adobe Flash — are not supported.

The absence of Flash is a bugaboo because Flash has been the technology behind much of the video on the web, though that landscape is changing. Even Adobe is pulling support for mobile versions of Flash.

Fortunately, Apple backs other increasingly popular standards — HTML5, CSS 3, and JavaScript. But the company was apparently sensitive enough to the issue that in the early days of the iPad, Apple made mention of several sites where video *would* play on the iPad. The list included CNN, The New York Times, Vimeo, Time, ESPN, Major League Baseball, NPR, The White House, Sports Illustrated, TED, Nike, CBS, Spin, and National Geographic. By now, of course, most popular videos are readily accessible, but know that from time to time you may still run into a snag.

With the appropriate utility software, you might also be able to convert some nonworking video to an iPad-friendly format on your computer. But if something doesn't play now, it may in the future because Apple has the capability to upgrade the iPad through software.

In the meantime, you can find a description of the video formats that iPad supports on Apple's website; point your browser to `www.apple.com/ipad/specs`.

Playing Video

Now that you know what you want to watch, here's how to watch it:

1. **On the Home screen, tap the Videos icon.**

   You see a tabbed interface for Movies, TV Shows and Music Videos. If Home Sharing is turned on your computer through iTunes, a Shared tab will also be visible.

2. **Tap the Movies tab.**

   For these steps, we walk you through watching a movie, but the steps for TV shows and music videos is similar.

   You see poster thumbnails for any movies you previously purchased through iTunes, as Figure 8-5 shows — even for those movies you haven't downloaded yet. (Some posters may only reveal a grayed-out box, showing the title of the movie, plus a filmstrip icon.)

   If you see the iCloud symbol on the video thumbnail you can stream the movie, provided you have a decent Internet connection.

   Tap Settings⇨Videos to choose whether to see thumbnails for all the videos you have stored in iCloud or on the device, or show only those that have been downloaded to your iPad.

3. **Tap the poster that represents the movie or other video you want to watch.**

   You are taken to a summary page for the movie revealing a larger movie poster, play button, and tabs for Details, Chapters, and Related, as shown in Figure 8-6.

   • Tap *Details* (if you're not already in that view) to see the plot summary, run time, and sundry other details about the movie in question.

   • Tap *Chapters* to jump to particular scenes or chapters in the movie and watch from that scene on. (If you're watching a TV show, you see the Episodes tab here instead.)

   • Tap *Related* to see posters representing other movies that are similar to this one, and that are (not so coincidentally) available to rent or buy in iTunes.

4. **To start playing a movie (or resume playing from where you left off), tap the Play button.**

   Alternatively, from the Chapters view (see Figure 8-7), tap any chapter to start playing from that point.

Movies

TV Shows

Videos

Figure 8-5: Choosing the movie, TV show, or music video to watch.

TIP

Tap Settings⇨Videos to change the setting to start playing from where you left off rather than to start playing from the beginning, or vice versa.

5. **(Optional) Rotate your iPad to landscape mode to maximize a movie's display.**

If you hold the iPad in portrait mode, you can see black bars on top of and below the screen where the movie is playing. Those bars remain when you rotate the device to its side, but the iPad plays the film in a wider-screen mode (depending on the video).

For movies, this is a great thing. You can watch flicks as the film-maker intended, in a cinematic *aspect ratio*.

Figure 8-6: Getting a description of the movie you're about to watch.

TECHNICAL STUFF

The iPad 2 doesn't give you a full high-definition presentation because that requires at least 1280-by-720-pixel resolution so the images are scaled down slightly. Having said that, we don't think you'll even notice the quality of the images — unless, that is, you place them beside an iPad with a Retina display, which now includes a version of the iPad mini, along with the svelte full-sized iPad Air.

Finding and Working the Video Controls

While a video is playing, tap the screen to display the controls shown in Figure 8-8. Then you can tap a control to activate it. Here's how to work the controls:

Figure 8-7: Start playing from any chapter.

Playhead   Scrubber bar

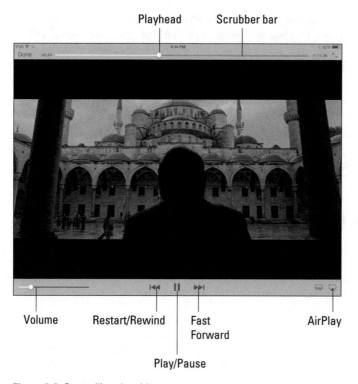

Volume   Restart/Rewind   Fast   AirPlay
                              Forward

Play/Pause

Figure 8-8: Controlling the video.

✔ **To play or pause the video,** tap the Play/Pause button.

✔ **To adjust the volume,** drag the volume slider to the right to raise the volume and to the left to lower it. The volume adjusts relative to how the physical Volume buttons are controlling audio levels.

✔ **To restart or go back,** tap the Restart/Rewind button to restart the video, or tap and hold the same button to rewind.

✔ **To skip forward,** tap and hold Fast Forward to advance the video. Or skip ahead by dragging the Playhead along the Scrubber bar.

✔ **To set how the video fills the screen,** tap the Scale button, which toggles between filling the entire screen with video or fitting the video to the screen. Alternatively, you can double-tap the video to go back and forth between fitting and filling the screen.

Fitting the video to the screen displays the film in its theatrical aspect ratio. Again, you may see black bars above and below the video (or to its sides), which some people don't like. The bars on the top and bottom are an example of *letterboxing;* on the sides, it's *pillarboxing. Filling* the entire screen with the video may crop or trim the sides or top of the picture, so you don't see the complete scene that the director shot.

✔ **To select language and subtitle settings,** tap the Audios and Subtitles button. You see options to select a different language, turn on or hide subtitles, and turn on or hide closed captioning. The control appears only if the movie supports any of these features or if you've turned on closed captioning by choosing Settings⇨Video.

✔ **To make the controls go away,** tap the screen again (or just wait for them to go away on their own).

✔ **To tell your iPad you're done watching a video,** tap Done. You return to the last Videos screen that was visible before you started watching the movie.

Watching Video on a Big TV

We love watching movies on the iPad, but we also recognize the limitations of a smaller screen, even one as stunning as the Retina display. Friends won't crowd around to watch with you, as good as it is, so Apple offers two ways to display video from your iPad to a TV:

✔ **AirPlay:** Through the AirPlay feature, you can wirelessly stream movies — commercial flicks or videos you shot — as well as photos and music from the iPad to an Apple TV box that's connected to an HDTV. Start watching the movie on the iPad and tap the AirPlay button that appears in the video controls. (Refer to Figure 8-8.) You can watch only one screen at a time. Tap Apple TV to stream to the TV through the Apple TV box. Tap iPad to watch on the iPad.

You can multitask while streaming a video. Therefore, while the kids are watching a flick on the TV, you can surf the web or catch up on e-mail.

Although you can stream from an iPad to an Apple TV and switch screens between the two, you can't stream a rented movie that you start watching on Apple TV to the iPad.

✔ **AV Adapter cables:** Apple sells two $39 cables — one each for digital AV (HDMI) and composite video connections — that let you connect your iPad to a standard (composite) or high-definition (HDMI) television, projector, or other device that has an HDMI or composite video inputs. Apple also sells Lightning–to–Digital AV and Lightning–to–VGA adapters at $49 each for use with the fourth-generation iPad and beyond.

If you have a more recent iPad, however, the appropriate Digital AV (HDMI) adapter also lets you *mirror* the iPad screen on the connected TV or projector. So not only can you watch a movie or video, but you can also view anything else that's on the iPad's screen: your Home screens, web pages, games, other apps, you name it.

Although the composite adapter has its cables built right in, the Digital AV adapter doesn't include an HDMI cable, so you have to supply one yourself. For more on accessories, check out Chapter 17.

Restricting Video Usage

If you've given an iPad to your kid or someone who works for you, you may not want that person spending time watching movies or television. You might want him or her to do something more productive, such as homework or the quarterly budget. That's where parental restrictions come in. Please note that the use of this iron-fist tool can make you really unpopular.

Tap Settings⬦General⬦Restrictions⬦Enable Restrictions. You're asked to establish or enter a previously established passcode. Twice. Having done so, you can set restrictions based on movie ratings (PG, R, and so on) and regulate access to TV shows, also based on ratings. You can also restrict FaceTime usage or use of the camera (which when turned off also turns off FaceTime). For more on restrictions, flip to Chapter 15, where we explain the settings for controlling (and loosening) access to iPad features.

Deleting Video from Your iPad

Video takes up space — lots of space. After the closing credits roll and you no longer want to keep a video on your iPad, here's what you need to know about deleting video:

- ✔ To delete a video manually, tap and hold its movie poster until the small circled *x* shows up on the poster. To confirm your intention, tap the larger Delete button that appears or tap Cancel if you change your mind.

- ✔ To remove a downloaded video from the device — the flick remains in iCloud—, tap Edit from the main Movies or TV Shows list screen, and tap the x-in-a-circle that appears on top of the movie poster. To confirm your intention, Apple asks whether you're sure you want to delete the video. If you're sure, tap Delete (or Cancel if you change your mind).

- ✔ If you delete a rented movie before watching it on your iPad, it's gone. You have to spend (more) loot if you hope to watch it in the future on the iPad.

Shooting Your Own Videos

The iPad 2 was the first iPad with a camera — um, two cameras, to be more precise. The rear camera can record video up to the high-definition techie standard of 720p and at 30 frames per second (fps), or as *full-motion video*. Come again? That's a fancy way to say that the video ought to play back smoothly. The front camera can also perform at 30 fps, but the VGA (*video graphics array*) quality isn't quite as good.

Apple equipped the later iPads with even better cameras. The 5-megapixel iSight camera takes terrific stills (see the next chapter) and lets you capture 1080p video, or the highest of the high-definition specifications. Another bonus is that it has built-in video stabilization, which helps compensate for a slightly jittery videographer.

Now that we've dispensed with that little piece of business, here's how to shoot video on the iPad:

1. **Tap the Camera icon on the Home screen.**

2. **Drag along the right edge of the screen until the Video mode is selected.**

   A dot will appear next to the word *Video,* which is highlighted in yellow. If either of your other options, Photo or Square, is selected, one of those will appear in yellow with a dot next to it instead.

   You can't switch from the front to the rear camera (or vice versa) while you're capturing a scene. So before shooting anything, think about which camera you want to use, and then tap the front/rear camera button in the top-right corner of the screen when you've made your choice.

3. **Tap the red Record button (labeled in Figure 8-9) on the middle-right side of the screen to begin shooting a scene.**

   We should point out that when you choose a non-videos shooting format — Photo or Square — the round shutter button will be white. In any case, while you're shooting a scene, the counter will tick off the seconds.

4. **Tap the red Record button again to stop recording.**

   Your video is automatically saved to the Camera Roll (represented by the small thumbnail below the camera modes) alongside any other saved videos and digital stills.

Front/Rear camera

Record button

Camera Roll

Figure 8-9: Lights, camera, action.

Editing what you shot

We assume that you captured some really great footage, but you probably shot some stuff that belongs on the cutting room floor as well. No big whoop — because you can perform simple edits right on your iPad. Tap the Camera Roll at the lower-right corner of the Camera app to find your recordings. Then:

1. **Tap a video recording to display the onscreen controls.**

2. **Drag the start and end points along the frame viewer at the top of the screen to select only the video you want to keep.**

   Hold your finger over the section to expand the frame viewer to make it easier to apply your edits. Tap the Play button to preview your surgery.

3. **Choose what to do with your trimmed clip. Tap Trim and then (as shown in Figure 8-10):**

   Figure 8-10: Getting a trim.

   - Tap *Trim Original* to permanently remove scenes from the original clip.

   - Tap *Save as New Clip* to create a newly trimmed video clip; the original video remains intact, and the new clip is stored in the Camera Roll.

   - Tap *Cancel* to start over.

   We should point out that this method will only let you edit footage captured on an iOS device, not video from a digital camcorder or camera, even if you sync it to the iPad.

For more ambitious editing on the iPad, consider iMovie for iPad, a $4.99 app (free to purchasers of new iOS 7 devices) that resembles a bare-bones version of iMovie for Mac computers. Through iMovie, you can export your finished video to YouTube, Vimeo, CNN iReport, and Facebook. And iMovie for iPad lets you produce Hollywood-style movie trailers, just like on a Mac.

Any video edited with the iOS version of iMovie has to have originated on an iOS device. You can't mix in footage shot with a digital camera or obtained elsewhere.

Sharing video

You can play back what you've just shot in portrait or landscape mode. And if the video is any good, you'll likely want to share it with a wider audience. To do so, open the Camera Roll and tap the thumbnail for the video in question. Tap the Action button, and you can e-mail the video (if the video file isn't too large) or send it as a Message (see Chapter 5). And there are many more options: You can save it to iCloud or share it in numerous other places, including Twitter, Facebook, Flickr, YouTube, Vimeo, and (if a Chinese keyboard was enabled) the Chinese services Youku and Tudou. You can also view your video as part of a slideshow (see Chapter 9) or, if you have an Apple TV box, dispatch it to a big-screen television via AirPlay.

Seeing Is Believing with FaceTime

We bet you can come up with a lengthy list of people you'd love to be able to eyeball in real time from afar. Maybe it's your old college roommate. Maybe it's your old college sweetheart. And maybe it's your grandparents, who've long since retired to warm climates somewhere.

That's the beauty of *FaceTime,* the video-chat app. FaceTime exploits the two cameras built into the devices, each serving a different purpose. The front camera lets you talk face to face. The back camera shows what you're seeing to the person you're talking to.

To take advantage of FaceTime, here's what you need:

- ✔ **Access to Wi-Fi or cellular:** And the people you're talking to need Internet access, too. On an iOS device, you need Wi-Fi or a cellular connection. If you want to go with the cell connection, you need at least a third-generation iPad running iOS 6. On a Mac, you need an upstream or downstream Internet connection of at least 128 Kbps. You also need at least a 1-Mbps upstream and downstream connection for HD-quality video calls.

  Using FaceTime over a cellular connection can quickly run through your monthly data allotment and prove hazardous to your budget. However, you can now do an audio-only FaceTime call, which can cut down significantly on your data usage.

- ✔ **FaceTime on recipient's device:** On your conversation partner's own iPad 2 or later, on an Intel-based Mac computer (OS X 10.6.6 or later), on a recent-model iPod touch, or on an iPhone 4 or later. (FaceTime first appeared on Apple's prized smartphone.)

Getting started with FaceTime

When you use FaceTime for the first time, after you tap the app's icon from the Home screen, you're required to sign in to FaceTime using your Apple ID, which can be your iTunes Store account, iCloud ID, or another Apple account. (You may have previously supplied this info during setup of your iPad.) If you don't have an account, tap Create New Apple ID to set one up within FaceTime. You also must supply an e-mail address or phone number that callers use to call you from their own FaceTime-capable iPads, Macs, iPhones, or iPod touches.

If this is the first time you've used a particular e-mail address for FaceTime, Apple sends an e-mail to that address to verify the account. Tap (or click) Verify Now and enter your Apple ID and password to complete the FaceTime setup. If the e-mail address resides in Mail on the iPad, you're already good to go.

If you have multiple e-mail addresses, callers can use any of them for FaceTime. To add an e-mail address after the initial setup, tap Settings⇨FaceTime⇨Add Another Email. And phone numbers (for your iPhone) work too with iOS 6.

In fact, it's often a good idea to allocate separate e-mail addresses for FaceTime, assuming you have more than one Apple product that can take advantage of it. That way, a call to you when you're on your Mac, for example, won't ring on the iPad instead.

You can turn FaceTime on or off within Settings, but if you don't turn it off, you don't have to sign back in when you launch the app.

Making a FaceTime call

Now the real fun begins — making an actual video call. (We say specifically "video call" because you can now also make FaceTime audio calls.)

Follow these steps:

1. **Start the FaceTime app from the Home screen or by asking Siri to open the app on your behalf.**

   You can check out what you look like in a window prior to making a FaceTime call. So powder your nose and put on a happy face.

2. **Choose someone to call.**

   Pick among the following:

   - *Your contacts:* Tap a name or number, and then tap the e-mail address or phone number that contact has associated with FaceTime. To add a contact, tap Contacts, and tap +.

   - *Your recent calls:* Tap Recents and then tap the appropriate number or name.

   - *Your favorites:* You can add frequent callers to a favorites list. Once again, merely tap a name to call.

3. **Check or change what you display on the screen, if a change is needed.**

When a call is underway, you can still see what you look like to the other person through a small picture-in-picture window that you can drag to any corner of the video call window. It's a great way to know whether your mug has dropped out of sight.

4. **(Optional) To toggle between the front and rear cameras, tap the Camera button that is also labeled in Figure 8-11.**

5. **Tap End when you're ready to hang up.**

While you're on a FaceTime call, the following tips are handy to know:

Call window shows who you're talking to   How you look to the other person

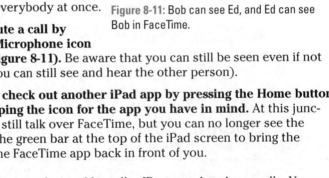

Switch cameras   Mute voice
End call

✔ **Rotate the iPad to its side to change the orientation.** In landscape mode, you're more likely to see everybody at once.

Figure 8-11: Bob can see Ed, and Ed can see Bob in FaceTime.

✔ **Silence or mute a call by tapping the Microphone icon (labeled in Figure 8-11).** Be aware that you can still be seen even if not heard (and you can still see and hear the other person).

✔ **Momentarily check out another iPad app by pressing the Home button and then tapping the icon for the app you have in mind.** At this juncture, you can still talk over FaceTime, but you can no longer see the person. Tap the green bar at the top of the iPad screen to bring the person and the FaceTime app back in front of you.

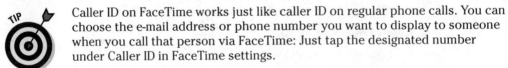

Caller ID on FaceTime works just like caller ID on regular phone calls. You can choose the e-mail address or phone number you want to display to someone when you call that person via FaceTime: Just tap the designated number under Caller ID in FaceTime settings.

Receiving a FaceTime call

Of course, you can get FaceTime calls as well as make them. FaceTime doesn't have to be open for you to receive a video call. Here's how incoming calls work:

✓ **Hearing the call:** When a call comes in, the caller's name (or e-mail address) prominently displays on the iPad's screen, as shown in Figure 8-12. You simultaneously hear the iPad ring.

✓ **Accepting or declining the call:** Tap Answer to answer the call or Decline if you'd rather not. If your iPad is locked when a FaceTime call comes in, slide the green arrow button to the right to answer. To decline it, do nothing and wait for the caller to give up.

✓ **Silencing the ring:** You can press the Sleep/Wake button at the top of the iPad to silence the incoming ring. If you know you don't want to be disturbed by FaceTime calls before you even hear the ring, flip the side switch on the iPad to

Figure 8-12: Tap Answer to answer the call.

mute. You may have to head to Settings (see Chapter 15) to change the function of this switch from Lock Rotation to mute. In Settings (or via Control Center), you can also turn on Do Not Disturb to silence incoming FaceTime calls.

✓ **Blocking unwanted callers:** If a person who keeps trying to FaceTime you (yep, we're treating it as a verb) becomes bothersome, you can block him or her. Go to Settings⊅FaceTime⊅Blocked, and choose the person's name from your Contacts.

With that, we hereby silence this chapter. But you can do more with the cameras on your iPad, and we get to that in Chapter 9.

9

You Oughta Be in Pictures

*T*hroughout this book, we sing the praises of the iPad's vibrant multitouch display. You'd be hard-pressed to find a more appealing portable screen for watching movies or playing games. As you might imagine, the iPad you have recently purchased (or are lusting after) is also a spectacular photo viewer. Images are crisp and vivid, at least those that you shot properly. (C'mon, we know Ansel Adams is a distant cousin.)

What's more, you can shoot some of those pictures directly with your prized tablet. The reasons, of course, are the front and rear cameras built into the device. If you read Chapter 8, you already know you can put those cameras to work capturing video. In this chapter, you get the big picture on shooting still images.

Okay, we need to get a couple of things out of the way: The iPad is never going to substitute for a point-and-shoot digital camera, much less a pricey digital SLR. As critics, we can quibble about the grainy images you get shooting in low light, or the fact that no flash is included. And shooting can be awkward.

But we're here, friends, to focus on the positive. And having cameras on your iPad may prove to be a godsend when no better option is available. Apple has jazzed up the cameras through the most recent iterations of the iPad. In the last chapter, we told you about the capability to capture full high-definition video up to what techies refer to as the 1080p standard.

In this chapter, we point out other optical enhancements in the most recent iPads. The 5-megapixel iSight camera has backside illumination and boasts what's known as an $f/2.4$ aperture and a five-element lens. It also has a hybrid infrared filter like what you'd find on an SLR, that helps lead to more uniform colors. Oh, and face detection makes sure the balance and focus are just right for up to ten faces on the screen.

All these features are photographer-speak for potentially snapping darn sweet pictures.

And we can think of certain circumstances — selling real estate, say, or shopping for a new home — where tablet cameras are quite convenient.

Apple has also made finding the pictures in your stash an easier task, too, with an organizational structure in iOS 7 that arranges photos in the Photos app by collections, moments, and years.

Meanwhile, you're in for a real treat if you're new to *Photo Booth,* a yuk-it-up Mac program that is also on the iPad. That may be the best, or at least the most fun, use of the cameras yet.

We get to Photo Booth at the end of this chapter. But over the next few pages, you discover the best ways to make the digital photos on the iPad come alive, no matter how they managed to arrive on your machine.

Shooting Pictures

There are a few ways to start shooting pictures on the iPad. So we're going to cut to the chase immediately:

1. **Fire up the camera itself. Choose one of the following:**
   - On the Home screen, tap the Camera app icon.
   - From the Lock screen, drag the Camera icon from the bottom-right corner in an upward motion.
   - Drag Control Center up from the bottom of the screen and tap the Camera app icon.
   - Ask Siri (read Chapter 14) to open the Camera app for you.

   However you get here, your iPad has turned into the tablet equivalent of a Kodak Instamatic, minus the film, of course, and in a form factor that is obviously much bigger. You're now effectively peering through one of the largest viewfinders imaginable in the near-10-inch display on full-size iPad models. And yea, the near-8-inch screen on the iPad mini provides a pretty sweet viewfinder as well.

TIP

If you're using a version of iOS prior to iOS 7 with your iPad, make sure the switch at the bottom-right corner of the screen is set to camera mode rather than video mode.

2. **Keep your eyes peeled on the iPad display, and use the viewfinder to frame your image.**

   We marvel at the display throughout this book; the Camera app gives us another reason to do so.

3. **Select a shooting format:**

   • *Photo:* Think snapshot.

   • *Square:* This gives you a picture formatted to make nice with the popular Instagram photo-sharing app.

   • *Video:* We kindly refer you to the previous chapter.

   You move from one format to another by swiping up or down along the right edge of the screen so that the format you've chosen is highlighted in yellow, with a yellow dot next to it.

4. **Snap your image:**

   • *Tap the white round camera button.* The button is at the middle-right edge of the screen whether you are holding the iPad in portrait mode or landscape mode (see Figure 9-1). As we show you in a moment, you'll be able to change the point of focus if necessary.

Front/Rear camera

Shutter release button

Camera Roll

Figure 9-1: Using the iPad as a camera.

- *Press the physical volume-up or volume-down button.* These buttons are on the side of the tablet (portrait mode) or at the top of the device (landscape mode). Just be careful not to cover the lens with your fingers.

The image you shoot lands in the Camera Roll in the lower-right corner of the screen. We explain what you can do with the images on the iPad later in this chapter.

Here are some tips for working with the Camera app:

- **Adjust the focal point.** Tap the portion of the screen in which you see the face or object you want as the image's focal point.

  A small rectangle (not shown in Figure 9-1) surrounds your selection, and the iPad automatically adjusts the exposure and focus of that part of the image.

- **Zoom in or out.** Tap the screen with two fingers and spread (unpinch) to zoom in or pinch to zoom out.

  The iPad has a 5X digital zoom, which basically crops and resizes an image. Such zooms are nowhere near as effective quality-wise as optical zooms on many digital cameras. Be aware that zooming works only with the rear camera still in Camera mode; it doesn't work with the front camera or when you shoot video.

- **See grid lines to help you compose your picture.** Tap Settings⇨Photos & Camera⇨Camera and tap the Grid switch to turn it on (green instead of gray will be showing).

  Grid lines can help you frame a shot using the photographic principle known as the Rule of Thirds.

- **Toggle between the front and rear cameras.** Tap the Front/Rear Camera button (see Figure 9-1) on the upper-right corner of the screen.

  We should point out that the front camera is of lower quality than its rear cousin, but it's perfectly adequate for the kinds of demands you put on it, including FaceTime and Photo Booth.

- **Shoot in HDR.** To exploit a feature known as *HDR,* or *high dynamic range,* photography, tap the HDR button (labeled in Figure 9-1).

  The HDR feature takes three separate exposures (long, normal, short) and blends the best parts of the three shots into a single image. In Settings (under Photos & Camera), you can choose to keep the "normal" photo along with your HDR result or just hang on to the latter.

- **Geotag your photos.** The iPad is pretty smart when it comes to geography. Turn on Location Services and the specific location settings for the camera appear in Settings. Pictures you take with the iPad cameras are *geotagged,* or identified by where they were shot.

Think long and hard before permitting images to be geotagged if you plan on sharing those images with people from whom you want to keep your address and other locations private — especially photos you're planning on sharing online.

Importing Pictures

You're not always going to use the iPad to take pictures, of course. Fortunately, there are several other methods for adding pictures to your prized tablet. Alas, one of these involves buying an accessory. We zoom in in the following sections.

Syncing pix

We devote an entire chapter (see Chapter 3) to synchronizing data with the iPad, so we don't dwell on it here. But because syncing pictures is still the most common way to import images to the iPad, we'd be remiss if we didn't mention it in this chapter. (The assumption in this section is that you already know how to get pictures onto your computer.)

When the iPad is connected to your computer, click the Photos tab on the iPad Device page in iTunes on the Mac or PC. Then select a source from the Sync Photos From pop-up menu.

Quickie reminder: On a Mac, you can sync photos (and videos) via iPhoto software version 6.06 or later and Aperture 3.02 or later. On a PC, you can sync with Adobe Photoshop Elements 8.0 or later. Alternatively, with both computers, you can sync with any folder that contains pictures.

Photo Stream: Sync photos among your devices effortlessly

The Photo Stream feature, when enabled, uploads and stores up to 1,000 photos from the last 30 days on iCloud and automatically downloads them to all your devices that have Photo Stream enabled when connected to Wi-Fi.

You need to enable two settings if you want to use your Photo Stream. First, instruct your iPad's camera to send photos *to* your Photo Stream by following these steps:

1. **Tap Settings on your Home screen.**

2. **Tap iCloud on the left side of the screen.**

3. **Tap Photos.**

4. **Tap the switch to turn on Photo Stream.**

Second, if you want to see your Photo Stream in the Photos app, do this:

1. **Tap Settings on your Home screen.**
2. **Tap Photos & Camera on the left side of the screen.**
3. **Tap the switch to turn on My Photo Stream.**

That's it. Turn it on, and you'll always have access to your last 30 days of pictures.

If you're a Mac user, iPhoto '11 (versions 9.2 and later) supports Photo Stream. To enable it, launch iPhoto on your Mac and do this:

1. **Choose iPhoto⇨Preferences.**
2. **Click the Photo Stream tab at the top of the Preferences window.**
3. **Select the My Photo Stream check box.**

A bit later in this chapter, we tell you about a cool variation that lets you share Photo Streams with friends and family.

Connecting a digital camera or memory card

Almost all the digital cameras we're aware of come with a USB cable that you can use to transfer images to a computer. Of course, the iPad isn't a regular computer, and it isn't equipped with a USB port.

Instead, Apple sells an optional $29 iPad Camera Connection Kit for iPad 2s and third-generation iPads, and separate ($29 each) Lightning-to-USB Camera Adapter and Lightning-to-SD Card Camera Reader cables for more recent iPad models. Here's how it works:

1. **Connect your camera to your iPad, using one of the two connectors in the kit.**

   Two small connectors are included in the Camera Connection, and each fits into the iPad's dock connector at the bottom of the machine. One connector has a USB port; the other, an SD slot. If you have a fourth-generation iPad or later, use the Lightning–to–USB Camera connector for your camera and the Lightning–to–SD Card cable to work with the card.

   If you're going the USB route, kindly use the cable that comes with your camera because no such cable comes with Apple's kit.

2. **Make sure that the iPad is unlocked.**

3. **If you haven't already done so, turn on the camera and ensure that it's set to transfer pictures.**

   Consult the manual that came with the camera if you're unsure which setting to use.

The Photos app on the iPad opens and displays the pictures that you can import from the camera.

4. **Tap Import All to select the entire bunch, or tap the individual pictures you want to include if you'd rather cherry-pick.**

   A check mark appears next to each image you select. And that's pretty much it: The iPad organizes the pictures into albums and such, as we describe later in this chapter.

At this point, you're free to erase the pictures from your camera.

The SD Card Reader connector accommodates the SD memory cards common to so many digital camera models. The procedure works almost identically to the USB connector, except that you're inserting the SD gizmo into the dock or Lightning connector port rather than the USB connector mentioned previously. Just be careful to insert the SD gently to prevent any damage.

The Camera Connection Kit and the Lightning connectors support many common photo formats, including JPEG and Raw. The latter is a format favored by photo enthusiasts.

We were surprised to discover that the USB connector in this kit can also be used with certain USB computer keyboards, MIDI keyboards, microphones, and even some USB memory card readers. No guarantee your USB device will be compatible, but it never hurts to try.

Saving images from e-mails and the web

You can save pictures that arrive in e-mails or pictures that you come across on the web very easily: Just press and hold your finger against the image, and then tap Save Image when the menu pops up a second later. Pictures are stored in the Camera Roll. You can also tap Copy to paste said image into another app on your device.

Where Have All My Pictures Gone?

So where exactly do your pictures hang out on the iPad? Well, we explain in the preceding section what happens to images saved from e-mails and the Internet: They reside in the Camera Roll. (We wanted to see whether you were paying attention.)

In the Photos app, you will also find pictures you've shared with friends (as well as pictures they've shared with you) through the Shared Stream feature that is part of iCloud. The photos you imported are readily available too and are grouped in the same albums they were in on the computer.

In this section, we show you not only where to find these pictures, but also how to display them and share them with others — and how to dispose of the duds that don't measure up to your lofty photographic standards.

Get ready to literally get your fingers on the pics (without having to worry about smudging them). You can get to your pictures from the Photos app or the Camera app. However, in the Camera app, you can see only the pictures and videos stored in Camera Roll; in the Photos app, you can view all the pictures and videos you've imported as well.

Open the Photos app by tapping its icon on the Home screen. Then take a gander at the trio of tabs at the bottom of the screen: Photos, Shared, Albums, shown in Figure 9-2. We take these on one by one.

Figure 9-2: Camera Roll tops your list of Photos albums.

Choosing albums

Tapping Albums lists all the albums you have on your iPad, with Camera Roll sitting on the upper left. Apple has kindly supplied a couple of additional premade albums: Panoramas, for all the panoramic scenes you've captured (on other devices because the feature isn't available on the iPad, at least not without third-party apps), and Videos. (The process of shooting videos is described in the previous chapter.)

Albums that were synced from your Macintosh computer carry the From My Mac tag. These include the Events album and the Faces album, which used to have dedicated buttons in iOS, but no more. Another album that used to have its own dedicated button is Places, but it's not visible in this view.

Tap an album listing to open it. When you do, you see the minimalistic interface, shown in Figure 9-3, which reveals the by-now-familiar Camera Roll.

Browse the thumbnails until you find the picture or video you want, and then tap it. We soon show you all the cool things you can do from there.

You'll know when a thumbnail represents a video rather than a still image because the thumbnail displays a tiny movie camera icon accompanied by the length of the video.

If you can't locate the thumbnail for a photo you have in mind, flick up or down to scroll through the pictures rapidly, or use a slower dragging motion to pore over the images more deliberately. We're certain you will find the one you're looking for soon enough.

To return to the list of albums, tap Albums at the upper-left corner of the screen.

After backing out, you can create a new album from the albums view by tapping the + in the upper-left corner (refer to Figure 9-2) and choosing a name for the album. Type that name and tap Save. To select pictures (or videos) to add to your newly minted album, tap their thumbnails.

Shortly, we show you how to add pictures to an *existing* album.

 Albums you create on the iPad reside only on the iPad. They can't be synced or copied to your PC or Mac.

The Photos tab

Placing pictures into photo albums seems to us like it's been the way of the world forever. But albums per se are not the only organizing structure that makes sense.

Select for action items or to add selected images to albums.

This thumbnail represents a video.

Return to Albums.

View by years, collections, or moments.

View photos you shared or others shared with you.

View by albums.

Figure 9-3: Digging into Camera Roll.

As part of iOS 7, Apple cooked up a simple but ingenious interface for presenting pictures that is essentially a timeline of photos, grouped by years, collections, and moments (see Figure 9-4):

- **Years:** Pictures categorized by years are indeed all the pictures taken in a given year. Your photos appear as a grid of Lilliputian thumbnails; in the case of years, you can barely make out any of the pictures.

- **Collections:** The collections category is a subset within a year, such as your holiday pictures in Las Vegas. Tap the Years view, and slightly bigger thumbnails appear as part of the Collections view.

✔ **Moments:** Within the collections category is another subset called *moments* — the pictures, say, that you took by the dancing fountains at the Bellagio Hotel. Tap the collections view, and the thumbnails get just a little bit bigger in the moments view; and you can more easily make out who and what is in them, though the thumbnails are still compact.

Years   Collections

Moments

Figure 9-4: View your photos by years (top left), collections (top right), and moments (bottom left).

Here's how you work in the views:

- **Select a photo.** In the years and collections views, you can press and drag your finger across the grid to quickly skim all the pictures — as you do so, the thumbnails swell again in size, one by one. Lift your finger, and that last thumbnail takes over a chunk of the screen, ready for you to admire it, edit it, or share it. In moments view, you can also tap a thumbnail to select it.

- **Edit a photo.** Select an image, and at the upper right (see Figure 9-5) you see Edit, which you can tap to tweak the picture. We tell you all about the editing maneuvers you can take in the "Touching up photos" section later in this chapter.

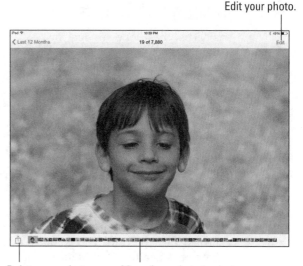

Edit your photo.

Delete your photo.   Move from photo to photo.

Figure 9-5: You can edit, share, or discard a photo.

- **Share your photo:** Tap the Action icon, which gives you a variety of options for sharing the image, copying it, including it in a slideshow, and more.

- **Move from picture to picture.** At the very bottom edge of the display is a skimming bar for quickly moving from picture to picture. We get to all of that shortly.

- **See every photo in your library for a particular view.** Apple summarizes photos in the collections and years views by showing you only a representative sample for those collections and years. To see every photo in your library that fits those views, go to Settings⇨Photos & Camera and turn on Summarize Photos by tapping the switch to make it green.

- **Find location information.** Through all three views, you'll see location information headings that get a tad more specific as you move from years to collections to moments, assuming your iPad knows where the pictures were taken. If you tap a place location, Apple will fire up a map and show you how many pictures were taken in the area, as shown in Figure 9-6.

TIP

You can spread your fingers on a map to enlarge it and narrow the pictures taken to a particular area, town, or even neighborhood. For more on Maps, flip to Chapter 6.

Swimming in Photo Stream

As part of the iCloud service, any photo you take with the iPad or with another iOS device dating back to iOS 5 can be automatically pushed to all your other devices, specifically your Mac, PC, iPod touch, Apple TV (third-generation or later), or iPhone. The transfer takes place through the magic of *Photo Stream,* the antidote to the endless problem of "I've snapped a picture; now what?"

Figure 9-6: Finding pictures on a map.

You need not fret about storage space when using Photo Stream. The last 1,000 pictures you've taken over up to 30 days are held in a special Photo Stream album for 30 days — enough time, Apple figures, for all your devices to connect and grab those images, because a Wi-Fi connection is your only requirement. All the pictures you've taken remain on your Mac or PC, because those machines have more capacious storage. You can always manually move images from the Photo Stream album into other albums on your iPad or other iOS devices and computers.

Photos taken on the iPad aren't whisked away into Photo Stream until you leave the Camera app. In that way, you get a chance to delete pictures that you'd rather not have turn up everywhere.

But once you leave the Camera app, all the photos there are saved in My Photo Stream (found in the list of Albums in the Photos app). The Camera Roll also includes pictures that arrived as e-mail attachments and eventually landed in there because you saved them. Screen captures taken on the iPad are there as well.

You can save pictures in the My Photo Stream album to any other album on the tablet. Choose the images you have in mind, and tap the Action icon in the bottom-left corner of the screen. Then tap Save to Camera Roll.

If you delete pictures from My Photo Stream, they are removed also from the stream on your other devices. But the pictures safely remain in Camera Roll in your iPad or whatever device you used to shoot them.

If (for some reason) the pictures you snap on the iPad are not being uploaded, go to Settings, scroll down, tap Photos & Camera, and make sure Photo Stream is turned on.

Sharing Photo Streams

The Photo Streams feature is a generally terrific and hassle-free way for you to make sure the pictures you've shot end up on your devices. But Apple, in its infinite wisdom, recognizes that you might also want to share your best images with friends and family and have those pictures automatically appear on those people's devices.

An impressive — and aptly named — solution called Shared Photo Streams arrived on the iPad, iPod touch, and iPhone with iOS 6 (and a bit earlier on Macs running OS X Mountain Lion). It was modified in iOS 7 and is now referred to as iCloud Sharing, or just *Shared Streams.* The feature enables you to share pictures and videos with other folks, and in turn lets you receive photo streams that they make available to you.

Here's how to get Shared Photo Streams up and running:

1. **On the Home screen, tap Settings.**

2. **Tap Photos & Camera.**

3. **If the Photo Sharing option isn't on, tap it to turn it on.**

4. **Open the Photos app, and then tap the Shared tab.**

5. **Tap New Shared Stream and then type a name for your stream in the New Stream dialog box that appears.**

   The name is entirely your call, but we recommend something fairly descriptive, along the lines of *My Trip to Tahiti* (and you should be so lucky).

6. **Tap Next, and choose who will receive your stream, as shown in Figure 9-7.**

   You can type a phone number, text address, or an e-mail address, or choose one of your contacts by tapping the + in a circle in the To field.

Figure 9-7: Inviting people to share in your stream.

7. **Tap Create.**

   The recipient will receive an e-mail similar to the one in Figure 9-8 and can choose to subscribe to the stream by tapping the button.

8. **Add photos to the shared stream, choosing them from years, collections, or moments.**

9. **(Optional) Enter a comment.**

10. **Tap Post.**

Subscribe to Edward Baig's "My Cool Vacation" Photo Stream?

You are invited to view this Photo Stream and post your own photos, videos, and comments.
Other subscribers will see your email address when you join.

Subscribe to this Photo Stream

iCloud

iCloud is a service provided by Apple. My Apple ID | Support | Terms and Conditions | Privacy Policy | Don't Send Me Photo Stream Emails
Copyright © 2013 Apple Inc. 1 Infinite Loop, Cupertino, CA 95014, United States. All rights reserved.

Figure 9-8: Inviting a friend to share a Photo Stream.

We recommend checking out the activity view at the top left of your Shared streams. It provides a nice summary of photos you and your pals posted.

You can share photos and videos with pretty much anyone who has online access — people don't need to join iCloud. If you want to share your stream with everyone, you can do so through a public gallery on iCloud.com. To do that, tap the Shared icon at the bottom of the Photos app and then tap the stream in question. Tap the People tab in the upper right, tap the Public Website switch to On, and then share the web link.

If the people you are sharing with have their own iCloud accounts and are on an iOS 6 account or later (or using a Macintosh computer running OS X Mountain Lion or Mavericks), they can not only glom on to your stream to view your photos, but also leave comments about them. Don't worry — you have the power to remove snarky remarks.

If the people you are sharing with have iOS 7, they can add their own photos and videos to the stream, provided that doing so is okay with you. If it is, turn on the Subscribers Can Post switch. At your discretion, you can also receive notifications when your subscribers weigh in with comments or add their own pictures or videos to the Shared stream.

If you're ultimately unhappy with the Shared stream itself — or the people with whom you are sharing it — you can kill the Shared stream or at minimum kick those people off the list. To kill the stream, tap the Delete Photo Stream button.

To remove a subscriber, tap the stream, tap the People tab, and then tap the name of the person with whom you are sharing the stream. Scroll down to the bottom and tap Remove Subscriber. You'll be asked to tap a Remove button just to make sure or tap Cancel if you have second thoughts. If you do remove a subscriber, you can always re-invite the person later.

Admiring Your Pictures

Photographs are meant to be seen, of course, not buried in the digital equivalent of a shoebox. The iPad affords you some neat ways to manipulate, view, and share your best photos.

You've already found out how to find individual pictures in albums, via iCloud, and in groupings of years, collections, and moments. You may already know (from previous sections in this chapter) how to display picture controls. But you can do a lot of maneuvering of your pictures without summoning those controls. Here are some options:

- **Skip ahead or view the preceding picture:** From a moments view, or after selecting a picture from within an album, flick your finger left or right.

- **Switch from landscape or portrait mode:** Here you see the iPad's wizardry (or, more specifically, the device's cool sensors) at work. When you turn the iPad sideways, the picture automatically reorients itself from portrait to landscape mode, as the images in Figure 9-9 show. Rotate the device back to portrait mode, and the picture readjusts accordingly.

- **Skim:** A bar appears at the bottom of the screen when you summon picture controls. Drag your finger across the bar in either direction to quickly view all the pictures in an open album.

Figure 9-9: The same picture in portrait (left) and landscape (right) modes.

- **Zoom:** Double-tap to zoom in on an image and make it larger. Do so again to zoom out and make it smaller. Alternatively, on the photo, pinch your thumb and index finger together to zoom in and unpinch them to zoom out.

- **Pan and scroll:** This cool little feature was once practically guaranteed to make you the life of the party. Now it's commonplace, if no less cool. After you zoom in on a picture, drag it around the screen with your finger. Besides impressing your friends, you can bring front and center the part of the image you most care about. That lets you zoom in on Fido's adorable face as opposed to, say, the unflattering picture of the person holding the dog in his lap.

Touching up photos

The iPad is never going to serve as a substitute for a high-end photo-editing program such as Adobe Photoshop. But you can do some relatively simple touch-ups, right from the Photos app.

Choose an image and tap Edit. At the bottom of the Edit Photo screen are five icons, shown in Figure 9-10:

Edit your photo
using these buttons.

Figure 9-10: Who says you can't improve the quality of the picture?

- ✔ **Rotate:** Rotate the image counterclockwise.

- ✔ **Enhance:** Let the iPad take a stab at making your image look better. Apple lightens or darkens the picture, tweaks color saturation, and more. Repeatedly tap the icon to turn this tool on or off. Tap Save if you like the result. Along the way, you can always tap Undo or Revert to Original.

- ✔ **Add a filter:** Tap Filters to choose a filter — Mono, Tonal, Noir, Fade, Chrome, Process, Transfer, and Instant. If you're not satisfied after applying a filter, tap None or Revert to Original to go back to the original photo.

- ✔ **Remove red-eye:** Get rid of that annoying red-eye. Tap Red-Eye, and tap each eye; tap again to undo. If the iPad doesn't actually find an eye to correct, a message pops up indicating that is the case.

- ✔ **Crop:** Crop the image. By tapping Crop and then Aspect Ratio, you can crop the image through many different options (Original, Square, 3 x 2, 3 x 5, 4 x 3, 4 x 6, 5 x 7, 8 x 10, 16 x 9). Drag the photo around the crop grid, pinch, and zoom. If necessary, choose Reset and pick a new aspect ratio. When you're satisfied with the result, tap Crop and then tap Save to save the image. Or tap Cancel to revert to the original or tap Revert to Original at the top of the screen to accomplish the same thing.

Deleting pictures

We told a tiny fib earlier by intimating that photographs are meant to be seen. We should have amended that statement by saying that *some* pictures are meant to be seen. Others you can't get rid of fast enough. Fortunately, the iPad makes it a cinch to bury the evidence:

1. **Tap the objectionable photograph.**

2. **Tap to display the picture controls, if they're not already displayed.**

3. **Tap the trashcan icon.**

4. **Tap Delete Photo.**

   The photo mercifully disappears. It's also deleted from Photo Stream across all your devices.

If you've applied more than one of the tools to your image, you can use the Undo button in the upper-left corner to step backward through time, undoing one step for each tap. Or tap the Revert to Original button to remove all the improvements at once.

Admiring pictures on the TV

The AirPlay feature that lets you stream music and videos wirelessly from the iPad to an Apple TV (see Chapter 8) works with photos, too. For wired connections to a TV, let us direct you to Chapter 17 on accessories.

To watch the slideshow or view individual pictures on a big screen TV via Apple TV, tap the AirPlay button shown that you can summon via Control Center and then tap Apple TV from the list. If the AirPlay button isn't visible, make sure that the iPad and Apple TV share the same Wi-Fi network. Tap the iPad button to view the slideshow again on the iPad. We can tell you the experience is very cool.

Launching Slideshows

Those of us who store a lot of photographs on computers are familiar with running slideshows of those images. You can easily replicate the experience on the iPad, and through AirPlay, stream the slideshow wirelessly to an Apple TV. Or you can use an optional cable that connects to a TV, projector, or even — you still got one of these? — a VCR. Follow these steps:

1. **Choose Camera Roll or another album in the albums list.**

   To do so, tap the Photos icon from the Home screen or tap the Camera Roll button in the Camera app.

2. **Do one of the following:**

   - *In the Photos app:* Select a picture from an album, tap it to summon the picture controls (as shown in Figure 9-11), and then tap the Action icon in the bottom left. At the top of the screen, the image you selected as the basis of your slideshow has a check mark, as shown in Figure 9-12. Scroll to the left or right to view other pictures in the album and tap any or all of those adjacent images to select them for the slideshow as well. Check marks appear as you do so. Tap any picture a second time to deselect it and remove the check mark.

Figure 9-11: Summoning picture controls.

• *In the Camera app:* Tap the image in the lower-right corner of the screen to display the most recent image in Camera Roll, and find a picture to include in your slideshow. From there, follow the preceding steps to tap and choose other images for the slideshow.

3. **Tap Slideshow.**

   You are taken to the Slideshow Options screen, as shown in Figure 9-13.

4. **Choose transition effects and the music (if any) that you'd like to accompany the slideshow:**

   • *Transitions:* You can change the effect you see when you move from one slide to the next. Your five choices: Cube, Dissolve, Ripple, Wipe, or a personal favorite of ours, *Origami,* in which the images fold out in ways similar to the Japanese folk art of paper folding. Why not try them all to see what you like?

Figure 9-12: Check off the pictures to add to your slideshow.

   • *Music:* Adding music to a slideshow couldn't be easier. From the Slideshow Options window, tap the Play Music option so that it's turned on. Then tap Music in the Slideshow Options overlay to choose your soundtrack from the playlists, artists, songs, or music albums on the device. Ed loves backing up slideshows with Sinatra, Sarah Vaughan, or Gershwin, among numerous other artists. Bob loves using songs by The Beatles or stately classical music.

TIP

Tap anywhere on the screen while a slideshow is playing to exit the slideshow.

Figure 9-13: Choose options for your slideshow.

5. **Choose where you get to see the slideshow.**

   You can see the slideshow on your iPad itself or have it beamed wirelessly to an Apple TV, should you own Apple's $99 set-top box.

6. **Tap Start Slideshow.**

   The slideshow ends automatically unless you've set it to repeat, as explained in the next section. Tap the screen to end it prematurely.

Your only obligation is to enjoy the show.

If you don't want to cherry-pick photos for a slideshow but instead want to include every picture in a given album, tap an album in Albums view so that the word *Slideshow* appears at the upper-right reaches of the screen. Tap Slideshow. You are taken to the Slideshow Options screen (see Step 3). From there, pick your transitions and/or music, and tap Start Slideshow. We still want you to enjoy the show.

You can alter the length of time each slide is shown, change the transition effects between pictures, and display images in random order.

From the Home screen, tap Settings and then scroll down and tap Photos & Camera. Then tap any of the following to make changes:

- ✔ **Play Each Slide For:** You have five choices (2 seconds, 3 seconds, 5 seconds, 10 seconds, 20 seconds). When you're finished, tap the Photos & Camera button to return to the main Settings screen for Photos.

- ✔ **Repeat:** If this option is turned on, the slideshow continues to loop until you stop it. If it's turned off, the slideshow for Camera Roll or your album plays just once.

- ✔ **Shuffle:** Turning on this switch plays slides in random order.

Press the Home button to leave the settings and return to the Home screen.

More (Not-So-) Stupid Picture Tricks

You can take advantage of the photos on the iPad in a few more ways. In each case, you tap the picture and make sure the picture controls are displayed. Then tap the Action icon at the bottom left to display the choices shown in Figure 9-14 (not all choices are visible).

Here's a rundown of each choice:

- ✔ **AirDrop:** AirDrop is a neat wireless method for sharing photos, videos, or other files with folks who happen to be nearby and also have a relatively recent iOS 7-capable device (fourth-generation or later iPad,

Choosing photos.

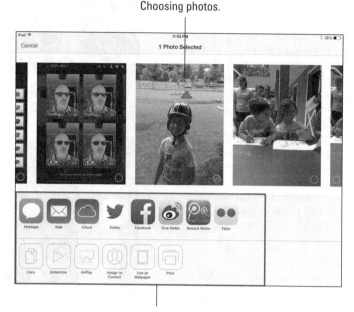

Actions you can take with
your selected photo.

Figure 9-14: Look at what else I can do!

iPhone 5 or later, and the most recent iPod touch). Tap a photo to select
it and then tap the icon representing the device owned by the person
with whom you are trying to share the image. That person will receive
an invitation to accept the photograph or reject it, as shown in
Figure 9-15. If the photo is accepted, the picture lands on the person's
Camera Roll almost immediately.

Turn on AirDrop in Control Center (see Chapter 14) and choose whether
to make your tablet discoverable to everyone or only to your contacts
who are in the vicinity.

✔ **Message:** You can also send a picture through the Message app. Tap the
Message option, and the picture is embedded in your outgoing message;
you merely need to enter the phone number or name of the person to
whom you're sending the picture. If that person is also using an iOS 5 or
later device, the photo will be sent as an iMessage, which doesn't count
against your texting allotment.

✔ **Mail:** Some photos are so precious that you just have to share them with
family members and friends. When you tap Mail, the picture is automatically embedded in the body of an outgoing e-mail message. Use the virtual
keyboard to enter the e-mail addresses, subject line, and any comments
you want to add — you know, something profound, such as "Isn't this

a great-looking photo?" After tapping Send to whisk picture and accompanying message on their way, you have the option to reduce the image size (small, medium, or large) or keep the actual size. Consider the trade-offs: A smaller image may get through any limits imposed by your (or the recipient's) Internet provider or company. But if you can get the largest image through, you will give the recipient the full picture (forgive the pun) in all its glory. (Check out Chapter 5 for more info on using e-mail.)

✓ **iCloud:** You can post pics to Apple's online cloud locker.

✓ **Twitter:** Lots of people send pictures with their tweets these days. The iPad makes it breeze. Tap Tweet, and your picture is embedded in an outgoing tweet. Just add your words, sticking to Twitter's character limit of 140, and tap Post.

✓ **Facebook:** And lots of people share photos on the world's largest social network. After your Facebook account is configured, you too can post there from your iPad.

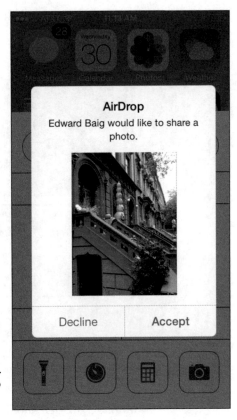

Figure 9-15: AirDrop lets you share a picture wirelessly with a friend who is nearby.

✓ **Sina Weibo and Tencent Weibo:** If you've enabled a Chinese keyboard, you'll see options for China's own social networks.

✓ **Flickr:** The Yahoo!-owned service is another popular photo-sharing destination.

✓ **Copy:** Tap to paste the image in an e-mail or elsewhere.

✓ **Slideshow:** As mentioned, this is your starting point for a slideshow, complete with an optional musical soundtrack.

✓ **AirPlay:** Own an Apple TV set-top box? You can use AirPlay to stream photos from the phone to the TV.

✓ **Save to Camera Roll:** If you didn't shoot the image in question on your iPad but want to add it to the device's Camera Roll, tap the Save to Camera Roll option.

- **Assign to Contact:** If you assign a picture to someone in your Contacts list, the picture you assign pops up whenever you receive a call from that person (on, say, your iPhone, since the iPad is not a phone) or receive a text. Tap Assign to Contact. Your list of contacts appears on the screen. Scroll through the list to find the person who matches the picture of the moment. As with the Use as Wallpaper option (described next), you can drag and resize the picture to get it just right. Then tap Set Photo.

  You can also assign a photo to a contact by starting out in Contacts. To change the picture you assigned to a person, tap his or her name in the Contacts list, tap Edit, and then tap the person's picture or the circle without a picture that carries the label Add Photo. From there, you can take another photo with one of the iPad's digital cameras, select another photo from one of your albums, or edit the photo you're already using (by resizing and dragging it to a new position). Of course, you are removing the photo you no longer want.

- **Use as Wallpaper:** Even with dramatic new dynamic designs, the background images on the iPad that Apple supplies can't measure up to your own pictures of your spouse, your kids, or your pet, perhaps? When you tap the Use as Wallpaper button, you see what the present image looks like as the iPad's background picture. In addition, you're given the opportunity to move the picture around and resize it, through the now-familiar action of dragging or pinching against the screen with your fingers. You can even see how the picture looks against the time and date that appear on the Lock screen, as Figure 9-16 shows. When you're satisfied with what the wallpaper looks like, tap the appropriate Set button. Options appear that let you use the photo as wallpaper for the Lock screen, the Home screen, or both. Per usual, you also have the option to tap Cancel. (You find out more about wallpaper in Chapter 15.)

- **Print:** In the 21st century, people are accustomed to viewing pictures on computer screens, digital frames, smartphones, and tablets. In the previous century, most viewed prints. But something is still special about printing pictures to give away, carry around, or place in an old-fashioned photo frame or album. If you have an AirPrint-capable printer, tap

Figure 9-16: Beautifying the iPad with wallpaper.

Print to print the photo, and the iPad tries to find the printer. When it does, you can choose how many copies of the print you wish to duplicate. If your printer has a tray for photo paper in addition to plain paper, the printer may automatically switch to that tray when you try to print a picture.

Sometimes you want to make decisions about multiple pictures at the same time, whether you're sharing them online, copying or printing them, adding them to a new album, or deleting them in bulk. Here's a convenient way to do so:

1. **Launch the Photos app, and either tap a specific album in the app or open to a moments view so that you see thumbnails of your pictures.**

2. **Tap Select at the upper right, and then tap each thumbnail on which you are planning to take action, so that a check mark appears.**

   As you do so, the count for each picture you select increases.

3. **Tap the Action icon and the action you want to take.**

   You can share pictures on a social network in bulk, e-mail them, send them via a message, or copy or print them. If you're not already in the Camera Roll, you can also save pictures there. The options that appear may vary depending on how many pictures you've selected — there's a limit on e-mailing too many photos, for example.

   You don't have to tap the Action icon to add pictures to a designated album or to delete them. After making your picture selections, look for Add To and the trashcan icon at the upper-left corner of the screen. Tap Add To and then, from the list that appears, tap the album where you want the pictures you've chosen to land. If you tap the trashcan icon instead, you can delete the selected photos.

Organizing Your Places, Faces, and Events

You've seen how pictures on the iPad can be organized into albums, years, collections, and moments. Apple has also added iPad support for the nifty Faces and Events features, which are familiar to Mac owners who use iPhoto software. In fact, Faces and Events that show up in your list of albums are accompanied by the words *From My Mac.*

Consult Chapter 3 on syncing for a refresher on getting data to and from a computer to your tablet and back, a process that is even simpler since the introduction of iCloud. When the iPad is connected to a Mac, you can sync photo events (pictures taken around birthdays, anniversaries, and so on) or faces (all the shots taken with a particular person in them). In Figure 9-17, all the pictures have Ed's mug in them.

The Faces feature requires that you sync to the iPad with iPhoto or Aperture on a Mac.

Entering the Photo Booth

Remember the old-fashioned photo booths at the local 5 and Dime? Remember the 5 and Dime? Okay, if you don't remember such variety stores, your parents probably do, and if they don't, their parents no doubt do. The point is that photo booths (which do still exist) are fun places to ham it up solo or with a friend as the machine captures and spits out wallet-size pictures.

Figure 9-17: Facing Ed in Faces.

With the Photo Booth app, Apple has cooked up a modern alternative to a real photo booth. The app is a close cousin to a similar application on the Mac. Here's how Photo Booth works:

1. **Tap the Photo Booth icon.**

    You get the tic-tac-toe-style grid shown in Figure 9-18.

2. **Point the front-facing camera at your face.**

    You see your mug through a prism of eight rather wacky special effects: Thermal Camera, Mirror, X-Ray, Kaleidoscope, Light Tunnel, Squeeze, Twirl, and Stretch. The center square (what is this, *Hollywood Squares?*) is the only one in which you come off looking normal — or, as we like to kid, like you're supposed to look. Some of the effects make you look scary; some, merely goofy.

    You can also use the rear camera in Photo Booth to subject your friends to this form of, um, visual abuse.

Figure 9-18: Photo booths of yesteryear weren't like this.

3. **Choose one of the special effects (or stick with Normal) by tapping one of the thumbnails.**

   Ed chose Mirror for the example shown in Figure 9-19 because, after all, two Eds are better than one. (Sorry, couldn't resist.)

   If you're not satisfied with the effect you've chosen, tap the icon at the lower-left corner of the app to return to the Photo Booth grid and select another.

4. **When you have your bizarre look just right, tap the shutter release on the screen to snap the picture.**

   Your pic lands (as do other pictures taken with the iPad cameras) in the Camera Roll album.

5. **(Optional) After choosing an effect and taking a picture, doctor things up even further by pinching or unpinching with your fingers.**

Figure 9-19: When one co-author just isn't enough.

From the Camera Roll album or from right here in the Photo Booth, pictures can be shared in all the usual places or — you might want to seriously consider this, given the distortions you've just applied to your face — deleted.

Nah, we're only kidding. Keep the image and take a lot more. Photo Booth may be a blast from the past, but we think it's just a blast.

Before leaving this photography section, we want to steer you to the App Store, which we explore in greater depth in Chapter 11. As of this writing, hundreds, probably thousands, of photography-related apps are available there, a whole host of them free. That's too many to mention here, but we know you'll find terrific photo apps just by wandering around the place.

And there you have it. You have just passed Photography 101 on the iPad. We trust that the coursework was, forgive the pun, a snap.

10

Curling Up with a Good iBook

Don't be surprised if you have to answer this question from an inquisitive child someday: "Is it true, Grandpa, that people once read books on paper?"

That time may still be a ways off, but it somehow doesn't seem far-fetched anymore. Apple is among the tech companies that are major proponents of the electronic-books revolution.

Don't get us wrong; we love physical books as much as anyone and are in no way urging their imminent demise. But we also recognize the real-world benefits behind Apple's digital publishing efforts — and those by companies like Amazon (which manufactures what is, for now, the market-leading Kindle electronic reader). As you discover in this chapter, the Kindle plays a role on the iPad as well.

For its part, the iPad makes a terrific electronic reader, with color and dazzling special effects, including pages that turn like those in a real book.

We open the page on this chapter to see how to find and purchase books for your iPad, and how to read them after they land on your virtual bookshelf. But first, we look at why you might want to read books and periodicals on your iPad.

Why E-Books?

We've run into plenty of skeptics who ask, "What's so wrong with the paper books that folks have only been reading for centuries that we now have to go digital?" The short answer is that nothing is wrong with physical books — except maybe that paper, over the long term, is fragile, and paper books tend to be bulky, a potential impediment for travelers.

On the other hand, when asked why he prefers paper books, Bob likes to drop one from shoulder height and ask, "Can your iPad (or Kindle) do that?"

Having said that, though, now consider the electronic advantages:

- **No more weight or bulk constraints:** You can cart a whole bunch of e-books around when you travel, without breaking your back. To the avid bookworm, this potentially changes the whole dynamic in the way you read. Because you can carry so many books wherever you go, you can read whatever type of book strikes your fancy at the moment, kind of like listening to a song that fits your current mood. You have no obligation to read a book from start to finish before opening a new bestseller just because that happens to be the one book you happen to have in your bag. In other words, weight constraints are out the window.

- **Feel like reading a trashy novel?** Go for it. Rather immerse yourself in classic literature? Go for that. You might read a textbook, cookbook, or biography. Or gaze in wonder at an illustrated beauty. What's more, you can switch among the various titles and styles of books at will before finishing any single title.

- **Flexible fonts and type sizes:** With e-books, or what Apple prefers to call *iBooks,* you can change the text size and fonts on the fly — quite useful for people with less than 20/20 vision.

- **Get the meaning of a word on the spot:** No more searching for a physical dictionary. You can look up an unfamiliar word on the spot.

- **Search with ease:** Need to do research on a particular subject? Enter a search term to find each and every mention of the subject in the book you're reading.

- **Read in the dark:** The iPad has a high-resolution backlit display so that you can read without a lamp nearby, which is useful in bed when your partner is trying to sleep.

- **See all the artwork in color:** Indeed, you're making no real visual sacrifices anymore. For example, the latest iBooks software from Apple lets you experience (within certain limits) the kind of stunning art book once reserved for a coffee table. Or you can display a colorful children's picture book.

Truth is, there are two sides to this backlit story. The grayscale electronic ink displays found on Amazon's Kindle and several other e-readers may be easier on the eyes and reduce fatigue, especially if you read for hours on end. And although you may indeed have to supply your own lighting source to read in low-light situations, at least on some of the devices, those screens are easier to see than the iPad screen when you're out and about in bright sunshine. And some newer E Ink-type readers include displays that actually do light up.

You can *buy* an iBook using iTunes on your Mac or PC, and with the arrival of Mac OS X Mavericks, you can now read that book on your Mac. You can also *read* iBooks on an iPhone, iPad, or iPod touch.

Beginning the iBook Story

To start reading iBooks on your iPad, you have to fetch the iBooks app in the App Store. (For more on the App Store, consult Chapter 11.)

As you might imagine, the app is free, and it comes with access to Apple's iBooks Store, of which we have more to say later in this chapter. For now, just know that iBooks Store is an inviting place to browse and shop for books 24 hours a day. All the other books you end up purchasing for your iPad library turn up on the handsome wooden bookshelf, as shown in Figure 10-1. The following basics help you navigate the iBooks main screen:

- **Change the view:** If you prefer to view a list of your books rather than use this Bookshelf view, tap the button toward the upper-right corner of the screen (labeled in Figure 10-1). In this view, you can sort the list by title, author, or category (as shown in Figure 10-2), or you can rearrange where books appear on the bookshelf.

- **Rearrange books in Bookshelf view:** Hold your finger on the book you want to move. Wait a second or two, and it will increase in size slightly to let you know it's now movable. Without lifting your finger, drag the book to its new location and then release.

- **Rearrange books in List view:** Tap Edit (in the upper-right corner) and then press the three horizontal lines to the right of the book you want to move. Now drag the book up or down the list.

View books by collection

Open iBooks Store

Tap a cover to open a book.

Bookshelf view

List view

Figure 10-1: You can read a book by its cover.

- **Remove a book from the bookshelf:** In either view, tap Edit and then tap the book(s) you want to remove. Each book you tap displays a check mark; tap the book again to remove the check mark and thus deselect the book. When all the books you want to delete have check marks, tap either the Delete This Copy or Delete From All Devices button at top left.

As with other content you purchase from Apple, you can restore (download) any book you've purchased from the Purchased tab of the iBooks Store.

✔ **Organize books by collections:** If you have a vast library of e-books, you might want to organize titles by genre or subject by creating collections of like-minded works. You might have collections of mysteries, classics, biographies, children's books, how-to's, textbooks, even all the *For Dummies* books you (hopefully) own. Apple has

Figure 10-2: Sort a list of your books by title, author, category, or bookshelf.

already created two collections on your behalf: Books for all titles and PDFs for the Adobe PDF files you may have on your iPad. (Apple doesn't let you edit or remove the premade Books or PDFs collections.) After you buy one or more titles through the store, Apple creates a Purchased Books collection. To create, rename, or remove a collection of your own, tap the Collections button (also labeled in Figure 10-1) to show off your current list of collections and choose from the following options:

- Tap New to add a new collection.

- Tap Edit and the red circle with the white dash to delete a collection. Tap Delete to finish the job.

  If the collection has books in it, you're asked whether you want to remove the contents of this collection from your iPad. If you choose not to remove them, they're returned to their original collections (Books, PDFs, or any other collection).

- If you want to change the name of a collection, tap its name.

- If you want to move a book or PDF to a collection, go to the bookshelf, tap Edit, tap each work you want to move, and then tap Move. Select the new collection for these titles.

A book can reside only in one collection at a time, with the noted exception of the Purchased Books collection.

Of course, here we are telling you how to move or get rid of a book before you've even had a chance to read it. How gauche. The next section helps you start reading.

Reading a Book

To start reading a book, tap it. The book leaps off the shelf, and at the same time, it opens to either the beginning of the book or the place where you left off. (And you may have left off on an iPhone, iPod touch, or another iPad because through your Apple ID, your virtual place in a book is transported from device to device as long as both devices have an Internet connection.)

Even from the very title page, you can appreciate the color and beauty of Apple's app as well as the navigation tools, as shown in Figure 10-3.

If you rotate the iPad to the side, the one-page book view becomes a two-page view, though all the navigational controls remain the same. On the newer multitouch books, you may have a scrolling view of a book rather than the typical one-page view.

While you're lounging around reading, and especially if you're lying down, we recommend that you use the Screen Rotation Lock (shown in Chapter 1) to stop the iPad from inadvertently rotating the display.

You can take advantage of the iPad's VoiceOver feature to have the iPad read to you out loud. It may not be quite like having Mom or Dad read you to sleep, but it can be a potential godsend for people with impaired vision. For more on the VoiceOver feature, consult Chapter 15.

The VoiceOver feature is useful under certain circumstances. But we're not at the point where the

Text Size,
Fonts,
Brightness

Table of Contents

Search

Add bookmark.

Slider

Figure 10-3: Books on the iPad offer handy reading and navigation tools.

iPad's loquacious virtual assistant Siri can read a book out loud. Maybe someday. For now, Siri can open the iBooks app, though. Read Chapter 14 for more on Siri.

Turning pages

You've been turning pages in books your entire life, so you don't want this simple feat to become a complicated ordeal just because you're now reading electronically. Fear not, it's not. You have no buttons to press.

Instead, to turn to the *next* page of a book, do any of the following:

- **Tap or flick your finger near the right margin of the page.** If you tap or flick, the page turns in a blink.

- **Drag your finger near the margin,** and the page folds down as it turns, as if you were turning pages in a real book.

- **Drag down from the upper-right corner of the book,** and the page curls from that spot. The effect is so authentic, you can make out the faint type bleeding from the previous page on the next folded-down page.

- **Drag up from the lower-right corner,** and the page curls up from that spot.

- **Drag from the middle-right margin,** and the entire page curls.

To turn to the *previous* page in a book, tap, flick, or drag your finger in a similar fashion, except now do so closer to the left margin. You'll witness the same cool page-turning effects.

That's what happens by default anyway. Tap Settings⊃Apps⊃iBooks; you have the option to go to the next page instead of the previous page when you tap near the left margin. So tapping either margin would advance you to the next page.

You can also flick to scroll through a book vertically rather than turning pages in portrait view. Tap the Font (little A and big A) button, and in the Themes dialog, switch from Book view (portrait) and Scroll view (vertical) There's also a Full Screen view that operates just like Book view, lacking the booklike adornments of page edges, hardbound binding, and so forth.

The iPad is smart, remembering where you left off. So if you close a book by tapping the Library button in the upper-left corner or by pressing the main Home button, you automatically return to this page when you reopen the book. It isn't necessary to bookmark the page (though you can, as we describe later in this chapter). The one proviso: You need an Internet connection when you "close" the book, because otherwise the server at Apple doesn't get the new bookmark info to pass on when you open the book on another device. And similarly, you need an Internet connection when you reopen it to retrieve the information that was passed on.

Jumping to a specific page

When you're reading a book, you often want to go to a specific page. Here's how:

1. **Tap anywhere near the center of the page you're reading to summon page navigator controls, if they're not already visible.**

   The controls are labeled in Figure 10-3.

2. **Drag your finger along the slider at the bottom of the screen until the chapter and page number you want appear.**

3. **Release your finger and *voilà* — that's where you are in the book. Tap "Back to page xx" at the bottom left corner of the screen to return to where you were. Or tap "Go to page xx" at the bottom right to go to the furthest point you've read in the book.**

Going to the Table of Contents

Most books you read on your iPad have Tables of Contents, just like many other books. Here's how you use a Table of Contents on your iPad:

1. **With a book open on your iPad, tap the Table of Contents button near the top of the screen.**

   The Table of Contents screen, as shown in Figure 10-4, appears.

2. **Tap the chapter, title page, or another entry to jump to that page.**

   Alternatively, tap the Resume button that appears at the upper-left corner of the screen to return to the previous location in the book.

Adding bookmarks

Moving around to a particular location on the iPad is almost as simple as moving around a real book, and as we explain in the earlier section "Turning pages," Apple kindly returns you to the last page you were reading when you closed a book.

Still, occasionally you want to bookmark a specific page so that you can easily return to it. To insert a bookmark somewhere, merely tap the Bookmark icon near the upper-right reaches of the screen. A red

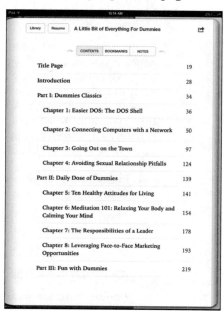

Figure 10-4: Perusing a Table of Contents.

ribbon slides down over the top of the Bookmark icon, signifying that a bookmark is in place. Tap the ribbon if you want to remove the bookmark. Simple as that.

After you set a bookmark, here's how to find it later:

1. **Tap the Table of Contents/Bookmark button.**

2. **Tap Bookmarks (if it's not already selected).**

   Your bookmark is listed along with the chapter and page citations, the date you bookmarked the page, and a phrase or two of surrounding text, as the example in Figure 10-5 shows.

3. **Tap your desired bookmark to return to that page in the book.**

You can also remove a bookmark from the Bookmarks list by swiping your finger to the left along a bookmark and then tapping the red Delete button that appears.

Adding highlights and notes

Bookmarks are great for jumping to pages you want to read again and again. Of course, you may instead want to highlight specific words or passages within a page. And some-

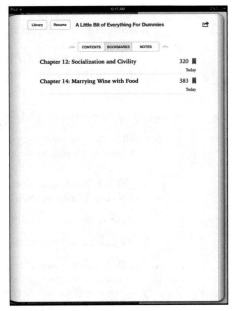

Figure 10-5: Finding the pages you bookmarked.

times you want to add your own annotations or comments as well, which is handy for school assignments. Pardon the pun, but Apple is on the same page. Here's how to do both:

1. **Press and hold your finger down against any text on a page. Then lift your finger to summon the Highlight and Note buttons.**

   These two buttons appear side by side, sandwiched along with Define and Search buttons that we address in a moment.

   You see grab points along the highlighted word.

2. **(Optional) Refine the highlighted section by expanding the grab points.**

3. **Choose a button to add a highlight or note:**

   • *When you tap the Highlight button,* the word or passage you selected is highlighted in color. You can later read the highlight by returning to the Table of Contents page in the same way that you find a bookmark. (See the preceding section and refer to Figure 10-5.)

- *Tap Note,* and a Post-it–like note appears on the screen. Using the virtual keyboard, type your note.

After you add a highlight or note, the following tips are handy to know:

- ✔ **Remove a highlight or note.** Tap the highlighted text or note, and on the toolbar that appears, tap the circle icon with a red line running diagonally inside. Alternatively, from the Highlights & Notes section under the Bookmarks list, swipe your finger in either direction along an entry and tap the red Delete button that appears.

- ✔ **Change the highlighted color of a highlight or note.** You can change the color from the default yellow to green, blue, pink, or purple. Touch the highlighted selection for a moment and lift your finger. From the toolbar, tap the icon with the color that you prefer.

- ✔ **Share or print notes.** From the Table of Contents page, in the upper-right corner of the screen, tap the Action icon (it looks like an arrow trying to escape a rectangle). Tap Email to e-mail your notes, or tap Print to print them (provided you have a compatible printer). You also have options to share via Message, or post on Twitter, Facebook, or the Chinese social network (if a Chinese keyboard is enabled) Sina Weibo. We don't know how that will play politically in China. See Chapter 2 for details about printing. Meanwhile, to see other possibilities for notes and iBooks generally, read the nearby sidebar "The iPad goes to school."

Changing the type size, font, and page color

If you want to enlarge the typeface size (or make it smaller), here's how:

1. **Tap the Text Size and Fonts button, labeled in Figure 10-3, at the upper-right corner of the screen.**

2. **Tap the uppercase *A*.**

   The text swells right before your eyes so that you can pick a size that's comfortable for you.

   To make the font smaller, tap the lowercase *a* instead.

If you want to change the fonts, tap the Fonts button and then tap Fonts and the font style you want to switch to. Your choices at this time are Athelas, Charter, Georgia, Iowan, Palatino, Seravek, and Times New Roman. We don't necessarily expect you to know what these look like just by the font names — fortunately, you get to examine the change right before your eyes. A check mark indicates the currently selected font style.

The iPad goes to school

Apple has been pushing iPads in K-12 and higher education. As part of its vision for the iPad and with iBooks 2 and beyond, the company is throwing its considerable weight behind digital textbooks, works that include interactive captions, quizzes, 3D objects, and video. Apple even unveiled free software for the Mac called iBooks Author to encourage teachers and others to produce their own interactive books for learning.

In the meantime, among the early high school textbooks produced for the iPad are titles that cover algebra, environmental sciences, physics, and other subjects.

E. O. Wilson's *Life on Earth* is an especially rich interactive digital biology textbook like none you've seen, from 3D models of DNA to animated maps of global photosynthesis. The introduction to the book was made available for free, after which you can purchase additional chapters as they're released, at $1.99 apiece as this book was being published. (In general, publishers will have to work out pricing on most of the emerging textbooks.) Wilson's book could only be viewed using iBooks 3.0 or later on an iPad running iOS 5.1 or later.

Meanwhile, if a book supports it, you can turn your notes into Study Cards — a great way for students to learn vocabulary or prepare for exams. (If the option is available, you'll see an icon that looks like a notepad just to the right of the Table of Contents button.) You can swipe the cards to move from one to another, or tap a card to see one side with glossary terms or material you've highlighted, on the other any notes you've supplied. At the time we wrote this book, there weren't a lot of new textbooks that supported Apple's vision. But with the backing of such prominent textbook publishers as Houghton Mifflin Harcourt, McGraw-Hill, and Pearson, it would appear to be only a matter of time. What's more, some third-party publishers such as Kno and Inkling are also producing some interesting interactive textbooks.

According to Apple, hundreds of thousands of books in the iBooks Store can be used in school curriculums, including novels for English or social studies. A world of educational content is also accessible via the iTunes U app.

As you consider these various efforts, we understand if you wish you'd had an iPad with digital textbooks back when you were in school.

We should also point out that while educational materials are a main impetus behind iBooks 3, there are other books rich in audio, video, and other interactive materials that take full advantage of Apple's latest software. One example: *George Harrison: Living In the Material World,* a handsome $14.99 book written by the ex-Beatle's widow, Olivia Harrison. You can only view it on an iPad with iBooks 2 or later.

To change the page color, tap Theme and pick White (the default), Sepia, or Night. As we mentioned earlier, while you're there, you can tap the Full Screen button if you want more of the content to stretch out across the entire page, or scroll if you want your content to operate like a digital scroll.

Searching inside and outside a book

If you want to find a passage in a book but just can't remember where it is, try searching for it. Here's how:

1. **Tap the magnifying-glass Search icon to enter a search word(s) or page number on the virtual keyboard that slides up from the bottom.**

   All the occurrences in the book turn up in a window under the Search icon, complete with a few lines of text and a page citation.

2. **Tap one of the items to jump to that portion of the book.**

   The words you were searching for are highlighted on that page.

You can also search the web (via Google) or the Wikipedia online encyclopedia by using the corresponding buttons at the bottom of the search results. If you do so, the iBooks app closes, and the Safari browser fires up Google or Wikipedia, with your search term already entered.

If you search Google or Wikipedia in this fashion, you are, for the moment, closing the iBooks application and opening Safari. To return to the book you're reading, you must reopen the app. Fortunately, you're brought back to the page in the book where you left off. And Google is still the search choice through iBooks, even if you selected another search engine in Safari.

Shopping for E-Books

We love browsing in a physical bookstore. But the experience of browsing Apple's iBooks Store, although certainly different, is equally pleasurable. Apple makes it a cinch to search for books you want to read, and even lets you peruse a sample prior to parting with your hard-earned dollars. To enter the store, tap the Store button in the upper-left corner of your virtual bookshelf or your library List view.

A few things to keep in mind: The iBooks Store operates in 155 countries as of this writing, with more than 1.8 million available books. By October 2012, more than 400 million books had been downloaded. Not all books are available in all markets, of course. Some works — Jay-Z's memoir *Decoded,* to take a single example — are enhanced with video. Meanwhile, the store includes titles from all six major trade publishers: Hachette Book Group, HarperCollins, Macmillan, Penguin Group, Simon & Schuster, and Random House, as well as several independents. John Wiley & Sons is also represented, of course. Random House had been the only holdout among big-name publishers when Apple first launched the store, but the largest trade-book publisher in the United States eventually came aboard.

Publishers, not Apple, set the prices. Many bestsellers in the joint cost $12.99, though some fetch $9.99 or less. *Dear Life* from Nobel Prize winner Alice Munro fetches $7.99. In fact, Apple runs specials from time to time. Leading up to Halloween, the store sold some picture books targeted at the trick-or-treating crowd for $3.99 or less. On the other hand, Anne Hillerman's *Spider Woman's Daughter* goes for $15.99. Free selections are also available.

Just browsing iBooks Store

You have several ways to browse for books in the iBook. The top portion of the screen shows ever-changing ads for books that fit a chosen category (Children & Teens in the example shown in Figure 10-6). But you can also browse Release Date in the particular category you have in mind. You can scroll to the left or right for more releases to peek at. Or tap See All for many more selections.

Look at the bottom of the screen. You see the following icons:

Figure 10-6: The featured page for Children & Teens.

- ✔ **Featured:** This is where you've been hanging out so far in this chapter. Featured works are the books being promoted in the store. These may include popular titles or an author spotlight from the likes of *Twilight* writer Stephenie Meyer. Swipe the featured books at the top of the screen for more choices. Do the same, if you wish, for the Fiction and Nonfiction sections. Or tap See All for more selections. Scroll all the way to bottom of the screen for Quick Links (Best of the Month, Award Winners, Sneak Peeks and more). In this area, you can also check out your iTunes account information, tap a button that transports you to iTunes customer service, and redeem any iTunes gift cards or gift certificates.

- ✔ **NYTimes:** Short for *The New York Times,* of course. These books make the newspaper's famous bestsellers lists, which are divided into fiction and nonfiction works. The top books in each list are initially shown. Scroll down to see more titles.

- ✔ **Top Charts:** Here Apple shows you the most popular books in the iBook Store. You find a list for Paid Books and Free Books. Scroll down to see more of the top books in each category.

- ✔ **Top Authors:** Tapping the Top Authors icon lets you find books by poring through a list of popular authors, shown in a scrollable pane on the left half of the screen. Flick your finger up or down to scroll the list, or tap one of the letters in the margin to jump to authors whose name begins with that letter. When you tap an author's name, a list of his or her available titles appears in a scrollable pane on the right.

- ✔ **Purchased:** Tapping here shows you the books you've already bought, which you can download onto your iPad.

Searching the iBooks Store

In the upper-right corner of the iBooks Store is a Search Store field, similar to the Search field you see in iTunes. Using the virtual keyboard, type an author name or title to find the book you seek.

If you like freebies, search for *free* in the iBooks Store. You'll find tons of (mostly classic) books that cost nothing, and you won't even have to import them. See the section "Finding free books outside the iBooks Store," later in this chapter, for more places to find free books. By Apple's count, free content is distributed in 155 countries. Off the top of our heads, we can't remember how many countries there are on Planet Earth. But it's fair to say that when it comes to digital books, Apple has most of them covered.

Deciding whether a book is worth it

To find out more about a book that you come across, you can check out the detail page and other readers' reviews or read a sample of the book:

- ✓ **Find the book's details.** Tap its cover. An information screen appears with Details highlighted by default. You can see when the book was published, read a description, see the number of pages, and more.

- ✓ **Find ratings and reviews.** Tap Ratings and Reviews to see the grades other readers bestowed on the book.

  You can throw in your own two cents, if you've already read it, by tapping Write a Review.

- ✓ **Find other books by the same author.** Tap Related to see the covers of other books written by the author. You can also check out other books that customers who bought this book also bought.

- ✓ **Share your interest in a book.** Tap the Action button in the upper-right corner of the information screen. You can then sing the praises of a book by tapping icons for Message, Mail, Twitter, and Facebook, as well as Chinese social networks Sina Weibo and Tencent Weibo (assuming you enabled a Chinese keyboard). You can also tap Copy Link.

Of course, the best thing you can do to determine whether a book is worth buying is to read a sample. Tap Sample, and the book cover almost immediately lands on your bookshelf. You can read it like any book, up until that juncture in the book where your free sample ends. Apple has placed a Buy button inside the pages of the book to make it easy to purchase it if you're hooked. The word *Sample* is plastered on the cover on the bookshelf to remind you that this book isn't quite yours — yet.

Buying a book from the iBooks Store

Assuming that the book meets or exceeds your lofty standards, and you're ready to purchase it, here's how to do so:

1. **Tap the price shown in the gray button on the book's information page.**

   Upon doing so, the dollar amount disappears, and the button becomes green and carries a green Buy Book label. If you tap a free book instead, the button is labeled Get Book.

2. **Tap the Buy Book/Get Book button.**

3. **Enter your iTunes password (if you're prompted) to proceed with the transaction.**

   The book appears on your bookshelf in an instant, ready for you to tap it and start reading. You get an e-mail receipt acknowledging your purchase via the same mail account in which you receive other receipts from iTunes for music, movies, and apps.

If you buy another book within 15 minutes of your initial purchase, you aren't prompted for your iTunes password again.

Buying books beyond Apple

The business world is full of examples where one company competes with another on some level, only to work with it as a partner on another level. When the iPad first burst onto the scene in early April 2010, pundits immediately compared it to Amazon's Kindle, the market-leading electronic reader. Sure, the iPad had the larger screen and color, but the Kindle had a few bragging points too, including a longer battery life (up to about a month on the latest Kindle, versus about 10 hours for the iPad), lighter weight, and a larger selection of books in its online bookstore.

But Amazon has long said that it wants Kindle books to be available for all sorts of electronic platforms, and the iPad, like the iPhone and iPod touch before it, is no exception. So we recommend taking a look at the free Kindle app for the iPad, especially if you've already purchased a number of books in Amazon's Kindle Store and want access to that wider selection of titles.

The Barnes & Noble NOOK app is also worth a look. In fact, both Barnes & Noble and Amazon are competing against the iPad with smaller, less-expensive tablets, the Nook Tablet and Kindle Fire and Kindle Fire HD and HDX, respectively. Google is doing the same with the Nexus 7 tablet (with its Google Play app). And there are numerous other players in the space.

Meanwhile, we haven't tried them all, and we know it's hard enough competing against Apple (or Amazon). But we'd be selling our readers short if we didn't at least mention that you can find several other e-book–type apps for the iPad in the App Store. As this book goes to press, you can have a look at the following apps, just to name a few:

- ✔ CloudReaders from Cloud Readers (free)
- ✔ Free e-books by Kobo
- ✔ Stanza from Lexcycle (free), acquired by Amazon in 2009. Regrettably, as of this writing Stanza was removed from the App Store. We're hoping it returns (but don't count on it).

See Chapter 11 for details about finding and downloading apps.

Finding free books outside the iBooks Store

Apple supports a technical standard — *ePub,* the underlying technology behind thousands of free public-domain books. You can import these to the iPad without shopping in the iBooks Store. Such titles must be *DRM-free,* which means that they're free of digital rights restrictions.

To import ePub titles, you can download them to your Mac or PC (assuming that they're not already there) and then sync them to the iPad through iTunes. There are other methods. If you have Dropbox, for example, you can bring an ePub into your account, and from Dropbox you can share the title with iBooks. You can also e-mail them as an attachment.

You can find ePub titles at numerous cyberspace destinations, among them

- ✔ **Feedbooks:** www.feedbooks.com
- ✔ **Google Play:** Not all the books here are free, and Google has a downloadable app. http://play.google.com/store/books
- ✔ **Project Gutenberg:** www.gutenberg.us
- ✔ **Smashwords:** www.smashwords.com
- ✔ **Baen:** www.baen.com

Also, check out the free titles that you can find through the apps mentioned in the previous section.

Reading Newspapers and Magazines

People in the newspaper business know that it's been tough sledding in recent years. The Internet, as it has in so many areas, has proved to be a disruptive force in media.

It remains to be seen what role Apple generally, and the iPad specifically, will play in the future of electronic periodicals or in helping to turn around sagging media enterprises. It's also uncertain which pricing models will make the most sense from a business perspective.

What we can tell you is that reading newspapers and magazines on the iPad is not like reading newspapers and magazines in any other electronic form. The experience is really slick, but only you can decide whether it's worth paying the tab (in the cases where you do have to pay).

There are two paths you might follow to subscribe to or read a single issue of a newspaper or magazine. The first path includes several fine publishing apps worth checking out, including *USA TODAY* (where Ed works), *The Wall Street Journal, TIME* magazine, *The New York Times, The New Yorker, Reuters News Pro, BBC News, Vanity Fair,* and *Popular Science.* We also highly recommend fetching the free Zinio app, which offers more than 5,000 digital publications including *Rolling Stone, The Economist, Macworld, PC World, Car and Driver, Maxim, National Geographic Interactive, Spin, Bloomberg Businessweek,* and many more. You can buy single issues of a magazine or subscribe, and you can sample and share some articles without a subscription.

In some cases, you have to pay handsomely or subscribe to some of these newspapers and magazines, which you find not in the iBooks Store but in the regular App Store, which we cover in Chapter 11. You also see ads (somebody has to pay the freight).

The second path, Newsstand, was new in iOS 5. This handy icon on your Home screen purports to gather all your newspaper and magazine subscriptions in a single place. Newsstand is actually a special type of folder rather than an app.

You purchase subscriptions in a section of the App Store, which you can also get to by tapping Newsstand on your Home screen and then tapping the Store button, which opens the App Store (see Chapter 11) to the new Subscriptions section.

Numerous publications have adopted the Newsstand paradigm, though some choose custom apps or Zinio, and many do both.

Part IV
The iPad at Work

In this part...

- Learn how to shop 'til you drop in the App Store, an emporium replete with a gaggle of neat little programs and applications. Best of all, unlike most of the stores you shop in, a good number of the items can be had for free.

- Get down to business and explore staying on top of your appointments and people with the Calendar and Contacts.

- Discover utilities such as the Reminders, Notes, and Clock apps.

- Take control of your iPad with Notification Center and Control Center.

- Get to know Siri, your (mostly) intelligent assistant. She responds to your voice and can do some amazing things including sending messages, scheduling appointments and reminders, searching the web, playing a specific song or artist, and so much more.

11

Apply Here (To Find Out about iPad Apps)

*O*ne of the best things about the iPad is that you can download and install apps created by third parties, which is to say apps not created by Apple (the first party) or you (the second party). At the time of this writing, more than 850,000 apps are available in the iTunes App Store. Furthermore, iPhone, iPod touch, and iPad owners have downloaded more than 50,000,000,000 (yes, 50 *billion*) apps.

Many apps are free, but others cost money; some apps are useful, but others are lame; and most apps are perfectly well-behaved, but others quit unexpectedly (or worse). The point is that among the many apps, some are better than others.

In this chapter, we take a broad look at apps that you can use with your iPad. You discover how to find apps on your computer or your iPad, and you find some basics for managing your apps. Don't worry: We have plenty to say about specific third-party apps in Chapters 18 and 19.

Tapping the Magic of Apps

Apps enable you to use your iPad as a game console, a streaming Netflix player, a recipe finder, a sketchbook, and much, much more. You can run three categories of apps on your iPad:

✓ **Apps made exclusively for the iPad:** This is the newest kind, so you find fewer of these than the other two types. These apps won't run on an iPhone or iPod touch, so you can't even install them on either device.

✓ **Apps made to work properly on an iPad, iPhone, or iPod touch:** These so-called *universal apps* can run on any of the three device types at full resolution. What is the full-screen resolution for each device? Glad you asked. For older iPhones and iPod touches, it's 960 x 640 pixels; for the iPhone 5 or later, it's 1136 x 640; for the iPad 2 and iPad mini, it's 1024 x 768 pixels; and the Retina display in the later iPad is a whopping 2048 x 1536 pixels.

✓ **Apps made for the iPhone and iPod touch:** These apps run on your iPad but only at iPhone/iPod touch resolution (960 x 640) rather than the full resolution of your iPad (1024 x 768 or 2048 x 1536).

You can double the size of an iPhone/iPod touch app by tapping the little 2x button in the lower-right corner of the screen; to return it to its native size, tap the 1x button. Figure 11-1 shows you what this looks like.

Frankly, most iPhone/iPod apps look pretty good at 2x size, but we've seen a few that have jagged graphics and don't look as nice. Still, with 700,000 or more to choose from, we're sure that you can find a few that make you happy.

Figure 11-1: iPhone/iPod touch apps run at a smaller size (left), but can be increased to double size (right).

You can obtain apps for your iPad in two ways:

- ✔ On your computer
- ✔ On your iPad

To use the App Store on your iPad, it must be connected to the Internet. Also, if you obtain an app on your computer, it isn't available on your iPad until you either sync the iPad with your computer or download the app from iCloud from the Purchased tab, covered later in this chapter. See Chapter 3 for details about syncing.

After you've obtained an app from the App Store on your computer or iPad, you can download it from iCloud to up to ten iOS devices.

But before you can use the App Store on your iPad or your computer, you first need an iTunes Store account. If you don't already have one, we suggest that you launch iTunes on your computer or the App Store or iTunes Store app on your iPad. Here's how:

- ✔ **On your computer:** Launch iTunes, click Sign In near the upper-left corner of the iTunes window, click Create Apple ID, and follow the onscreen instructions.

- ✔ **On your iPad:** Tap Settings⇨iTunes & App Store⇨Sign In⇨Create New Account and follow the onscreen instructions.

If you don't have an iTunes Store account, you can't download a single cool app — not even the free ones — for your iPad. 'Nuff said.

Using Your Computer to Find Apps

Okay, start by finding cool iPad apps using iTunes on your computer. Follow these steps:

1. **Launch iTunes.**

2. **Click the iTunes Store button near the upper-right corner of the iTunes window, or click iTunes Store in the sidebar.**

   If the sidebar isn't showing and you'd like it to show, choose View⇨Show/Hide Sidebar or press ⌘+Option+S (Mac).

   Either way, the result is that you'll be looking at the landing page of the iTunes Store.

3. **Click the App Store link.**

   The iTunes App Store appears, as shown in Figure 11-2.

iTunes Store   App Store link   Search iTunes Store

iPhone tab

App Store drop-down menu

Scroll bar

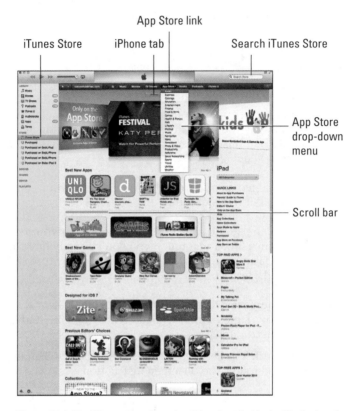

Figure 11-2: The iTunes App Store in all its glory (with the iPad tab selected).

If you wish to look at a specific department of the App Store, instead of clicking, press and hold on the App Store link and select a department (it's Books in Figure 11-2) from the drop-down menu.

4. **(Optional) If you want to look only for apps designed to run at the full resolution of your iPad, click the iPad tab at the top of the window (hidden by the App Store drop-down menu in Figure 11-2).**

Now you're ready to browse, search, and download apps, as we explain in the following sections.

Browsing the App Store from your computer

After you have the iTunes App Store on your screen, you have a couple of options for exploring its virtual aisles. Allow us to introduce you to the various "departments" available from the main screen.

The main departments are featured in the middle of the screen, and ancillary departments appear on either side of them. We start with the ones in the middle:

- The **Best New Apps** department is displaying six icons (and a sliver of a seventh) in Figure 11-2. These represent apps that are — what else? — the best new apps according to Apple's curators.

  Only six icons are visible, but the Best New Apps department actually has more than that. Look way over to the right of the words *Best New Apps*. See where it says, *See All?* Click that link to see *all* apps in this department at once. Or click and drag the scroll bar below the icons to see more.

- The **Best New Games** department also displays six icons, as shown in Figure 11-2, representing the best new games available today. Again, you can see more of these icons by clicking the See All link or dragging the scroll bar.

- The **Previous Editors' Choices** department appears below the Best New Games department. These are apps that were featured previously in a "best" category. Same deal here: See more by clicking See All or dragging the scroll bar.

Apple has a habit of redecorating (or even reconfiguring) the iTunes Store every so often, so allow us to apologize in advance if things aren't exactly as described here when you visit.

Separating the Best New Apps department and Best New Games department are ads (Dinorama, Games, and iTunes Radio Station Guide in Figure 11-2), with more ads between the Best New Games department and Previous Editors' Choices department (Designed for iOS 7: Zite, Shazam, and Open Table in Figure 11-2). Click an ad to learn more.

Three other departments appear to the right, under the Top Charts heading: Paid Apps; one of our favorite departments, Free Apps; and Top Grossing Apps (which isn't visible in Figure 11-2). The number-one app in each department displays both its icon and its name; the next nine apps show text links only.

Using the Search field in the iTunes Store

Browsing the screen is helpful, but if you know exactly what you're looking for, searching is faster. Follow these steps to search for an app:

1. **Type a word or phrase into the Search field in the upper-right corner of the main iTunes window. Press Return or Enter to initiate the search.**

In Figure 11-3, we searched for *photos.* You see results for the entire iTunes Store, which includes music, television shows, movies, and other stuff in addition to iPad apps.

Figure 11-3: We want to do cool stuff with our iPad camera, so we searched for *photo.*

2. **Among your search results, find the category for iPad Apps. (Refer to Figure 11-3.)**

   Because the screen displays results from Albums, Songs, Movies, TV Shows, Music Videos, and more, you might have to scroll down to see the iPad Apps section.

   Fortunately, you can also easily filter by media type. Just tap iPad Apps in the list near the upper-right corner of the screen, and everything but iPad apps disappears from the screen. Sweet!

3. **Click the See All link to the right of the words *iPad Apps*. (Refer to Figure 11-3.)**

   All the iPad apps that match your search word or phrase appear on a single screen.

One last thing: The little triangle to the right of each item's price is another drop-down menu, as shown for the Adobe Photoshop Express app in Figure 11-3. This drop-down menu lets you give this app to someone as a gift, add it to your wish list, send an e-mail to a friend with a link to it (shown selected in Figure 11-3), copy the link to this product to the Clipboard so that you can paste it elsewhere, or share this item on Facebook or Twitter.

Getting more information about an app in the iTunes Store

Now that you know how to find apps in the App Store, this section delves a little deeper and shows you how to find out more about an application that interests you.

To find out more about an app, just click its icon or text link. A detail screen like the one shown in Figure 11-4 appears.

This screen tells you most of what you need to know about the application, such as basic product information and a narrative description, what's new in this version, the language it's presented in, and the system requirements to run it. In the following sections, you take a closer look at the various areas on the screen.

Finding the full app description

Notice the blue More link in the lower-right corner of the Description section in Figure 11-4; click it to see a much longer description of the app.

Figure 11-4: The detail screen for SketchBook Pro, a nifty drawing and painting app for your iPad.

Bear in mind that the application description on this screen was written by the application's developer and may be somewhat biased. Never fear, gentle reader: In an upcoming section, we show you how to find reviews of the application — written by people who have used it (and, unfortunately, sometimes people who haven't).

Understanding the app rating

Notice that the SketchBook Pro app is rated 4+, as you can see below the Buy App button in the upper-left corner of the screen shown in Figure 11-4. The rating means that this app contains no objectionable material. Here are the other possible ratings:

- ✔ **9+:** May contain mild or infrequent occurrences of cartoon, fantasy, or realistic violence; or infrequent or mild mature, suggestive, or horror-themed content that may not be suitable for children younger than the age of 9.

- ✔ **12+:** May contain infrequent mildly offensive language; frequent or intense cartoon, fantasy, or realistic violence; mild or infrequent mature or suggestive themes; or simulated gambling that may not be suitable for children younger than the age of 12.

- ✔ **17+:** May contain frequent and intense offensive language; frequent and intense cartoon, fantasy, or realistic violence; mature, frequent, and intense mature, suggestive, or horror-themed content; sexual content; nudity; or depictions of alcohol, tobacco, or drugs that may not be suitable for children younger than the age of 17. You must be at least 17 years old to purchase games with this rating.

Checking requirements and device support for the app

Last but not least, remember the three categories of apps we mention earlier in the chapter, in the section "Tapping the Magic of Apps"? If you look below the Information heading in Figure 11-4 (below the Description and What's New sections), you can see the requirements for this particular app. It says `Requires iOS 6 or later. Compatible with iPad.` Note that it doesn't mention the iPhone or iPod touch. That's 'cause this app falls into the first category — apps made exclusively for the iPad. Another clue that it falls into the first category is that it says iPad Screenshots above the two pictures shown in Figure 11-4.

If the app belonged to the second or third category — apps made to work properly on an iPad, iPhone, or iPod touch, or apps made for the iPhone or iPod touch — it would say `Compatible with iPhone, iPod touch, and iPad` rather than `Compatible with iPad`.

Now you're probably wondering how you can tell whether an app falls into the second or third category. The first clue is the little gray plus sign next to the price, which appears for many of the apps shown in Figure 11-3. Apps with this symbol are universal and run at full resolution on iPhones and iPads. Another clue is to look at the screen shots. If you see *two* tabs — iPhone and iPad — after *Screenshots,* the app will work at the full resolution of an iPad, iPhone, or iPod touch. Conversely, if you only see one tab that says `iPhone Screenshots`, the app will run at iPhone/iPod touch resolution on your iPad.

One way to ensure that you look only for apps that take advantage of your iPad's big screen is to click the iPad tab on the front page of the App Store (shown earlier in Figure 11-2). All the apps displayed under the iPad tab are of the first or second type and are designed to take advantage of your iPad's larger screen.

Reading reviews

If you tap Ratings and Reviews below the product's name near the top of the screen, you'll see reviews written by users of this app. Each review includes a star rating, from zero to five. If an app is rated four stars or higher (SketchBook Pro is ranked five stars), you're safe to assume that most users are happy with this app.

In Figure 11-4, you can see that this application has an average rating for the current version of 5 stars based on 6 user ratings. You can tap Ratings and Reviews to see the average rating for all versions (4 stars based on 4,381 user ratings for SketchBook Pro). That means it's probably a pretty good app.

Finally, at the top of the Customer Reviews section is a pop-up menu that says Most Helpful in Figure 11-4. This menu lets you sort the customer reviews by your choice of Most Helpful, Most Favorable, Most Critical, or Most Recent.

Don't believe everything you read in reviews. Some people buy an app without reading its description, or they try to use it without following the included instructions. Then, when the app doesn't do what they expected, they give it a low rating. The point is, take the ratings and reviews with a grain of salt.

Downloading an app from the iTunes Store

This part is simple. When you find an app you want to try while browsing the App Store on your computer, just click the app's Free App or Buy App button. When you do so, you have to log on to your iTunes Store account, even if the app is free.

After you log on, the app begins downloading. When it's finished, it appears in the Apps section of your iTunes Library, as shown in Figure 11-5.

If an app costs money, you'll get a receipt for it via e-mail, usually within 24 hours.

Downloading an app to your iTunes Library is only the first half of getting it onto your iPad. After you download an app, you can sync your iPad so the app will be available on it. Chapter 3 covers syncing in detail. You can also get the app via the App Store's Purchased tab (described later in this chapter) or by enabling automatic downloads on the Settings app's Store pane or the iTunes Preferences Store tab on your computer.

Figure 11-5: Apps that you download appear in the Apps section of your iTunes Library.

If you want apps to download to your iPad automatically, regardless of which device you used to purchase the app, you can set that up:

- **On a computer:** Connect your iPad via either USB cable or Wi-Fi. Launch iTunes and click the iPad button near the upper-right corner of the iTunes window, or click your iPad's name in the sidebar on the left. Click the Apps tab and enable the Automatically Sync New Apps check box.

- **On your iPad:** Tap Settings⇨Store. Then turn on the switch for Apps in the Automatic Downloads section.

You can enable Automatic Downloads for Music and Books on your iPad (but not in iTunes).

By the way, if your iTunes App library doesn't look like ours (with big icons in a grid pattern), you've probably clicked the List tab; the All, iPhone/iPod touch, iPad, and Updates tabs display icons as shown in Figure 11-5.

Updating an app from the iTunes Store

Every so often, the developer of an iPad app releases an update. Sometimes these updates add new features to the app, sometimes they squash bugs, and sometimes they do both. In any event, updates are usually good things for you and your iPad, so it makes sense to check for them every so often.

To do this in iTunes: Select Apps in the Library pop-up menu, as shown in Figure 11-5 (or select Apps in the sidebar if you prefer). Click the Updates tab and then click the Update All Apps button in the lower-right corner of the screen.

Note that when updates are available, the Apps item in the pop-up menu tells you exactly how many updates are waiting for you (66 in Figure 11-5). The same number appears next to the Apps item in Update All Apps button or the Update button that appears when you click any app icon. After you download an update this way, it replaces the older version in your iTunes Library and on your iPad automatically the next time you sync. Or, if you've enabled automatic downloads for apps as described earlier in the chapter, the new app replaces the old app automatically the next time you're connected to the Internet.

Using Your iPad to Find Apps

Finding apps with your iPad is almost as easy as finding them by using iTunes. The only requirement is that you have an Internet connection of some sort — Wi-Fi or wireless data network — so that you can access the iTunes App Store and browse, search, download, and install apps.

Browsing the App Store on your iPad

 To get started, tap the App Store icon on your iPad's Home screen. After you launch the App Store, you see five icons at the bottom of the screen, representing five ways to interact with the store, as shown in Figure 11-6. The first four icons at the bottom of the screen — Featured, Top Charts, Near Me, and Purchased — offer four different ways to browse the virtual shelves of the App Store. (The fifth icon we cover a little later, in the section "Updating an app from the App Store.")

The first four icons are described as follows:

✔ The **Featured** section has five tabs at the top of the screen: All Categories, Games, Kids, Newsstand, and More (see Figure 11-6) in portrait mode. In landscape mode, the Newsstand category is missing.

✔ The **Top Charts** section offers lists of the Top Paid iPad apps and the Top Free iPad apps. These are, of course, the most popular apps that either cost money or don't. The Top Grossing apps also appear here. If you wonder how a free app can appear on this list, the gross includes revenue from in-app purchases.

In the upper-left corner of the Top Charts screen is a Categories button. Tap it and you see a list of categories such as Books, Education, Games, Music, News, and Productivity, to name a few. Tap one of these categories to see the Top Paid and Top Free iPad apps for that category.

Figure 11-6: The icons across the bottom represent the five sections of the App Store.

✔ The **Near Me** section is kind of cool. In it you'll find apps with local content, such as newspaper, television, and public transit apps. It's nice at home but even more useful when you're out of town. (Note that you must have Location Services enabled in Settings⇨Privacy for this to work.)

✔ The **Purchased** section displays all your iPad apps — the ones currently installed on this iPad and any that you've purchased that aren't installed. To the right of each app, you see either Installed or iCloud (as shown in the margin). To install an uninstalled app, tap its iCloud button and then type your password.

Most pages in the App Store display more apps than can fit on the screen at once. For example, the Best New Apps section in Figure 11-6 contains more than the nine apps you can see. A few tools help you navigate the multiple pages of apps:

✔ **Swipe from right to left** to see more apps in a category.

✔ **Swipe up the screen** to see additional categories.

✔ **Tap the See All link** at the top of most sections to (what else?) see all the apps in that section on the same screen.

Using the Search field in the App Store

If you know exactly what you're looking for (or even approximately what you're looking for), rather than simply browsing, you can tap the Search field in the upper-right corner of the iPad screen and type a word or phrase; then tap the Search key on the keyboard to initiate the search.

Finding details about an app in the App Store

Now that you know how to find apps in the App Store, the following sections show you how to find out more about a particular app. After tapping an app icon as you browse the store or in a search result, your iPad displays a detail screen like the one shown in Figure 11-7.

The app description on this screen was written by the developer and may be somewhat biased.

The information you find on the detail tab for an app on your iPad is similar to that info on the iTunes screen on your computer. The links, rating, and requirements simply appear in slightly different places on your iPad screen. (See the section "Getting more information about an app in the iTunes Store," earlier in this chapter, for explanations of the main onscreen items.)

Figure 11-7: Infinity Blade III is a gorgeous "let's kill some monsters" game.

To read reviews from your iPad, tap the Reviews tab. If you scroll to the bottom of the page and see a More Reviews button (not visible in Figure 11-7), tap it to see (what else?) more reviews.

Downloading an app from the App Store

To download an app to your iPad (while using your iPad), follow these steps:

1. **Tap the blue price (or free) button near the top of its detail screen.**

   In Figure 11-7, it says $6.99. Once tapped, the button transforms into a green Buy button.

2. **Tap the Buy button.**

3. **When prompted, type your iTunes Store account password.**

   After you do, the App Store closes, and you see the Home screen where the new app's icon will reside. The new app's icon is slightly dimmed and has the word Loading beneath it, with a blue progress bar near its bottom to indicate how much of the app remains to be downloaded, as shown in the margin.

4. **If necessary, if the app is rated 17+, click OK on the warning screen that appears after you type your password to confirm that you're 17 or older before the app downloads.**

The app is now on your iPad, but it isn't copied to your iTunes Library on your Mac or PC until your next sync unless you've enabled automatic downloads. If your iPad suddenly loses its memory (unlikely) or if you delete the app from your iPad before you sync (as we describe later in this chapter, in the section "Deleting an app"), that app is gone. That's the bad news. The good news is that you can download it again from the Purchased tab as described earlier in the chapter. Or the app will reappear spontaneously on your iPad if you've enabled automatic downloads.

Updating an app from the App Store

As we mention earlier in this chapter, every so often the developer of an iPad application releases an update. If an update awaits you, a little number in a circle appears on the Updates icon at the bottom of the iPad screen or in iTunes drop-down Library menu (where that number happens to be 66 in Figure 11-5). Follow these steps to update your apps from your iPad:

1. **Tap the Updates icon if any of your apps needs updating.**

   If you tap the Updates button and see (in the middle of the screen) a message that says All Apps Are Up to Date, none of the apps on your iPad requires an update at this time. If apps need updating, they appear with Update buttons next to them.

2. **Tap the Update button that appears next to any app to update it.**

   If more than one app needs updating, you can update them all at once by tapping the Update All button in the upper-right corner of the screen.

If you try to update an app purchased from any iTunes Store account except your own, you're prompted for that account's ID and password. If you can't provide them, you can't download the update.

Downloading other content on your iPad

You may have noticed that the App Store app on your iPad offers nothing but apps. iTunes on your computer, on the other hand, includes sections for music, movies, TV shows, books, podcasts, and iTunes U.

On your iPad, you obtain music, movies, and TV shows with the iTunes Store app, and magazines with the Newsstand app, which are both included with your iPad. To download books, podcasts, or iTunes U content, however, you'll need the iBooks, Podcasts, or iTunes U apps, which (curiously) are not included with your iPad out of the box.

The good news is that these apps are free in the App Store, so if you want to shop for books, podcasts, or iTunes U content on your iPad, you should probably go download one or more apps now.

All these apps work pretty much the same, so when you understand how to navigate the App Store app, you also know how to use all the store apps.

Working with Apps

Most of what you need to know about apps involves simply installing third-party apps on your iPad. However, you might find it helpful to know how to delete and review an app.

Deleting an app

The preinstalled apps that came on your iPad can't be removed, but you have two ways to delete any other app: in iTunes on your computer or directly from your iPad.

You can, however, hide certain preinstalled apps by choosing Settings⇨General⇨Restrictions.

To delete an app in iTunes (that is, from your computer), choose Apps from the Library pop-up menu or select Apps in the sidebar and then do one of the following:

- ✒ Click the app to select it and press the Delete or Backspace key on the keyboard.
- ✒ Click the app to select it and then choose Edit⇨Delete.
- ✒ Right-click the app and choose Delete.

After taking any of the actions in this list, you see a dialog that asks whether you're sure that you want to remove the selected app. If you click the Remove button, the app is removed from your iTunes Library as well as from any iPad that syncs with your iTunes Library.

Here's how to delete an app on your iPad:

1. **Press and hold any icon until all the icons begin to wiggle.**

2. **Tap the little *x* in the upper-left corner of the app that you want to delete.**

   A dialog appears, informing you that deleting this app also deletes all its data, as shown in Figure 11-8.

3. **Tap the Delete button.**

   You can't delete any of the bundled apps that came with your iPad.

4. **To stop the icons from wiggling, press the Home or Sleep/Wake button.**

Figure 11-8: Tap an app's little *x* and then tap Delete to remove the app from your iPad.

You also make icons wiggle to move them around on the screen or move them from page to page. To rearrange wiggling icons, press and drag them one at a time. If you drag an icon to the left or right edge of the screen, it moves to the next or previous Home screen. You can also drag two additional icons to the Dock (where Safari, Mail, Photos, and Music live) and have a total of six apps available from every Home screen.

Friendly reminder: Rearranging your icons in iTunes is faster and easier than making them wiggle and move on the iPad. See Chapter 3 to find out how.

Writing an app review

Sometimes you love or hate an app so much that you want to tell the world about it. In that case, you should write a review. You can do this in two ways: in iTunes on your computer or directly from your iPad.

To write a review using iTunes on your computer, follow these steps:

1. **Navigate to the detail page for the app in the iTunes App Store.**

2. **Click the Ratings and Reviews tab and then click the Write a Review button.**

   You may or may not have to type your iTunes Store password.

3. **Click the button for the star rating (1 to 5) you want to give the app.**

4. **In the Title field, type a title for your review, and in the Review field, type your review.**

5. **Click the Submit button when you're finished.**

   The Preview screen appears. If the review looks good to you, you're done. If you want to change something, click the Edit button.

To write a review from your iPad, follow these steps:

1. **Tap the App Store icon to launch the App Store.**

2. **Navigate to the detail screen for the app.**

3. **Scroll down the page and tap the Write a Review link.**

   You probably have to type your iTunes Store password.

4. **Tap one to five of the stars at the top of the Write a Review screen to rate the app.**

5. **In the Title field, type a title for your review, and in the Review field, type your review.**

6. **Tap the Submit button in the upper-right corner of the screen.**

Whichever way you submit your review, Apple reviews your submission. As long as the review doesn't violate the (unpublished) rules of conduct for app reviews, it appears in a day or two in the App Store, in the Reviews section for the particular app.

People, Places, and Appointments

*W*e hate to break the news to you, but your iPad isn't all fun and games; it has a serious side. The iPad can remind you of appointments and help you keep all your contacts straight. If you purchased a new iPad (or iPhone or iPod touch) after October 22, 2013, you also received the iWork suite, which includes Numbers (a first-class spreadsheet), Pages (a terrific word processor), and Keynote (the best presentation program we know), as well as the iLife suite (iPhoto, iMovie, and GarageBand).

In this chapter, we explore Calendar and Contacts, a pair of apps that aren't particularly flashy but can be remarkably useful. Space constraints prohibit us from covering iWork and iLife in this book, but check out our online coverage.

Working with the Calendar

The Calendar program lets you keep on top of your appointments and events (birthdays, anniversaries, and the like). You open it by tapping the Calendar icon on the Home screen. The icon is smart in its own right because it changes daily, displaying the day of the week and the date.

The app underwent a makeover as part of iOS 7. You can display five main calendar views: by year, by month, by day, by week, and by a searchable List view that shows current and future appointments.

Tap one of the four tabs at the top of the screen — Day, Week, Month, or Year — to choose a view. There's a Today button in the lower-left corner of the screen, which returns you to the current date in any view. (Also at the bottom of the screen are the Calendars button and Inbox button, which we get to shortly.)

To get to List view, tap the search icon — a little magnifying glass — in the upper-right corner of the screen.

We take a closer look at these views in the following sections.

Year view

There's not much to the yearly view (see Figure 12-1), but at a glance you can see the current calendar year with today's date (October 9 in Figure 12-1) circled in red. You can scroll up or down to see prior or future years, but unfortunately, you can't tell on which days you have appointments in this view.

Month view

Tap any of the months visible in the yearly view to jump to that specific month, as shown in Figure 12-2. When your iPad is in Month view, you can see which days have appointments or scheduled events. Tap a day to see the list of activities on the agenda for that day, which leads nicely into the next section.

Day view

As we just mentioned, you have to tap a date to see what you have going on in a 24-hour period — though to see an entire day's worth of entries, you'll have to scroll up or down. You can swipe to the left to advance to the next day of the week and beyond; swipe to the right to retreat one or more days; or tap a day near the top of the screen to jump to it.

In this Day view, all-day events, birthdays, and events pulled from your Facebook account (if you provide

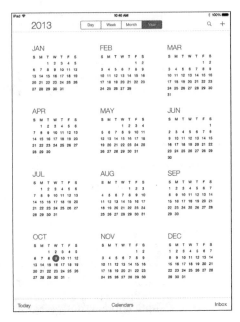

Figure 12-1: Calendar Year view.

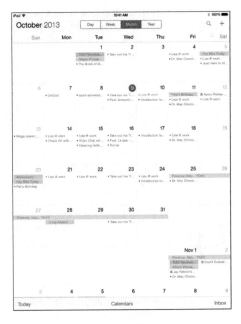

Figure 12-2: The Calendar Month view.

your Facebook credentials) appear in a narrow strip above the timeline for the day, as shown for Florence, Italy, in Figure 12-3.

Your daily appointments span the entire time in which they've been scheduled on your calendar. For example, if an appointment runs from 11:00 a.m. to 1:00 p.m., those two hours will be blocked off on the calendar.

You find out how to create calendar entries in a moment, but for now know that you can hold down on an event and drag it to a new time slot should your plans change. If you have overlapping appointments, you'll see more than a single entry claim a given time slot.

Calendars are color-coded according to the calendar in which you scheduled the appointment to help you distinguish an appointment you made on your travel calendar versus, say, a work, family, or Facebook calendar.

Figure 12-3: The Calendar Day view.

Week view

In this view, shown in Figure 12-4, you can see an entire week at a glance. The current day is circled in red. You can arrange to start your weekly view on any day of the week. Tap Settings⇨Mail, Contacts, Calendars⇨Start Week On, and then tap the day on which you want to start your week (Sunday is the default in the United States.)

List view

List view isn't complicated. You can get to the List view by tapping the search (magnifying-glass) icon near the upper-right corner of the screen.

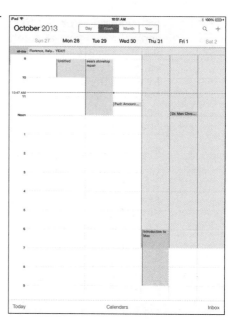

Figure 12-4: What's going on in the week ahead?

Syncing calendars with your desktop

The iPad can display the color-coding you assigned in Calendar (formerly iCal) in Mountain Lion or Mavericks on a Mac. Cool, huh?

If you're a Mac user who uses Calendar, you can create multiple calendars and choose which ones to sync with your iPad. What's more, you can choose to display any or all of your calendars. Calendar entries you create on your iPad are synchronized with the calendar(s) you specified in the iTunes Info pane. You can also sync calendars with Microsoft Outlook on a Mac or versions of Microsoft Outlook (dating all the way back to Outlook 2003) on a PC.

The best solution we've found is to use iCloud to keep calendars updated and in sync across all your iOS devices and computers. On the iPad, tap Settings➪iCloud and make sure the Calendars option is turned on (green).

One last thing: If you're a Mac user running OS X 10.9 Mavericks or later, iCloud is the *only* way you can sync data, as we mention in Chapter 3.

As you would expect, all your calendar appointments are listed chronologically, as shown in Figure 12-5. If you have a lengthy list, drag up or down with your finger or flick to rapidly scroll through your appointments. If you're looking for a specific calendar entry, you can search for appointments by typing the titles, invitee names, locations, or notes in the search box above your list of entries (or employ Spotlight to help you search).

Tap any of the listings to get meeting or appointment details for that entry. If you tap a person's birthday, you see his or her contact information. Sorry, but you just ran out of excuses for not sending a card at least.

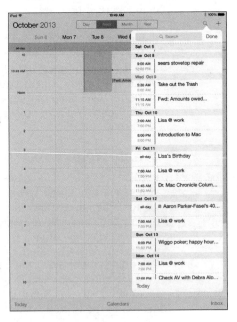

Figure 12-5: The Calendar List view.

Adding Calendar Entries

In Chapter 3, you discover pretty much everything there is to know about syncing your iPad, including syncing calendar entries from your Windows machine (using the likes of Microsoft Outlook) or Mac (using Calendar, Microsoft Entourage, or Outlook). You can also add calendar entries from iCloud.

In addition, any calendar entries in Facebook can automatically show up in the Calendar app. You will have to visit Settings, enter your username and password, and then make sure the Calendar app in the Facebook setting is turned on.

In plenty of situations, you enter appointments on the fly. Adding appointments directly to the iPad is easy:

1. **Tap the Calendar icon at the top of the screen, and launch the Year, Month, or Day view.**

2. **Tap the + button in the upper-right corner of the screen.**

   Tapping it displays the Add Event screen, shown in Figure 12-6.

3. **Tap the Title and Location fields in turn (second-generation iPads don't have a Location field) and finger-type as much or as little information as you feel is necessary.**

   Tapping displays the virtual keyboard (if it's not already shown).

    If your iPad includes dictation or Siri, you can use either of those features here to add a calendar entry. See Chapter 14 for more on dictation and Siri.

4. **To add a start time or end time (or both):**

   a. *Tap the Starts or Ends field.*

      A carousel wheel, like the one shown for the End time in Figure 12-7, appears below the field you tapped.

   b. *Choose the time the event starts.*

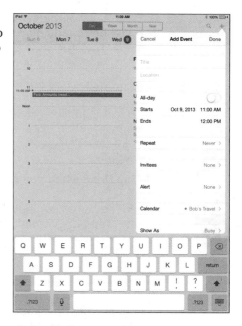

Figure 12-6: The screen looks like this just before you add an event to your iPad.

Figure 12-7: Controlling the Starts and Ends fields is like manipulating a bike lock.

Use your finger to roll separate carousel controls for the date, hour, and minute (in 1-minute intervals) and to specify AM or PM. The process is a little like manipulating a combination bicycle lock or an old-fashioned date stamp used with an inkpad.

c. Repeat the two preceding steps for the end time, if needed.

To enter an all-day milestone (such as a birthday), tap the All-Day switch to turn it on. (Green will be showing.) Because the time is no longer relevant for an all-day entry, you won't see Starts, Ends, or Time Zone options.

5. Tap Done when you're finished.

If your iPad comes equipped with Siri, we can't think of any easier way to add an entry. You can instruct Siri along the lines of "Set a lunch appointment for tomorrow at noon with the Smiths." Siri is pleased to comply.

That's the minimum you have to do to set up an event. But we bet you want to do more. The Calendar app makes it easy:

- **Change the time zone.** If the correct location isn't already present, tap the Time Zone field and type the name of the city where the appointment is taking place.

- **Set up a recurring entry.** Tap the Repeat field. Tap to indicate how often the event in question recurs. This setting is good for everything from a weekly appointment, such as an allergy shot, to a yearly event, such as an anniversary.

  The options are Every Day, Every Week, Every 2 Weeks, Every Month, and Every Year. Tap Never if you are planning to never repeat this entry again.

- **Invite people to join you.** Tap Invitees to specify who among your Contacts will be attending the event.

- **Set a reminder or alert for the entry.** Tap Alert and tap a time.

  Alerts can be set to arrive at the actual time of an event, or 1 week before, 2 days before, 1 day before, 2 hours before, 1 hour before, 30 minutes before, 15 minutes before, or 5 minutes before the event. If it's an all-day entry, you can request alerts 1 day before (at 9:00 a.m.), 2 days before (at 9:00 a.m.), or 1 week before.

  When the appointment time rolls around, you hear a sound and see a message like the one shown in Figure 12-8.

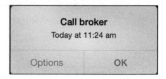

Figure 12-8: Alerts make it hard to forget.

If you're the kind of person who needs an extra nudge, set another reminder by tapping the Second Alert field (which you'll see only if a first alert is already set).

- **Assign the entry to a particular calendar.** Tap Calendar, and then tap the calendar you have in mind (Home or Work, for example).

- **Indicate whether you're busy or free by tapping Show As.** If you're invited to an event, you can tap Availability and then tap Free (if it's shown on your iPad).

- **Enter a web address.** Tap the URL field (at the bottom of the Add Event screen) and type the web address.

- **Enter notes about the appointment or event.** Tap the Notes field (bottom of the screen) and type your note.

Tap Done after you finish entering everything.

Managing your calendars

When you have the hang of creating calendar entries, you can make the task much easier with these tips:

- **Choose a default calendar.** Tap Settings⇨Mail, Contacts, Calendars, and then flick the screen until the Calendar section appears. Tap Default Calendar and select the calendar that you want to show up regularly.

- **Make events appear according to whichever time zone you selected for your calendars.** In the Calendar settings, tap Time Zone Support to turn it on, and then tap Time Zone. Type the time zone's location, using the keyboard that appears. If you travel long distances for your job, this setting comes in handy.

When Time Zone Support is turned off, events are displayed according to the time zone of your current location.

- **Turn off a calendar alert.** Tap Settings⇨Sounds, and then make sure that the selected alert tone is set to None. (You see only the last calendar alert sound that you selected. To see your other choices, tap Calendar Alerts.) You can also set default alert times for birthdays, all-day events, or certain other events. Tap Settings⇨Mail, Contacts, Calendars, and scroll down to Default Alert Times. For birthdays or all-day events, you can choose to be alerted at 9:00 a.m. on the day of the event, at 9:00 a.m. one day before, at 9:00 a.m. two days before, or a week before. For other alerts, you can choose a default alert time at the time of event, 5 minutes before, 15 minutes before, 30 minutes before, 1 hour before, 2 hours before, 1 day before, 2 days before, or 1 week before the event.

- **Modify an existing calendar entry.** Tap the entry, tap Edit, and then make whichever changes need to be made.

- **Wipe out a calendar entry.** Tap Edit⇨Delete Event. You have a chance to confirm your choice by tapping either Delete Event (again) or Cancel.

Letting your calendar push you around

If you work for a company that uses Microsoft Exchange ActiveSync, calendar entries and meeting invitations from co-workers can be *pushed* to your device so that they show up on the screen moments after they're entered, even if they're entered on computers at work. Setting up an account to facilitate this pushing of calendar entries to your iPad is a breeze, although you should check with your company's tech or IT department to make sure that your employer allows it. Then follow these steps:

1. **Tap Settings⇨Mail, Contacts, Calendars⇨Add Account.**

2. **From the Add Account list, tap Microsoft Exchange.**

3. **Fill in the e-mail address, username, password, and description fields, and then tap Next.**

4. **If required, enter your server address on the next screen that appears.**

   The iPad supports something called the Microsoft Autodiscovery service, which uses your name and password to automatically determine the address of the Exchange server. The rest of the fields should be filled in with the e-mail address, username, password, and description you just entered.

5. **Tap Next.**

6. **Tap the switch to turn on each information type that you want to synchronize using Microsoft Exchange.**

   The options are Mail, Contacts, Calendars, and Reminders. You should be good to go now, although some employers may require you to add passcodes to safeguard company secrets.

If you have a business-issued iPad and it is lost or stolen — or it turns out that you're a double-agent working for a rival company — your employer's IT administrators can remotely wipe your device clean.

Calendar entries can also be pushed as part of iCloud.

Displaying multiple calendars

By tapping the Calendars button at the bottom of the yearly, monthly, or daily view, you can choose the calendar or calendars to display on your phone. Merely tap the calendar that you want to include so that a check mark appears next to it, as shown in Figure 12-9.

Figure 12-9: Choosing the calendars to display.

You can tap the Hide All Calendars button when you don't want any calendars to be visible, or conversely tap Show All Calendars when you want your entire schedule to be an open book. You can also turn on Facebook events (in Settings) to display those in your calendar, as well as display birthdays, including those of the people you've friended on the social network.

From the Calendars view, tap the *i*-in-a-circle for even more tricks. You can assign a color to your calendar, share the calendar with a given individual (tap Add Person to do so), make a calendar public (by flipping a switch), or delete the calendar.

Responding to meeting invitations

The iPad has one more important button in the Calendar app. It's the Inbox button, located at the bottom-right corner of the yearly, monthly, and daily views. If you partake in iCloud, have a Microsoft Exchange account, or have a calendar that adheres to the CalDAV Internet standard, you can send and receive a meeting invitation, though you also need a compatible e-mail application that understands CalDAV and lets you not only receive but also respond to the invitation.

If you have any pending invitations, you'll see them when you tap the Inbox, which is separated into new invitations and invitations to which you've already replied. You can tap any of the items in the list to see more details about the event to which you've been invited.

Suppose that a meeting invitation arrives from your boss. You can see who else is attending the shindig, check scheduling conflicts, and more. Tap Accept to let the meeting organizer know you're attending, tap Decline if you have something better to do (and aren't worried about upsetting the person who signs your paycheck), or tap Maybe if you're waiting for a better offer.

And as we point out previously, you can also invite other folks to attend an event that you yourself are putting together.

Meantime, if you run into a conflict, why not ask Siri to change your schedule? For that matter, you can also call upon Siri to remind you when you have your next appointment. Visit Chapter 14 for more on this clever feature.

 You can choose to receive an alert every time someone sends you an invitation. In the Calendar settings, tap New Invitation Alerts so that the switch is turned on.

As mentioned, if you take advantage of iCloud, you can keep calendar entries synchronized between your iPhone, iPad, iPod touch, and Mac or PC. When you make a scheduling change on your iPad, it's automatically updated on your computer and other devices, and vice versa. Choose iCloud from the Add Account screen to get started, assuming you didn't turn on iCloud when you first activated your iPad.

Subscribing to calendars

You can subscribe to calendars that adhere to the CalDAV and iCalendar (.ics) standards, which are supported by the popular Google and Yahoo! calendars and by the Mac's Calendar. Although you can read entries on the iPad from the calendars you subscribe to, you can't create entries from the iPad or edit the entries that are already present.

To subscribe to one of these calendars, tap Settings➪Mail, Contacts, Calendars➪Add Account➪Other. You then choose Add CalDAV Account or Add Subscribed Calendar. Next, enter the server where the iPad can find the calendar you have in mind, and if need be, a username, a password, and an optional description.

Sifting through Contacts

If you read the chapter on syncing (see Chapter 3), you know how to get the snail-mail addresses, e-mail addresses, and phone numbers that reside on your Mac or PC into the iPad. Assuming that you went through that drill already, all those addresses and phone numbers are hanging out in one place. Their not-so-secret hiding place is revealed when you tap the Contacts icon on the Home screen. The following sections guide you from the main screen to whatever you want to do with your contacts' information.

Adding and viewing contacts

To add contacts from within the Contacts app, tap the + button at the top of the screen and type as much or as little profile information as you have for the person. Tap Add Photo to add a picture from your photo albums or collections (or to take a snapshot with your iPad camera). You can edit the information later by tapping the Edit button when a contact's name is highlighted.

A list of your contacts appears on the left panel of the screen, with the one you're currently viewing shown in gray; see Figure 12-10. On the right, you can see a mug shot of your contact, plus any info you have: phone number, e-mail address, home and another address, and birthday (all blurred in Figure 12-10 to protect Jacob's privacy). You also find an area to scribble notes about a contact.

You have three ways to land on a specific contact:

- ✔ **Flick your finger so that the list of contacts on the left side scrolls rapidly up or down,** loosely reminiscent of the spinning Lucky 7s and other pictures on a Las Vegas slot machine. Think of the payout you'd get with that kind of power on a one-armed bandit.

- ✔ **Slide your thumb or another finger along the alphabet on the left edge of the contacts list or tap one of the teeny-tiny letters** to jump to names that begin with that letter.

✔ **Start to type the name of a contact in the Search field near the top of the contacts list. Or, type the name of the place your contact works.** When you're at or near the appropriate contact name, stop the scrolling by tapping the screen.

When you tap to stop the scrolling, that tap doesn't select an item in the list. This may seem counterintuitive the first few times you try it, but we got used to it and now we really like it this way. Just think of that first tap as applying the brakes to the scrolling list.

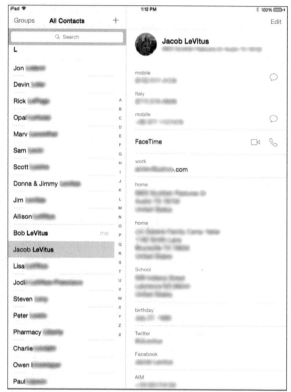

Figure 12-10: A view of all contacts.

You can change the way your contacts are displayed. Tap Settings⇨Mail, Contacts, Calendars. Then scroll down to Contacts settings on the right side of the screen, if it's not already visible. Tap Sort Order or Display Order, and for each one, choose the First, Last option or Last, First option to indicate whether you want to sort or display entries by a contact's first or last name.

Searching contacts

You can search contacts by entering a first or last name in the Search field or by entering a company name.

You can locate people on your iPad without actually opening the Contacts app. Type a name in the Spotlight Search field (see Chapter 2), and then tap the name in the search results. And if your iPad comes with Siri, you can not only ask her to find people for you, you can also have her compose and send them an e-mail or iMessage, or call them via FaceTime video or audio chat.

If you're searching contacts with a Microsoft Exchange account, you may be able to search your employer's *Global Address List* (GAL for short). This search typically works in one of two ways:

- ✔ Tap the Groups button in the upper-left corner of the All Contacts screen and tap the appropriate Exchange server name to find folks. Groups on your computer might reflect, say, different departments in your company, friends from work, friends from school, and so on.

- ✔ You can search a so-called LDAP *(Lightweight Directory Access Protocol)* server. It strikes us that nothing is "lightweight" about something called an LDAP server, but we digress. Similarly, if you have a CardDAV account, you can search for any contacts that have been synced to the iPad.

Contacting and sharing your contacts

You can initiate an e-mail from within Contacts by tapping an e-mail address under a contact's listings. Doing so fires up the Mail program on the iPad, with the person's name already in the To field. For more on the Mail app, we direct you to Chapter 5.

You can also share a contact's profile with another person. Tap the Share Contact button (you may have to scroll down to see it), and once again, the Mail program answers the call of duty. This time, the contact's vCard is embedded in the body of a new Mail message. Just address the message and send it on its merry way. A *vCard* is kind of like an electronic business card. You can identify it by its `.vcf` file format.

Finally, you can tap a contact's snail-mail address to launch the Maps app and see it pinned to a map.

Linking contacts

The people you know most likely have contact entries in more than one account, meaning that you might end up with redundant entries for the same person. The iPad solution is to *link* contacts. Find the contact in question, tap Edit, scroll to the bottom of the Edit screen and tap Link Contact. Choose the related contact entry and then tap Link. It's worth noting that the linked contacts in each account remain separate and aren't merged.

Removing a contact

Hey, it happens. A person falls out of favor. Maybe he's a jilted lover. Or maybe you just moved cross country and no longer will call on the services of your old gardener.

Removing a contact is easy, if unfortunate. Tap a contact and then tap Edit. Scroll to the bottom of the Edit screen and tap Delete Contact. You get one more chance to change your mind.

13

Indispensable iPad Utilities

In This Chapter

▶ Noting Notes

▶ Remembering with Reminders

▶ Negotiating Notification Center

▶ Punching the Clock app

▶ Sizing up the social media

▶ Using a hotspot

▶ Getting the drop on AirDrop

We'd venture to say that no one bought an iPad because of Notes, Clock, Reminders, or Game Center. Still, these apps help make the iPad indispensable on a daily basis.

In addition to the indispensable apps described in this chapter, as we also demonstrate how to create a Wi-Fi hotspot no matter where you are (all iPads with 4G features except the second generation) and how to share with AirDrop.

Taking Note of Notes

Notes is an app that creates text notes that you can save or send through e-mail. To create a note, follow these steps:

1. **Tap the Notes icon on the Home screen.**

2. **Tap the New Note button (shown in the margin) in the upper-right corner to start a new note.**

   The virtual keyboard appears.

3. **Type a note, such as the one shown in Figure 13-1.**

You can use Siri to set up and dictate your note by speaking if you're using any iPad except the second generation (you hear more about Siri in Chapter 14).

Other things you can do before you quit the Notes app include

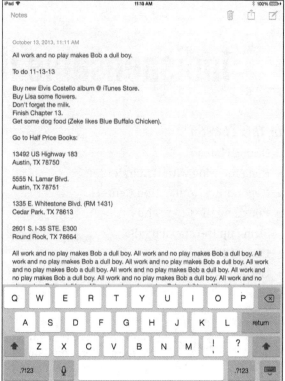

Figure 13-1: The Notes app revealed.

 ✔ Tap the Notes button in the upper-left corner of the screen if you're using portrait mode (short edges parallel to the ground) to see a list of all your notes. If you sync notes with more than one account, such as iCloud, Google, or Yahoo!, you'll see buttons for All Notes as well as buttons for notes synced with each service.

 ✔ When the list is onscreen (hint: It's always visible when you hold your iPad in landscape mode with the longer edges parallel to the ground), just tap a note to open and view, edit, or modify it.

 ✔ Tap the Action icon near the top-right corner of the screen (it looks like an arrow coming out of a square), to send the note using the Mail or Messages apps (see Chapter 5 for more about Mail and iMessages), copy the note to the clipboard (see Chapter 2 for the scoop on copy and paste), or print the note (see Chapter 2 for more about printing).

 ✔ Tap the Trash icon near the top-right corner of the screen to delete the note.

As with most iPad apps, your notes are saved automatically while you type them so that you can quit Notes at any time without losing a single character.

We'd be remiss if we didn't remind you that you can sync Notes with your Mac and other devices via iCloud. We'd also be remiss if we didn't mention that unlike other sync functions, you don't enable Notes syncing in iTunes. Instead, you enable it in Settings⇨iCloud on your iPad and System Preferences⇨iCloud on your Mac.

And that's all she wrote. You now know what you need to know about creating and managing notes with Notes.

Remembering with Reminders

You can find lots of good To-Do list apps in the App Store; if you don't believe us, try searching for *To-Do list,* and you'll find more than 100 offerings for the iPad. Many of them are free, but others sell (and sell briskly, we might add) at prices up to $30 or $40. Most of these third-party reminder apps have nothing to worry about from the Reminders app. Although some people may love it, we'd be remiss if we didn't point out your numerous other options if you desire features that aren't available from Reminders.

What you get for free is Reminders, a simple To-Do list app for making and organizing lists, with optional "reminders" available for items in your lists.

Tap the Reminders icon on your Home screen, and you'll see something that looks like Figure 13-2.

Reminders on the right side of the screen in Figure 13-2 belong to a list called *Next Actions* as indicated by it being highlighted in a lighter shade of blue on the left side of the screen.

Working with lists

To create a new list, tap Add List in the lower-left corner of the screen, type a name for the list on the virtual keyboard, and then tap Done. You can have as many or as few lists as you like.

To manage the lists you create, tap the Edit button at the bottom of the list,

Figure 13-2: The Reminders app.

shown in Figure 13-2. When you do, the left side of the screen goes into what we like to think of as Edit mode, as shown in Figure 13-3.

Here's a quick rundown of how it works (after you tap the Edit button):

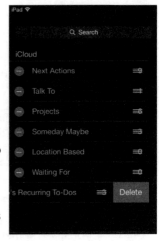

- **Delete a list:** Tap the red minus sign for the list. The list's name slides to the left and reveals a red Delete button (see Bob's Recurring To-Dos in Figure 13-3).

  You can also delete a list without first tapping the Edit button by swiping it from right to left. The red Delete button appears next to the list's name; tap it to delete the list or tap anywhere else to cancel and not delete it.

- **Reorder (move up or down) lists:** Press and hold your finger on the three horizontal lines (shown in the margin) to the right of a list's name in Edit mode, and then drag the name up or down. When the list's name is where you want it to be, lift your finger. Note that the number of items in the list is overlaid on the three horizontal lines (it's a 9 in the margin because it came from the Next Actions list).

Figure 13-3: Tap the Edit button to create, delete, or reorder your lists.

Setting up reminders

Reminders is a simple app; the steps for managing reminders are equally simple. Here's how to remind yourself of something with the Reminders app:

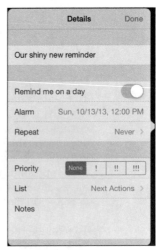

1. **To create a new reminder, tap the first blank item in the Reminder list.**

   The virtual keyboard appears.

2. **Type a title for the new reminder.**

   You can dictate your reminder instead of typing it if you're using any iPad except a second-generation. You can find out more about dictation in Chapter 15.

   The item appears in the current Reminders list.

   At this point, your reminder is bare-bones; its date, repeat, and priority options have not been activated.

Figure 13-4: Details for Our Shiny New Reminder.

3. **To activate any or all of these options, tap the reminder and then tap the little *i*-in-a-circle to reveal the Details overlay, as shown in Figure 13-4.**

Your options include the following:

- Tap Remind Me On A Day if you want to specify a day and time for this reminder.

  If you have an iPad with 3G or 4G, you can also set a location-based reminder. Just tap the At a Location switch (not shown in Figure 13-4 because that particular iPad is Wi-Fi only) to enable it, specify the location, and then choose When I Arrive, or When I Leave.

  Location-based reminders will suck your iPad battery dry faster than almost anything else. Remember to mark location-based reminders as completed by tapping their check boxes when you finish them or you'll be reminded of something you've already done every time you pass that location and drain your iPad battery unnecessarily.

  If you set a location-based reminder with an iPhone or iPad with 3G or 4G, or with the Reminders app in OS X Mountain Lion or Mavericks, the reminder syncs with your Wi-Fi-only iPad, but without the location. In fact, you won't even see the At a Location switch if your iPad is Wi-Fi-only (as in Figure 13-4).

- After you set a reminder, you'll notice that a Repeat button appears that wasn't there before. Tap it if you wish to set a second reminder for a different day or time.

- To specify a priority for this reminder, tap Priority. Select None, Low, Medium, or High.

- If you want this reminder to appear in a list other than the one it currently appears upon, tap List. Tap the list you want to move this reminder to.

- If you have anything else to add, you can type it into the Notes field.

4. **Tap the Done button in the upper-right corner after you've set all your options.**

Choose the list you want your new reminder to appear on *before* you create it.

Viewing and checking off reminders

After you create reminders, the app helps you see what you have and haven't done and offers a few other tools that are good to know about:

- ✔ **Check off reminders.** You probably noticed that every reminder you create includes a hollow circle to its left. Tap the circle to indicate that a task has been completed. When you do, the words Hide (or Show) Completed appear at the bottom of the list. Tap these words to hide or show tasks you've completed in this list.

✔ **Search reminders.** To search for a word or phrase in all your reminders, completed or not, tap the Search field at the upper left, type your word or phrase, and then tap the Search key. Or swipe down from the middle of any Home screen to search for it with Spotlight.

✔ **Keep reminders on your Mac or PC.** You can create reminders on your Mac or PC with To Do items in iCal (Lion) or Reminders (Mountain Lion or Mavericks) or Tasks in Outlook. And if you're using iCloud, your reminders will always be up to date on all your devices.

That's about it. The Reminders app isn't a bad effort. If it lacks a feature or two that you desire, we remind you to check out the myriad third-party To-Do list apps in the App Store.

Negotiating Notification Center

Notification Center, shown in Figure 13-5, drops down over whatever you're doing at the time so that you can easily see calendar entries, reminders, the weather forecast, and new e-mail messages. Notification Center works regardless of which app you're using. To summon Notification Center to the forefront of your iPad screen, all you need is the magical incantation — that is, a swipe from the top of the screen downward. Go ahead and give it a try. We'll wait.

Notification banners also appear on the Lock screen, as shown in Figure 13-6.

Banner notifications are sweet, and we're particularly fond of sliding our finger to view a particular item. But we digress. You find out how to enable or disable banner notifications (and alert notifications, too), but not until Chapter 15.

Here's what you need to know about navigating Notification Center:

✔ **Close Notification Center.** Swipe or flick the blue arrow that looks like a caret symbol (^) at the bottom of the list (refer to Figure 13-5) upward.

✔ **Open a notification.** Tap it, and it opens in the appropriate program.

✔ **Clear a single notification.** Tap the little circle to the left of the notification and it disappears.

Figure 13-5: Notification Center in all its splendor.

✔ **The Today, All, and Missed tabs at the top of the screen provide different filters for your notifications.** Tap them to see the way each presents information. Note that some details, such as today's weather and the "Tomorrow" section, only appear in the Today tab.

You can also swipe from left to right and right to left to switch among the Today, All, and Missed screens.

✔ **Clear all notifications from a particular app.** Tap the All tab at the top of the screen (refer to Figure 13-5); you can't clear all notifications from a particular app from the Today or Missed tabs.

Now tap the little *x* in a circle to the right of the app's name (Reminders, Calendar,

Figure 13-6: Banner notifications on the Lock screen; slide your finger on one to open it.

Messages, and such). The *x* turns it into a Clear button when you tap it. Tap the Clear button and all notifications from that app are cleared and the app's name disappears from Notification Center (but will reappear if and when the app needs to notify you again).

That's how to summon and use Notification Center. There's still a bit more — including how to change the notification settings for individual apps — but you'll have to wait until the settings chapter (which happens to be Chapter 15).

Punching the Clock

Well, yes, most tablets do have a clock. But not every tablet has a *world clock* that lets you display the time in multiple cities on multiple continents. And not every device also has an alarm, a stopwatch, and a timer to boot.

You can tap the Clock icon in Control Center to open your Clock app.

So tap the Clock icon on your Home screen or in Control Center and see what the Clock app is all about.

World clock

Want to know the time in Beijing or Bogota? Tapping World Clock (inside the Clock app) lets you display the time in numerous cities around the globe, as shown in Figure 13-7. When the clock face is dark, it's nighttime in the city you chose; if the face is white, it's daytime outside.

Tap the + in the middle of the clock in the upper-right corner of the screen (the one that says "Add") to add a new city, then use the virtual keyboard to start typing a city name, as shown in Figure 13-8.

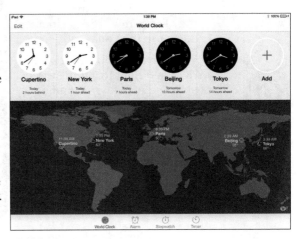

If there isn't a clock with a + in the upper-right corner, you probably have six or more clocks already. To see the rest of the clocks and the clock with the + button, swipe the clocks from right to left.

Figure 13-7: What time is it in Tokyo?

The moment you press the first letter, the iPad displays a list of cities or countries that begin with that letter. So, as Figure 13-8 shows, typing *V* brings up Andorra la Vella, Andora; Bantam Village, Cocos (Keeling) Islands; and Boa Vista, Brazil, among myriad other possibilities. You can create clocks for as many cities as you like, though only six cities at a time appear onscreen.

To remove a city from the list, tap Edit and then tap the red circle with the white horizontal line that appears to the left of the city you want to drop. Then tap Delete.

Figure 13-8: Clocking in around the world.

You can also rearrange the order of the cities displaying the time. Tap Edit, and then press your finger against the symbol with three horizontal lines to the right of the city you want to move up or down in the list. Then drag the city to its new spot.

Alarm

Ever try to set the alarm in a hotel room? It's remarkable how complicated setting an alarm can be, on even the most inexpensive clock radio. Like almost everything else, the procedure is dirt-simple on the iPad:

1. Tap Clock on the Home screen or Control Center to display the Clock app.

2. Tap the Alarm icon at the bottom of the screen.

3. Tap the + button in the upper-right corner of the screen.

4. Choose the time of the alarm by rotating the wheel in the bottom half of the screen.

   This step is similar to the action required to set the time that an event starts or ends on your calendar.

5. Tap Save when the alarm settings are to your liking.

That's what you can do with a regular alarm clock. What's the big deal, you say? Well, you can do even more with your iPad alarm:

- **Set the alarm to go off on other days.** Tap Repeat and then tell the iPad the days you want the alarm to be repeated, as in Every Monday, Every Tuesday, Every Wednesday, and so on.

- **Choose your own sound.** Tap Sound to choose the tone that will wake you up. You can even use songs from your Music library and any custom tones stored on your iPad.

   Your choice is a matter of personal preference, but we can tell you that the ringtone for the appropriately named Alarm managed to wake Ed from a deep sleep.

- **Set the snooze to sleep in.** Tap Snooze on (showing green) to display a Snooze button along with the alarm. Tap the Snooze button to shut down the alarm for nine minutes.

- **Name your alarm.** If you want to call the alarm something other than, um, Alarm, tap the Label field and use the virtual keyboard to type another descriptor.

Simple stuff, really. But if you want really simple and have anything except a second-generation iPad, you can ask Siri to set the alarm for you. See Chapter 14 for how to use Siri.

You know that an alarm has been set and activated because of the tiny status icon (surprise, surprise — it looks like a clock) that appears on the status bar in the upper-right corner of the screen.

An alarm takes precedence over any tracks you're listening to on your iPad. Songs momentarily pause when an alarm goes off and resume when you turn off the alarm (or press the Snooze button).

When your ring/silent switch is set to Silent, *your iPad still plays alarms from the Clock app.* It stays silent for FaceTime calls, alert sounds, or audio from apps. But it *will* play alarms from the Clock app.

Although it seems obvious, if you want to actually *hear* an alarm, you have to make sure that the iPad volume is turned up loud enough for you to hear.

Stopwatch

If you're helping a loved one train for a marathon, the iPad Stopwatch function can provide an assist. Open it by tapping Stopwatch in the Clock app.

Just tap Start to begin the count, and then tap Stop when your trainee arrives at the finish line. You can also tap the Lap button to monitor the times of individual laps.

Timer

Cooking a hard-boiled egg or Thanksgiving turkey? Again, the iPad comes to the rescue. Tap Timer (in the Clock app) and then rotate the hour and minute wheels until the length of time you desire is highlighted.

 Tap the Sounds button (shown in the margin) near the bottom of the screen to choose the ringtone that will signify time's up.

After you set up the length of the timer, tap Start when you're ready to begin. You can watch the minutes and seconds wind down on the screen, if you have nothing better to do. Or tap Pause to pause the countdown temporarily.

If you're doing anything else on the iPad — admiring photos, say — you hear the ringtone and see a *Timer Done* message on the screen at the appropriate moment. Tap OK to silence the ringtone.

Socializing with Social Media Apps

At first glance, it appears the iPad is light on social media support. What we mean is that Game Center is the only sign of social media on a brand new iPad.

Still, iOS 7 is much more friendly to social media than it appears at first glance. Although your iPad doesn't come with official Facebook or Twitter apps, support for the two most popular social networks is baked right into iOS 7.

You can find free apps for these social media networks (and many others) in the App Store, but iOS 7 lets you install the Facebook and Twitter apps without even having to visit the App Store. Just tap Settings➪Facebook (or Twitter), and then tap the Install button to install the app you've chosen.

 You don't necessarily need an app to participate in social networking. The networks we talk about in this section can be fully utilized using Safari on your iPad. And frankly, unlike the iPhone, where the Safari experience is hampered by the tiny screen and keyboard, the websites are eminently usable on your iPad. So, if you want to check them out and don't feel like downloading their apps, here are their URLs:

- ✔ **Facebook:** `www.facebook.com`
- ✔ **Twitter:** `http://twitter.com`

We'd be remiss if we didn't at least point out some of the niceties you get when you access one of these social media networks using an app instead of a browser, so the following sections offer a few of our insights.

If you use Facebook or Twitter, the first thing to do regardless of whether you intend to use the apps, is to tap Settings⇨Facebook and Settings⇨Twitter and provide your username and password for each service you intend to use. This will let you share photos, maps and directions, videos, URLs, and much more by tapping the Share button and then tapping the icon for Facebook or Twitter.

Facebook

The Facebook iPad app, as shown in Figure 13-9, makes it easy to access the most popular Facebook features with a single finger tap.

Note that the Facebook iPad app has a slick interface with quick access to many popular Facebook features, as shown on the left in Figure 13-9.

Figure 13-9: Bob's Facebook News Feed, as shown in the Facebook iPad app (left) and Safari (right); you can use either (or both) to get your Facebook fix.

On the other hand, Safari can't provide push notifications for Facebook events such as messages, Timeline posts, friend requests and confirmations, photo tags, events, or comments, whereas the iPad app does all that and more.

The bottom line is that there's nothing to prevent having the best of both worlds. So if you're a heavy Facebook user, consider using the Facebook iPad app for some things (such as push notifications and status updates) and Safari for others (such as reading your Wall or News Feeds).

Twitter

Twitter puts a slightly different spin on social networking. Unlike Facebook, it doesn't try to be all-encompassing or offer dozens of features, hoping that some of them will appeal to you. Instead, Twitter does one thing and does it well. That thing is letting its users post short messages, or *tweets,* quickly and easily from a variety of platforms, including web browsers, mobile phones, smartphones, and other devices.

Twitter users then have the option of following any other Twitter user's tweets. The result is a stream of short messages like the ones shown in Figure 13-10.

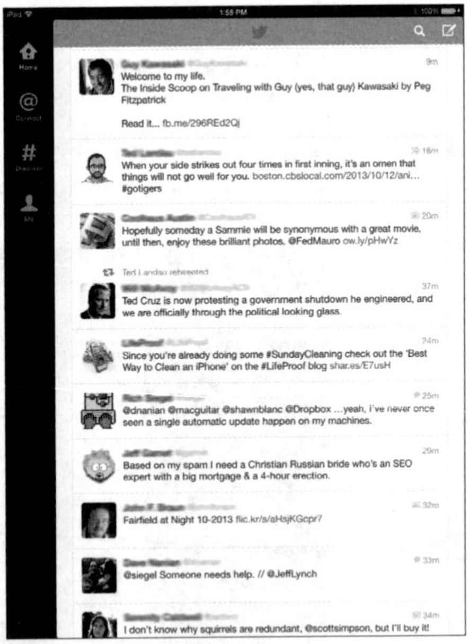

A tweet is 140 characters or fewer (including spaces). This tip, for example, is precisely 140 characters. Bottom line: omit needless words.

Game Center

Game Center is the odd duck of the bunch. Unlike the other apps we cover in this section, Game Center has no website; you have to use the Game Center app that came with your iPad. And unlike the others, which are broad-based and aimed at anyone and everyone, Game Center is designed for a specific segment of the iPad (and iPhone and iPod touch) universe — namely, users who have one or more games on their iPads (or other devices).

Figure 13-10: The official Twitter iPad app through the eyes of Bob (@LeVitus).

Mac users can get in on the fun, too, as long as they're using Mountain Lion or Mavericks, which include a Game Center app very similar to the one on your iPad.

Game Center acts as a match-up service, letting you challenge your friends or use its Auto-Match Invite Friend button to challenge a stranger who also happens to be looking for someone to play against.

Game Center supports thousands upon thousands of games these days, some of which are shown in Figure 13-11.

Figure 13-11: Some of the games with Game Center support.

The games include many top sellers, such as *Angry Birds, Real Racing 2 HD, Fairway Solitaire,* and Bob's current game obsession, the stunning *Infinity Blade III.*

Sharing Your Connection (Personal Hotspot)

If you have a newer iPad (anything but a second-generation iPad), the personal hotspot is a feature that lets your iPad with Wi-Fi + 4G share its cellular high-speed data connection with other devices, including computers, iPod touches, and other iPads.

To enable your personal hotspot and share your cellular data connection with others:

1. **Tap Settings on your Home screen.**
2. **Tap Personal Hotspot.**
3. **Tap the Personal Hotspot switch to enable it (it will turn green).**
4. **Tap Wi-Fi Password to create or change the password for the Wi-Fi network you create.**

Now Wi-Fi, Bluetooth, or USB-enabled devices can join your hotspot network and share your iPad's cellular data connection.

Your personal hotspot network adopts your iPad's name, which is *Bob L's iPad 64 (3d-gen)* in Figure 13-12.

At the time we wrote this, most carriers offered support for personal hotspots in some or all of their data plans in the USA. There are still some that don't, so check with your carrier if you don't see a Personal Hotspot option in the Settings app (and, of course, your iPad has 4G).

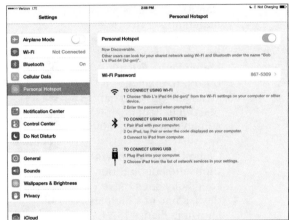

Verizon doesn't charge extra for this feature, but the data used by connected devices counts against your monthly data plan allotment.

Figure 13-12: Devices can join this network via Wi-Fi, Bluetooth, or USB by following the appropriate connection instructions.

To see how much data you're using, tap Settings⇨General⇨Usage⇨Cellular Usage.

Dropping In on AirDrop

At various points when you're using your iPad, you encounter AirDrop, a fast, safe, and secure (through encryption) wireless method of sharing photos, videos, contacts, documents, and more with people you are close to physically.

You just tap the Action icon when it is available in an app. AirDrop exploits both Wi-Fi and Bluetooth. No advanced setup is required.

To be part of an AirDrop exchange, you and the recipient must be using iOS 7 and have an iPhone 5 or later, a fourth-generation iPad or later, an iPad mini, or a fifth-generation iPod touch.

Taking advantage of this clever feature involves three simple steps:

1. **Turn on the AirDrop feature (if it's not on already) in Control Center.**

   You have the option to make your phone visible to Everyone (within the vicinity) or just to your contacts.

2. **Tap the Action icon when it presents itself in an app and choose the file or files that you want to share.**

3. **Choose the recipients of those items by tapping the circle for the person, as shown in Figure 13-13.**

Yes, you can choose more than one person. People in range who are eligible to receive the file are represented on your iPad by a circle. (The circles may even contain their pictures.)

The AirDrop process hath begun. The people on the receiving end will get a prompt asking them to accept the picture, video, or whatever it is you're offering them. Assuming they take kindly to your offer and grant permission (by tapping Accept rather than Decline), the file

Figure 13-13: Bob is about to receive a note via AirDrop.

lands on their devices in short order, where it is routed to its proper location. That is, a picture or video ends up in the Photos app, a contact in the Contacts app, and the Passbook pass in the Passbook app.

If you use a Mac computer, you're probably familiar with an OS X feature that carries the same name and operates similarly. But with the iOS 7 version of AirDrop, unlike the version on the Mac, folks can transfer files even if they don't share the same wireless network. And the two AirDrop implementations do not interact, at least at the time of this writing.

14

Taking iPad Controls Siri-ously

In This Chapter

▶ Using Control Center

▶ Calling Siri

▶ Determining what you can say

▶ Editing mistakes

▶ Using dictation

▶ Making Siri better

*H*ow could you not love Siri? The intelligent, voice-activated virtual personal assistant living like a genie inside the iPad mini and in iPads since the third generation not only *hears* what you have to say but also attempts to figure out the intent of your words. Siri then does her darnedest to respond to your wishes. She — yes, it's a female voice (at least until you change it) — can help you dictate and send a message, get directions, call a friend, discover who won the ballgame, tell you when a movie is playing, arrange a wake-up call, search the web, find a decent place to eat, and lots more. Siri talks back, too, sometimes with humor and other times with attitude. When Ed told Siri he was tired, she responded with, "That's fine. I just hope you're not doing anything dangerous."

Siri isn't perfect. Sometimes Siri mishears us, occasionally more often than we'd like, and other times she doesn't quite know what we have in mind. But blemishes and all, we think she's pretty special — and she's become smarter along the way.

Come to think of it, we should probably stop referring to Siri as *she,* even though she, um, started that way. You can now choose a male or female voice to represent Siri — and yes, we'll resist making any other transgender references. We'll also resist saying much more about Siri until later in this chapter because we want to get to one of the best new features that arrived with iOS 7: Control Center, which Apple correctly points out is merely a swipe away.

Controlling Control Center

As its name suggests, Control Center is a single repository for the controls, apps, and settings you frequently call upon. Indeed, you will almost certainly spend a lot more time in Control Center than in Settings.

To access Control Center, swipe up from the bottom of the screen — any screen. The beauty of Control Center is that it's always available when you need it.

Now, take a gander at Figure 14-1 to get an immediate handle on all the things that Control Center lets you get at right away.

We start the Control Center tour on the upper row and move from left to right. You see controls for any music you might be playing at the time, as shown in Figure 14-1. The song can be playing on the iPad's own Music app, or through a third-party app such as Spotify — which is, in fact, how the song is playing in this example.

Next, you see icons for Airplane mode (see Chapter 15 for more), Wi-Fi, Bluetooth, Do Not Disturb, the screen's orientation lock, the time (as part of the Clock app), and the camera.

Drop down a row, and you've got volume and brightness controls.

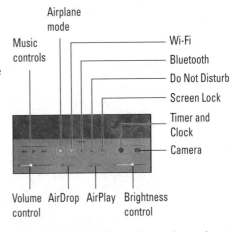

Figure 14-1: Control Center is merely a swipe away.

You also may see controls for AirDrop and AirPlay. The former is a way to share pictures, videos, and other files wirelessly with folks nearby who have iOS 7 devices of their own and Bluetooth turned on. AirDrop requires an iPhone 5 or later, a fourth-generation iPad or later, or an iPad mini. By contrast, AirPlay is a way to stream music and movies wirelessly via Wi-Fi to Apple TVs and to compatible AirPlay-enabled speakers and receivers. We discuss AirPlay in greater depth in Chapter 8.

You can permit access to Control Center on the Lock screen — or deny that access — inside Settings. You can also allow or refuse access to Control Center from within apps.

Either way, Apple assumes that you'll use Control Center all the time. We agree.

Summoning Siri

When you first set up the iPad, you have the option of turning on Siri. If you did so, you're good to go. If you didn't, tap Settings⇨General⇨Siri, and flip the switch so that On is showing.

To call Siri into action, press and hold the Home button until you hear a tone. Pretty simple, eh? The question, "What can I help you with?" appears onscreen, as shown in Figure 14-2. Start talking, and your question appears onscreen.

Siri also responds when you press a button on a Bluetooth headset.

 We should point out that having Siri turned on is a prerequisite to using dictation on your iPad, discussed later in this chapter.

What can I help you with?

What happens next is up to you. You can ask a wide range of questions or issue voice commands. If you didn't get your words out fast enough or you were misunderstood, tap the Microphone icon at the bottom of the screen and try again.

Figure 14-2: Siri is eager to respond.

Siri relies on voice recognition and artificial intelligence (hers, not yours). The voice genie responds in a conversational (if still ever-so-slightly robotic) manner. But using Siri isn't entirely a hands-free experience. Spoken words are supplemented by information on the iPad screen (as you see in the next section).

Just where does Siri get that information? By tapping into Location Services and seeking answers from the web using sources such as Bing, Wikipedia, Yelp, Yahoo!, Open Table, Twitter, and WolframAlpha, which you can learn more about in the nearby sidebar.

And Siri on the iPad can open apps — Apple's own as well as third-party apps. Indeed, from your contacts, Siri might be able to determine who your spouse, co-workers, and friends are, as well as knowing where you live. You might ask, "How do I get home from here?" and Siri will fire up Maps to help you on your way. Or you can say, "Find a good Italian restaurant near Barbara's house," and Siri will serve up a list, sorted by Yelp rating. Using Open Table, Siri can even make a restaurant reservation.

Making your iPad (and other computers) really smart

Chances are you haven't heard of WolframAlpha. But if you want to know the gross domestic product of France or find events that happened on the day you were born, WolframAlpha can deliver such facts. You don't search the web per se on WolframAlpha as you would using a service such as Google. WolframAlpha describes itself as a "new way to get knowledge . . . by doing dynamic computations based on a vast collection of built-in data, algorithms, and methods." It taps into knowledge curated by human

"experts." So you can get nutritional information for peanut M&Ms or compute a growth chart for your 4-foot 7-inch ten-year old daughter.

There's a reason that Siri relies on this "computational knowledge engine," which was driven over a period of nearly 30 years by really smart guy Stephen Wolfram. We also recommend checking out the $2.99 WolframAlpha app for your iPad, which gives you broader access to the knowledge engine, beyond where Siri goes.

Siri requires Internet access. A lot of factors go into accuracy, including surrounding noises and unfamiliar accents. And you also need to be comfortable with the fact that Apple is recording what you say.

Figuring Out What to Ask

The beauty of Siri is that there's no designated protocol you must follow when talking to her. Asking, "Will I need an umbrella tomorrow?" produces the same result as "What is the weather forecast around here?" (See Figure 14-3.)

If you're not sure what to ask, tap the circled *?* to list sample questions or commands, as shown in Figure 14-4. You can actually tap any of these examples to see even more samples.

Here are some ways Siri can lend a hand . . . um, we mean a voice:

- **FaceTime:** "FaceTime *phone number* my wife."

- **Music:** "Play Frank Sinatra" or "Play iTunes Radio."

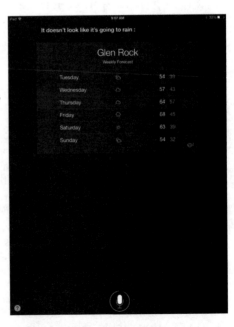

Figure 14-3: Siri can find you help.

- **Messages:** "Send a message to Nancy to reschedule lunch."

- **Calendar:** "Set up a meeting for 9 A.M. to discuss funding."

- **Reminders:** "Remind me to take my medicine at 8 A.M. tomorrow."

- **Maps:** "Find an ATM near here."

- **Mail:** "Mail the tenant about the recent rent check."

- **Stocks:** "What's Apple's stock price?"

- **Web search:** "Who was the 19th president of the United States?"

- **WolframAlpha:** "How many calories are in a blueberry muffin?"

- **Clock:** "Wake me up at 8:30 in the morning."

- **Sports:** "Who is pitching for the Yankees tonight?

- **Trivia:** "Who won the Academy Award for Best Actor in 2003?"

- **Twitter:** "Send tweet, 'Going on vacation,' smiley-face emoticon'" or "What is trending on Twitter?"

Figure 14-4: Siri can help out in many ways.

Correcting Mistakes

As we point out earlier, as good as Siri is, she sometimes needs to be corrected. Fortunately, you can correct her mistakes fairly easily. The simplest way is to tap the Microphone icon and try your query again. You can say something along the lines of, "I meant Botswana."

You can also tap your question to edit or fix what Siri thinks you said. You can make edits by using the keyboard or by voice. If a word is underlined, you can use the keyboard to make a correction.

Siri seeks your permission before sending a dictated message. That's a safeguard you come to appreciate. If you need to modify the message, you can do so by saying such things as, "Change Tuesday to Wednesday" or "Add: I'm excited to see you, exclamation mark" — indeed, *I'm excited to see you* and an *!* will be added.

Using Dictation

All iPads from the third generation on offer a Dictation function, so you can speak to your iPad and have the words you say translated into text. It's easy and usually works pretty well. Even if you're a pretty good virtual-keyboard typist or use a Bluetooth keyboard (see Chapter 17), dictation is often the fastest way to get your words into your iPad.

Dictation is part of Siri. If you need to set up Siri, turn to the earlier section "Summoning Siri."

When it's enabled, you see the microphone key on the virtual keyboard when it appears onscreen. Just tap the microphone key on the keyboard and begin speaking when the Microphone icon pops out of the key, as shown in Figure 14-5.

Dictation only works if you're connected to the Internet. If you're not connected, the microphone key will be grayed out.

Most apps display the microphone key on the keyboard, but there are some that don't. If you don't see a microphone key, the app doesn't accept dictated input.

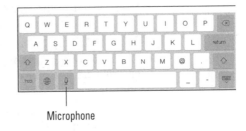

Microphone

Figure 14-5: Tap the microphone key to begin dictation; tap anywhere onscreen to end it.

Tap Done to end the dictation. Your iPad cogitates for a moment, displaying a spinning circle where your words will be in a few more seconds. Then your words magically appear.

Here are a couple of ways you can improve your Dictation experience:

- You can speak punctuation by saying it. So remember to say, "period," "question mark," or whatever at the end of your sentences. You can also insert commas, semicolons, dashes, and other punctuation by saying their names.

- The better your iPad hears you, the better your results will be:

  - A wired headset with a microphone is great when you have a lot of ambient noise nearby.

  - A Bluetooth headset may be better than the built-in microphone.

  - If you use the iPad's built-in mic, make sure the iPad case or your fingers aren't covering it.

Making Siri Smarter

From Settings, you can tell Siri which language you want to converse in. Out of the gate, Siri is available in English (United States, United Kingdom, or Australian), as well as versions of Chinese, French, German, Italian, Japanese, Korean, and Spanish.

You can also request voice feedback from Siri all the time, or just when you're using a hands-free headset.

In the My Info field in Settings, you can tell Siri who you are. When you tap My Info, your Contacts list appears. Tap your own name in Contacts.

With iOS 7, you can even choose whether Siri has either a male or female voice.

You can call upon Siri even from the Lock screen. (That's the default setting, anyway.) Consider this feature a mixed blessing. Not having to type a passcode to get Siri to do her thing is convenient. On the other hand, if your iPad ends up with the wrong person, he or she would be able to use Siri to send an e-mail or message in your name, post to Facebook, or tweet, bypassing whatever passcode security you thought was in place. If you find this potential scenario scary, tap Settings⇨General⇨Passcode Lock. Then enter your passcode and switch the Siri option under Allow Access When Locked from on (green is showing) to off (gray). For more on Settings, read Chapter 15.

Part V
The Undiscovered iPad

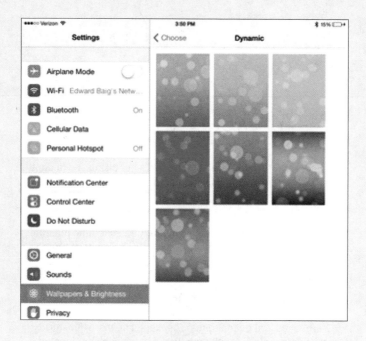

Find out what other content you can download to your iPad at www.dummies.com/extras/ipad.

In this part...

✔ Explore every single iPad setting that's not discussed in depth elsewhere in the book; by the time you finish reading Chapter 15, you'll know how to customize every part of your iPad that *can* be customized.

✔ Peruse our comprehensive guide to troubleshooting the iPad, which details what to do when almost anything goes wrong complete with step-by-step instructions for specific situations.

✔ Gaze longingly at some of the iPad accessories we use and recommend including carrying cases, physical keyboards, earphones and headphones, speakers, and more. No, this stuff's not included with your iPad, but we consider most of it essential just the same.

15

Setting You Straight on Settings

*D*o you consider yourself a control freak? The type of person who has to have it your way? Boy, have you landed in the right chapter.

Settings is kind of the makeover factory for the iPad. You open Settings by tapping its Home screen icon; from there, you can do things like change the tablet's background or wallpaper and specify Google, Yahoo!, or Bing as the search engine of choice. You can also alter security settings in Safari, tailor e-mail to your liking (among other modifications), and get a handle on how to fetch or push new data.

The Settings area on the iPad is roughly analogous to System Preferences on a Mac or the Control Panel in Windows, with a hearty serving of application preferences thrown in for good measure.

One of the key feature additions to iOS 7 is Control Center, which grants you immediate access to some settings that used to require a separate visit to the Settings complex. But even with Control Center, expect to make some tweaks in Settings from time to time.

Because we cover some settings elsewhere in this book, we don't dwell on every setting here. But you still have plenty to digest to help you make the iPad your own.

Checking Out the Settings Screen

When you first open Settings, you see a display that looks something like Figure 15-1, with a scrollable list on the left side of the screen and a pane on the right that corresponds to whichever setting is highlighted in blue. We say "something like this" because the Settings on your iPad may differ slightly from those of your neighbor's. Plus, you must scroll down to see the entire list.

One other general thought to keep in mind: If you see a greater-than symbol (>) appear to the right of a listing, the listing has a bunch of options. Throughout this chapter, you tap the > symbol to check out those options.

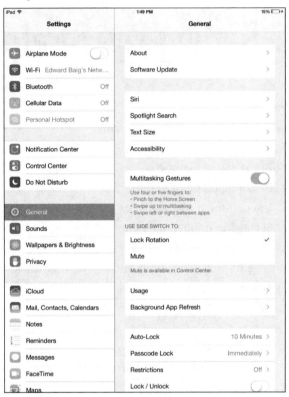

Figure 15-1: Your list of settings.

As you scroll to the bottom of the list on the left, you come to all the settings that pertain to some of the specific third-party apps you've added to the iPad. (See Chapter 11.) Everybody has a different collection of apps on his iPad, so any settings related to those programs will also obviously be different.

Flying with Sky-High Settings

Your iPad offers settings to keep you on the good side of air-traffic communications systems. No matter which iPad you have — Wi-Fi only or 3G and 4G — you have Airplane mode.

Using a cellular radio on an airplane is a no-no. Wi-Fi is too, some of the time. But nothing is verboten about using an iPad on a plane to listen to music, watch videos, and peek at pictures — at least, after the craft has reached cruising altitude.

So how do you take advantage of the iPad's built-in iPod (among other capabilities) at 30,000 feet, while temporarily turning off your wireless gateway to e-mail and Internet functions? The answer is, by turning on Airplane mode.

To do so, merely tap Airplane Mode on the Settings screen to enable the setting. You'll know it's on rather than off when you see green instead of gray on the switch.

That act disables each of the iPad's wireless radios (depending on the model): Wi-Fi, cellular, and Bluetooth. While your iPad is in Airplane mode, you can't surf the web, get a map location, send or receive e-mails, sync through iCloud, use the iTunes or App Store, or do anything else that requires an Internet connection. If a silver lining exists here, it's that the iPad's long-lasting battery ought to last even longer — good news if the flight you're on is taking you halfway around the planet.

 The appearance of a tiny Airplane icon on the status bar at the upper-left corner of the screen reminds you that Airplane mode is turned on. Just remember to turn it off when you're back on the ground.

 If in-flight Wi-Fi is available on your flight, you can turn on Wi-Fi independently, leaving the rest of your iPad's wireless radio safely disabled. And it's a breeze to do by toggling the setting in Control Center.

Controlling Wi-Fi Connections

As we mention in Chapter 4, Wi-Fi is typically the fastest wireless network that you can use to surf the web, send e-mail, and perform other Internet tricks on the iPad. You use the Wi-Fi setting to determine which Wi-Fi networks are available to you and which one to exploit based on its signal.

Tap Wi-Fi so that the setting is on, and all Wi-Fi networks in range display, as shown in Figure 15-2.

 Tap the Wi-Fi switch to Off whenever you don't have access to a network and don't want to drain the battery. You can easily toggle Wi-Fi on and off in Control Center.

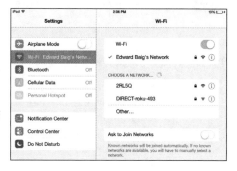

Figure 15-2: Check out your Wi-Fi options.

A signal-strength indicator can help you choose the network to connect to if more than one is listed; tap the appropriate Wi-Fi network when you reach a decision. If a network is password-protected, you see a Lock icon and need the passcode to access it.

You can also turn the Ask to Join Networks setting on or off. Networks that the iPad is already familiar with are joined automatically, regardless of which one you choose. If the Ask feature is off and no known networks are available, you have to select a new network manually. If the Ask feature is on, you're asked before joining a new network. Either way, you see a list with the same Wi-Fi networks in range.

If you used a particular network automatically in the past but you no longer want your iPad to join it, tap the "i" in a circle symbol next to the network in question (within Wi-Fi settings) and then tap Forget This Network. The iPad develops a quick case of selective amnesia.

In some instances, you have to supply other technical information about a network you hope to glom on to. You encounter a bunch of nasty-sounding terms: DHCP, BootP, Static IP Address, Subnet Mask, Router, DNS, Search Domains, Client ID, HTTP Proxy, and Renew Lease. (At least this last one has nothing to do with renting an apartment or the vehicle you're driving.) Chances are none of this info is on the tip of your tongue — but that's okay. For one thing, it's a good bet that you'll never need to know this stuff. What's more, even if you *do* have to fill in or adjust these settings, a network administrator or techie friend can probably help you.

Sometimes you may want to connect to a network that's closed and not shown on the Wi-Fi list. If that's the case, tap Other and use the keyboard to enter the network name. Then tap to choose the type of security setting the network is using (if any). Your choices are WEP, WPA, WPA2, WPA Enterprise, and WPA2 Enterprise. Again, it's not exactly the friendliest terminology in the world, but we figure that someone nearby can lend a hand.

If no Wi-Fi network is available, you have to rely on 4G, 3G, or a slower cellular connection if you have capable models. If you don't — or you're out of reach of a cellular network — you can't rocket into cyberspace until you regain access to a network.

Getting Fired Up over Bluetooth

Of all the peculiar terms you may encounter in techdom, *Bluetooth* is one of our favorites. The name is derived from Harald Blåtand, a tenth-century Danish monarch, who, the story goes, helped unite warring factions. And, we're told, *Blåtand* translates to *Bluetooth* in English. (Bluetooth is all about collaboration between different types of devices — get it?)

Blåtand was obviously ahead of his time. Although we can't imagine that he ever used a tablet computer, he now has an entire short-range wireless technology named in his honor. On the iPad, you can use

Bluetooth to communicate wirelessly with a compatible Bluetooth headset or to use an optional wireless keyboard. Such accessories are made by Apple and many others.

To ensure that the iPad works with a device, it has to be wirelessly *paired*, or coupled, with the chosen device. If you're using a third-party accessory, follow the instructions that came with that headset or keyboard so that it becomes *discoverable*, or ready to be paired with your iPad. Then turn on Bluetooth (on the Settings screen) so that the iPad can find such nearby devices and the device can find the iPad.

Bluetooth Pairing Request
Enter the code "6109" on "Edward Baig's Keyboard", followed by the return or enter key.

Cancel

In Figure 15-3, an Apple Wireless Keyboard and the iPad are successfully paired when you enter a designated passkey on the keyboard. You won't need a passkey to pair every kind of device, though. You can't, for example, enter a passkey when pairing the iPad with a wireless speaker. Bluetooth works up to a range of about 30 feet.

Figure 15-3: Pairing an Apple Wireless Keyboard with the iPad.

You know Bluetooth is turned on when you see the Bluetooth icon on the status bar. If the symbol is white, the iPad is communicating wirelessly with a connected device. If it's gray, Bluetooth is turned on in the iPad, *but* a paired device isn't nearby or isn't turned on. If you don't see a Bluetooth icon, the setting is turned off.

To unpair a device, select it from the device list and tap Forget this Device. We guess breaking up *isn't* hard to do.

The iPad supports stereo Bluetooth headphones, so you can now stream stereo audio from the iPad to those devices.

The iPad can tap into Bluetooth in other ways. One is through *peer-to-peer* connectivity, so you can engage in multiplayer games with other nearby iPad, iPhone, or iPod touch users. You can also do such things as exchange business cards, share pictures, and send short notes. In addition, you don't even have to pair the devices as you do with a headset or wireless keyboard.

You can't use Bluetooth to exchange files or sync between an iPad and a computer. Nor can you use it to print stuff from the iPad on a Bluetooth printer (although the AirPrint feature handles that chore in some instances). That's because the iPad doesn't support any of the Bluetooth profiles (or specifications) required to allow such wireless stunts to take place — at least not as of this writing. We think that's a shame.

Roaming among Cellular Data Options

You see another set of settings only if you have a Wi-Fi + 3G or + 4G iPad. The options appear on the right pane of the Settings screen when you highlight Cellular Data on the left:

- **Cellular Data:** If you know you don't need the cellular network when you're out and about or are in an area where you don't have access to the network, turn it off. Your battery will thank you later. But even if you have access to a speedy cellular network, be prudent; in a 4G environment where you can easily consume gobs of data, your data allowance may run out all too quickly.

- **Data Roaming:** You may unwittingly rack up lofty roaming fees when exchanging e-mail, surfing with Safari, or engaging in other data-heavy activities while traveling abroad. Turn off Data Roaming to avoid such potential charges. You will see the Data Roaming option only if you have turned on Cellular Data.

- **Account Information:** Tap View Account to see or edit your account information or to add more data.

- **Add a SIM PIN:** The tiny *SIM,* or *Subscriber Identity Module,* card inside your iPad with cellular holds important data about your account. To add a PIN or a passcode to lock your SIM card, tap SIM PIN. That way, if someone gets hold of your SIM, she can't use it in another iPad without the passcode.

  If you assign a PIN to your SIM, you have to enter it to turn the iPad on or off, which some might consider a minor hassle. And be aware that the SIM PIN is different from and may be in addition to any passcode you set for the iPad, as described later in this chapter.

- **Personal Hotspot:** Tap Personal Hotspot to share your iPad's data connection with any other devices you carry: perhaps a computer or smartphone. Just know that extra charges may apply and even if it doesn't you will rack up that much extra data. You or the owner of the device piggybacking on your Internet connection have to enter the designated password generated by the iPad for the Hotspot connection to make nice. You can use the Hotspot feature via Wi-Fi or Bluetooth, or by connecting a USB cable. See Chapter 13 to find out how to use Personal Hotspot.

- **Enable LTE:** LTE stands for Long Term Evolution. What it really stands for is speed. Turn Enable LTE on for the fastest possible cellular data connection if you're in range. The biggest downside is you can eat up data awfully fast.

- **Use Cellular Data For:** You can use your cellular connection for iCloud documents, iTunes, a Safari Reading List, and certain third-party apps. You can see just how much data you're using on your apps and, if need be, shut down an app that's sucking up way too much.

✔ **Cellular Data Usage:** This lists how much cellular data you've consumed for the current period. You also can see whether you're using up data while roaming. Overall, you'll know if you're closing in on your monthly data allowance.

Managing Notifications

Through Apple's Push Notification service, app developers can send you alerts related to programs you've installed on your iPad. Such alerts are typically in text form but may include sounds as well. The idea is that you'll receive notifications even when the app they apply to isn't running. Notifications may also appear as numbered "badges" on their corresponding Home screen icon.

The downside to keeping Push notifications turned on is that they can curtail battery life (although honestly, we've been pretty satisfied with the iPad's staying power, even when Push notifications are active). And you may find notifications distracting at times.

You no longer find a global On/Off switch for Notifications; beginning with iOS 5, you have to manage them on an app-by-app basis. To do so, tap Notification Center on the left side of the Settings screen, as shown in Figure 15-4, and then tap the app you want to manage.

All installed apps that take advantage of Notification Center (see Chapter 13) appear on the right side of the panel, as shown in Figure 15-4, with the enabled apps displayed in the upper section (Include) and disabled apps in the lower section (Do Not Include; not shown).

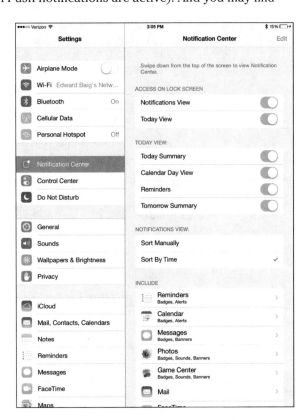

Figure 15-4: Notify the iPad of your notification intentions.

Tap any app to adjust its settings, as shown in Figure 15-5.

Figure 15-5 shows Notification settings for the Mail app (more specifically, Gmail). Some apps offer other options, including sound alerts, and other apps may offer fewer options, but we think you'll figure it out. To help you get started, here's a rundown of the options shown in Figure 15-5, starting at the top:

Figure 15-5: Notification settings for the Mail app.

- ✔ **Alert Style:** Tap to select the style of alert you want to see:

  - *None:* Choose None, and notifications won't appear spontaneously. They'll still be available in Notification Center (swipe down from the top of the screen; see Chapter 13) but won't interrupt your work (or play).

  - *Banners:* Choose Banners to display alerts as banners at the top of the screen and have them go away automatically, as opposed to . . .

  - *Alerts:* Choose Alerts to display alerts that require action before proceeding.

- ✔ **Badge App Icon:** Enable this to display the number of pending alerts on the app's icon on your Home screen.

- ✔ **Alert Sound:** Tap this setting to choose the sound that accompanies notifications of new mail messages. (The Ding sound is selected in Figure 15-5.) But you can pick from a lengthy list of sound and ringtone alternatives and tap each possible choice to hear what the sound snippet sounds like. Or select None if you're in the mood for total quiet.

- ✔ **Show in Notification Center:** Tap the switch to enable or disable notifications for this app in Notification Center. Straightforward enough.

- ✔ **Show on Lock Screen:** Enable this option if you want to see notifications for this app when your iPad screen is locked.

- ✔ **Show Preview:** Enable this to see the first part of the mail or iMessage as part of notification in Notification Center.

Apps that don't take advantage of the iOS Notification Center can still offer notifications, but you'll have to scroll down to the Apps section on the left side of

Settings and tap the app you want to alter. Note that the app you hope to fiddle with doesn't always appear in the Apps section of Settings. For that matter, many of the apps that do appear in the list don't offer notifications anyway.

The broader point we're trying to make is that we urge you to check out the settings for *all* the apps you see in this list. You'll never know about many useful options if you don't.

If you find you went overboard with notifications at first to the point where they become annoying or distracting, don't fret. You can always go back and redo some or all of notifications that you've set up.

You have a lot to say about Notification Center itself. You can determine whether to view it on the Lock screen, display the Today view, and (if you're displaying that view) what to show in there (Today's Summary, Calendar Day View, Reminders, Tomorrow Summary).

Apple understands that sometimes you don't want to be bothered by notifications or other distractions, no matter how unobtrusive they might be. The result is a feature aptly named Do Not Disturb. Flip the switch so the setting is turned to On, and a moon icon appears in the status bar. Then you can rest assured that your alerts are silenced until you turn the setting back to the Off position. Of course, it's even easier to turn this setting on or off in Control Center.

Controlling Control Center

We've already sung the praises of Control Center, the convenient utility that is no farther away than an upward swipe from the bottom of the screen. In Settings, you get to decide whether to make Control Center accessible from the Lock screen and whether you can access it within apps. The switches for making these determinations are pretty straightforward.

Location, Location, Location Services

By using the onboard Maps or Camera apps (or any number of third-party apps), the iPad makes good use of knowing where you are. The iPads with 3G or 4G exploit built-in GPS. The Wi-Fi–only iPad can find your general whereabouts (by *triangulating* signals from Wi-Fi base stations and cellular towers).

If that statement creeps you out a little, don't fret. To protect your right to privacy, individual apps pop up quick messages (similar to the two warnings presented by Google Maps, shown in Figure 15-6) asking whether you want them to use your current location. But you can also turn off Location Services in Settings: Tap Privacy and then tap Locations Services to turn the setting off.

Not only is your privacy shielded, but you also keep your iPad battery juiced a little longer.

While visiting the Privacy setting, you may want to consult the Privacy listings for individual apps on your iPad — Contacts, Calendars, Reminders, Photos, Bluetooth Sharing, and the Microphone. If any third-party apps request access to these apps, they show up here.

From time to time on the iPad, you can land in the same destination multiple ways, so you can access the same Privacy settings via the Restrictions settings that we address later in this chapter.

Figure 15-6: Google Maps wants to know where you are.

Settings for Your Senses

The next bunch of settings control what the iPad looks like and sounds like.

Brightening your day

Who doesn't want a bright, vibrant screen? Alas, the brightest screens exact a trade-off: Before you drag the brightness slider shown in Figure 15-7 to the max, remember that brighter screens sap the life from your battery more quickly. The control appears when Wallpapers & Brightness is highlighted.

Figure 15-7: Sliding this control adjusts screen brightness.

That's why we recommend tapping the Auto-Brightness control so that it's on. The control automatically adjusts the screen according to the lighting environment in which you're using the iPad — while at the same time being considerate of your battery. And the Auto-Brightness control is one reason to adjust the brightness here, as opposed to Control Center: Auto Brightness is not available in Control Center.

Wallpaper

Choosing wallpaper is a neat way to dress up the iPad according to your aesthetic preferences. iOS 7 includes colorful dynamic animated wallpapers with floating bubbles that add a subtle dizzying effect. But stunning as they are, these images may not hold a candle to the masterpieces in your own photo albums (more about those in Chapter 9).

You can sample the pretty patterns and dynamic designs that the iPad has already chosen for you, as follows:

1. **Tap Wallpapers & Brightness and then tap the two iPads below the words *Choose Wallpaper*.**

   A list of photo albums appears with Wallpaper, a photo album of lovely images included with your iPad.

2. **Tap Apple Wallpaper (Dynamic or Stills) or one of your own photo albums in the list.**

   Thumbnails of the images in that album appear, as shown in Figure 15-8.

Figure 15-8: Choosing a majestic background.

3. **Tap a thumbnail image.**

   That image fills the screen.

4. **When an image is full-screen, choose one of the options that appear at the bottom of the screen:**

   • *Set Lock Screen* makes your selected image the wallpaper of choice when the iPad is locked.

   • *Set Home Screen* makes the wallpaper decorate only your Home screen.

- *Set Both* makes your image the wallpaper for both the Lock screen and the Home screen.

- *Cancel* takes you back to the thumbnail page without changing your Home or Lock screen.

Sounds

Consider the Sounds settings area the iPad's soundstage. There, you can turn audio alerts on or off for a variety of functions: ringtones, text tones, new e-mail, sent mail, calendar and reminder alerts, Facebook posts, and tweets. You can also decide whether you want to hear lock sounds and keyboard clicks.

You can alter the ringtone you hear for FaceTime calls and the text tones you hear for iMessages, and visit the iTunes store to buy more text tones or ringtones if you're not satisfied with those that Apple supplies, for $0.99 and $1.29 a pop. (Mac owners can create their own by using GarageBand, as can folks who use GarageBand on an iPad. And the app is now free for folks who purchase new iOS 7 devices.) To set a custom tone for individuals in the Contacts app, tap the Edit button and then either the Ringtone or Text Tone option.

To raise the decibel level of alerts, drag the volume slider to the right. Drag in the opposite direction to bring down the noise. An alternative way to adjust sound levels is to use the physical Volume buttons on the side of the iPad for this purpose, as long as you're not already using the iPad's iPod to listen to music or watch video.

You can enable and disable this feature with the Change with Buttons switch, right below the volume slider.

Exploring Settings in General

Certain miscellaneous settings are difficult to pigeonhole. Apple wisely lumped these under the General settings moniker. Here's a closer look at your options.

About About

You aren't seeing double. This section, as shown in Figure 15-9, is all about the About setting. And About is full of trivial (and not-so-trivial) information *about* the device. What you find here is straightforward.

- ✔ **Network you use (3G or 4G only):** AT&T, Sprint, T-Mobile, or Verizon

- ✔ **Number of songs stored on the device**

✔ **Number of videos**

✔ **Number of photos**

✔ **Number of apps**

✔ **Storage capacity used and available:** Because of the way the device is formatted, you always have a little less storage than the advertised amount of flash memory.

✔ **Software version:** As this book goes to press, we're up to version 7.03. But as the software is tweaked and updated, your device takes on a new build identifier, indicating that it's just a little bit further along than some previous build. So you see, in parentheses next to the version number, a string of numbers and letters that looks like 11B511 and tells you more precisely what software version you have. The number/letter string changes whenever the iPad's software is updated and is potentially useful to some tech-support person who might need to know the precise version you're working with.

Figure 15-9: You find info about your iPad under About.

✔ **Carrier and cellular data (Wi-Fi + 3G or + 4G versions only):** Yep, that's AT&T, Sprint, T-Mobile, or Verizon in the United States.

✔ **Serial and model numbers**

✔ **Cellular Data Number (for billing purposes only)**

✔ **Wi-Fi address**

✔ **Bluetooth address:** See the earlier section to find out more about this setting.

✔ **IMEI, ICCID, and MEID:** These stand for *International Mobile Equipment Identifier, International Circuit Card Identifier,* and *Mobile Equipment Identifier,* respectively. They live up to their geeky acronyms by helping to identify your specific device.

✔ **Modern Firmware:** The version of your iPad's firmware, which is a combination of hardware and software, that helps your iPad function as an iPad.

✔ **Diagnostics & Usage:** Choose whether to send diagnostic data automatically to Apple.

✔ **Legal Notices, License, Regulatory and Trusted Certificates:** You had to know that the lawyers would get in their two cents somehow. You find all the fine print here. And *fine print* it is because you can't unpinch to enlarge the text (not that we can imagine more than a handful will bother to read this legal mumbo jumbo).

Software Update

Pretty self-explanatory. When Apple unleashes an update, such as the one that moved the device from iOS 6 to iOS 7, you can find it here.

Siri

We love that Siri, the chatty personal digital assistant who can remind you whether to take an umbrella or clue you in on how the Giants are faring in the NFL, has found her way to the iPad from her original hangout spot on the iPhone 4S. You can talk to Siri by pressing and holding the Home button and speaking out loud. Siri will talk back.

But sometimes, well — there's no way to say this kindly — you want to shut Siri up. To do that, just turn the Siri setting from On to Off. If you do disable Siri, be aware that the information she uses to respond to your requests is removed from Apple's servers. So if you call Siri back into duty later, it may take a little bit of time for the feature to re-send information. Don't fret if you don't remember any of this. Apple reminds you ahead of your silencing Siri.

Other Siri settings to take note of:

✔ **Default language:** You can choose the language in which she will speak to you. The default is U.S. English.

✔ **Voice gender:** Siri is no longer just a she. You can switch from a female to a male voice or vice versa.

✔ **Voice feedback:** You can select whether to always get voice feedback from Siri, as opposed to only when you're in a "hands-free" situation.

✔ **Your info:** And you can let Siri know who you are by choosing your name (if not already shown) in the My Info section of Siri settings. If for some reason you want to pick another name, you can do so from your list of Contacts.

Spotlight Search

Tell the iPad the apps that you want to search. Touch the three horizontal lines next to an app that you want to include in your search and drag it up or down to rearrange the search order.

Accessibility

The Accessibility or Universal Access Features tools on your iPad are targeted at helping people with certain disabilities. The following sections explain each one in turn.

VoiceOver

This screen reader describes aloud what's on the screen. It can read e-mail messages, web pages, and more. With VoiceOver active, you tap an item on the screen to select it. VoiceOver places a black rectangle around it and either speaks the name or describes an item. For example, if you tap, say, Wallpapers & Brightness, the VoiceOver voice speaks the words "Wallpapers & Brightness button." VoiceOver even lets you know when you alternately position the iPad in landscape or portrait mode or when your screen is locked or unlocked.

Within the VoiceOver setting, you have several options. For instance, if you turn on Speak Hints, VoiceOver may provide instructions on what to do next, along the lines of "double-tap to open." You can drag a Speaking Rate slider to speed up or slow down the speech. You can also determine the kind of typing feedback you get, from among characters, words, characters and words, or no feedback. Additional controls let you turn on Phonetics and Pitch Change and choose the voice.

The voice you hear speaks in the language you specified in International settings, which we explain earlier.

You have to know a whole new set of finger gestures when VoiceOver is on, which may seem difficult, especially when you first start using VoiceOver. When you stop to think about it, this makes a lot of sense. You want to be able to hear descriptions on the screen before you actually activate buttons. Different VoiceOver gestures use different numbers of fingers. Here's a rundown on many of these:

- **Tap:** Speak the item.

- **Flick right or left:** Select the next or previous item.

- **Flick up or down:** This gesture has multiple outcomes that depend on how you set the so-called "rotor control" gesture. Think of the rotor control as you'd think about turning a dial: You rotate two fingertips on the screen. The purpose is to switch to a different set of commands or features. This leads us back to the flick-up or flick-down gestures. Suppose you're reading text in an e-mail. By alternately spinning the rotor, you can switch between hearing the body of a message read aloud word by word or character by character. After you set the parameters, flick up or down to hear stuff read back. The flicking-up-or-down gestures serve a different purpose when you type an e-mail: The gestures move the cursor left or right within the text.

- **Two-finger tap:** Stop speaking.

- **Two-finger flick up:** Read everything from the top of the screen.

- **Two-finger flick down:** Read everything from your current position on the screen.

- **Three-finger flick up or down:** Scroll a page.

- **Three-finger flick right or left:** Go to the next or previous page.

- **Three-finger tap:** Lets you know which page or rows are on the screen.

- **Three-finger swipe down after selecting an item in the status bar:** Opens Notification Center.

- **Three-finger swipe up after selecting an item in the status bar:** Opens Control Center.

- **Four-finger flick up or down:** Go to the first or last part of the page.

- **Four-finger flick right or left:** Go to the next or previous section.

- **Double-tap:** Activate a selected icon or button to launch an app, turn a switch from on to off, and more.

- **Touch an item with one finger and tap the screen with another:** Otherwise known as *split-tapping,* when you touch an item, a voice identifies what you touched (for example, "Safari button" or "Notifications on button"). A tap with the second finger selects whatever was identified with the first finger (that is, "Safari button selected" or "Notifications on button selected"). Now you can double-tap to launch the button or whatever else was selected.

- **Double-tap, hold for a second, and then add a standard gesture:** Tell the iPad to go back to using standard gestures for your next move. You can also use standard gestures with VoiceOver by double-tapping and holding the screen. You hear tones that remind you that standard gestures are now in effect. They stay that way until you lift your finger.

- **Two-finger double-tap:** Play or pause. You use the double-tap in the Music, YouTube, and Photos apps.

- **Three-finger double-tap:** Mute or unmute the voice.

- **Three-finger triple-tap:** Turn the display on or off.

As part of iOS 6, Apple brought VoiceOver to Maps, AssistiveTouch, and Zoom.

Zoom

The Zoom feature offers a screen magnifier for those who are visually challenged. To zoom by 200 percent, double-tap the screen with *three* fingers. Drag three fingers to move around the screen. To increase magnification, use three fingers to tap and drag up. Tap with three fingers and drag down to decrease magnification.

The Zoom feature does have a downside: When magnified, the characters on the screen aren't as crisp (although the Retina display is still pretty sharp), and you can't display as much in a single view.

Large Type

You can make text larger in the Mail, Contacts, Calendars, Messages, and Notes apps. Drag the slider from left to right or from the small "A" toward a larger "A." You can turn on a Larger Dynamic Type switch to enlarge the text even more in certain supported apps.

Bold Text

Not everyone took kindly to the design changes brought by iOS 7. Some people don't think the text is bold or bright enough. These people should consider turning on the Bold Text switch. Note that doing so (or turning it off again) requires that you restart your iPad.

Increase Contrast

This setting is another effort to bolster legibility. Turn this contrast switch on and see whether it makes a positive difference to your eyes.

Invert Colors

The colors on the iPad can be reversed to provide a higher contrast for people with poor eyesight. The screen resembles a film negative.

Mono Audio

If you suffer hearing loss in one ear, the iPad can combine the right and left audio channels so that both channels can be heard in either earbud of any headset you plug in. A slider control can adjust how much audio is combined and to which ear it is directed.

The iPad, unlike its cousins the iPhone and the iPod touch, doesn't come with earbuds or headphones. You have to supply your own.

Speak Selection

When this setting is on, the iPad speaks any text you select. You also find a slider control to adjust the speaking rate. And you can highlight words as they are spoken.

Speak Auto-Text

When this setting is on, the iPad automatically speaks auto-corrections and capitalizations.

Reduce Motion

We think the parallax effect of icons and alerts added with iOS 7 is pretty cool, but your neighbor may not agree. By turning this switch on, you can reduce the parallax effect and be fairly confident that your wallpaper will remain still.

On/Off labels

Throughout this book, you read that when certain switches are on, you'll see green showing. If you turn on this particular switch, you'll still see green, but you'll also see a nerdy 1 when the setting or switch is turned on or a little 0 when the switch is off.

Guided Access

Parents of autistic kids know how challenging it can be to keep the child focused on a given task. The Guided Access setting that can limit iPad usage to a single app and also restrict touch input on certain areas of the screen. You can turn the feature on or off by employing Triple-Click Home, the very next setting.

Switch Control

Several controls are represented under the Switch Control setting. The general idea is that you can use a single switch or multiple switches to select text, tap, drag, type, and perform other functions. However, turning on Switch Control changes the gestures that you use to control your tablet and are presumably already familiar with. Switch Control makes use of different techniques. For example, the iPad can scan by or highlight items on the screen until you select one. Or you can choose to take advantage of scanning crosshairs to select a location on the screen. You can also manually move from item to item using multiple switches, with each switch set to handle a specific action.

AssistiveTouch

Turn on this setting if you need to use an adaptive accessory, such as a joystick, because of difficulties touching the screen. Plus, when this setting is on, you can create your own custom gestures.

Home-click speed

Slow down the speed required to double or triple-click the Home button, which is next on the list of Accessibility options.

Accessibility shortcut

Double-pressing the Home button launches multitasking. But you can set up the iPad so that triple-tapping the button (tapping three times really fast) turns on certain Accessibility features. (This tool used to be called Triple-Click Home.) By doing so, you can turn on or off VoiceOver, Invert Colors, Zoom, Switch Control, and AssistiveTouch.

Subtitles & Captioning

To turn on closed captioning or subtitles for a movie or video in which they're available, tap this setting. You can also choose a style for your subtitles.

Multitasking gestures

Enable this option if you want to use four or five fingers to

- ✔ Pinch to the Home screen.
- ✔ Swipe up to multitask.
- ✔ Swipe left or right to switch among open apps.

By all means, enable this option if it isn't enabled. The gestures really improve the multitasking experience, and we recommend you give them a try. If, for some reason, you hate them, you know where to go to turn them off.

Usage settings

The About setting (covered earlier) gives you a lot of information about your device. But after you back out of About and return to the main General settings, you can find other settings for statistics on iPad usage:

- ✔ **Battery percentage:** You almost always see a little battery meter in the upper-right corner of the screen, except for certain instances, such as when you watch videos and the whole top bar disappears. If you also want to see your battery life presented in percentage terms, make sure that the Battery Percentage setting is turned on.

- ✔ **iCloud:** Shows the amount of total and available storage. Tap Manage Storage to, well, manage your iCloud storage, taking note of all your iOS backups. If, need be, of course, you can buy more storage. Tap Change Storage Plan to get started. The 10GB $20/year plan actually gives you 15GB of storage; the 20GB $40/year plan actually gives you 25GB of storage; and the 50GB $100/year plan actually gives you 55GB. You can also downgrade to a free 5GB plan.

- ✔ **Storage (for the device):** Lets you check out which apps on your iPad are hogging the most storage and to delete those you're no longer using.

Auto-Lock

Tap Auto-Lock in the General settings pane, and you can set the amount of time that elapses before the iPad automatically locks or turns off the display. Your choices are 15 minutes before, 10 minutes, 5 minutes, or 2 minutes. Or you can set it so that the iPad never locks automatically.

If you work for a company that insists on a passcode (see the next section), the Never Auto-Lock option isn't in the list that your iPad shows you.

Don't worry about whether the iPad is locked. You can still receive notification alerts and adjust the volume.

Passcode Lock

If you want to prevent others from using your iPad, you can set a passcode by tapping Passcode Lock and then tapping Turn Passcode On. By default, you use the virtual keypad to enter and confirm a four-digit passcode. If you'd prefer a longer, stronger passcode, tap the Simple Passcode switch to turn it off. Now provide your current passcode, and then enter and confirm your new passcode, which can be almost any combination of the letters, numbers, and symbols that are available on the standard virtual keyboard.

You can also determine whether a passcode is required immediately, after 1 minute, after 5 minutes, 15 minutes, 1 hour, or 4 hours. Shorter times are more secure, of course. On the topic of security, the iPad can be set to automatically erase your data if someone makes ten failed passcode attempts.

You can also change the passcode or turn it off later (unless your employer dictates otherwise), but you need to know the present passcode to apply any changes. If you forget the passcode, you have to restore the iPad software, as we describe in Chapter 16.

Restrictions

Parents and bosses may love the Restrictions tools, but kids and employees usually think otherwise. You can clamp down, er, provide proper parental guidance to your children by preventing them (at least some of the time) from using the Safari browser, Camera, FaceTime, iTunes Store, iBooks Store, Siri, or Game Center. Or you might not let them install new apps or make purchases inside the apps you do allow — or (conversely) let them delete apps. When restrictions are in place, icons for off-limit functions can no longer be seen. Tap Enable Restrictions, set or enter your passcode — you have to enter it twice if you are setting up the passcode — and tap the button next to each item in the Allow or Allowed Content lists that you plan to restrict. Their corresponding settings should be off (gray is showing rather than green).

You can also restrict the use of explicit language when you dictate text. An asterisk (*) replaces a naughty word.

Moreover, parents have more controls to work with. For instance, you can allow Junior to watch a movie on the iPad but prevent him from watching a flick that carries an R or NC-17 rating. You can also restrict access to certain TV shows, explicit songs and podcasts, and apps based on age-appropriate ratings. In Game Center, you can decide whether your kid can play a multiplayer game or add friends. Apple lets you choose whether to let the kids read books with explicit sexual content. You can also restrict access to websites that have adult content.

Stop feeling guilty: You have your users' best interests at heart.

If guilt gets the better of you, you can turn off Restrictions. Open the Restrictions setting by again typing your passcode. Then switch the setting on for each item you are freeing up. Tap Disable Restrictions. You have to enter your passcode one more time before your kids and office underlings return you to their good graces.

Under Restrictions settings, you'll find privacy controls as well. And in this area, you can allow or restrict changes made to your accounts, Find My Friends, cellular use, background app refreshes, even volume limits.

There's a lot here, and even if you're rather liberal about policing your kids' activities, we recommend you poke around and consider all your options.

Cover Lock/Unlock

You have the choice to automatically lock and unlock your iPad when you close and open the clever iPad Smart Cover, Apple's Smart Case, or some other covers. If you set a passcode, you still have to enter it to wake the iPad from siesta-land.

Side Switch

You can use the side switch for one of two purposes: You can lock the rotation so that the screen orientation doesn't change when you turn the iPad to the side, or you can mute certain sounds. Here's where you get to make that choice.

Date & Time

In our neck of the woods, the time is reported as 11:32 p.m. (or whatever time it happens to be). But in some circles, it's reported as 23:32. If you prefer the latter format on the iPad's status bar, tap the 24-Hour Time setting (under Date & Time) so that it's on.

This setting is just one that you can adjust under Date & Time. You can also have the iPad set the time in your time zone. Here's how:

1. **Tap Date & Time.**

   You see fields for setting the time zone and the date and time.

2. **Tap the Time Zone field and make sure Set Automatically is turned off.**

   The current time zone and virtual keyboard are shown.

3. **Tap X to remove the city currently shown in the Time Zone field, and tap the letters of the city or country whose time zone you want to enter until the one you have in mind appears. Then tap the name of that city or country.**

   The Time Zone field is automatically filled in for that city.

4. **Tap the Set Date & Time field so that the time is shown; then roll the carousel controls until the proper time displays.**

5. **Roll the carousel controls to choose the proper month, day, and year until the correct date appears.**

6. **Tap General to return to the main Date & Time settings screen.**

You can also dispense with these settings and just have the iPad set the time automatically, based on its knowledge of where you happen to be: Just make sure the Set Automatically option is set to On.

Keyboard

Under Keyboard settings, you have the following options:

- **Auto-Capitalization:** You can turn Auto-Capitalization on or off.

  Auto-Capitalization, which the iPad turns on by default, means that the first letter of the first word you type after ending the preceding sentence with a period, a question mark, or an exclamation point is capitalized.

- **Auto-Correction:** When turned on, the iPad takes a stab at what it thinks you meant to type.

- **Check Spelling:** When on, the keyboard can check spelling while you type.

- **Enable Caps Lock:** If Caps Lock is enabled, all letters are uppercased LIKE THIS if you double-tap the Shift key. (The Shift key is the one with the arrow pointing up.) Tap Shift again to exit Caps Lock.

- **"." Shortcut:** You can also turn on this keyboard setting, which inserts a period followed by a space when you double-tap the spacebar. This setting is turned on by default; if you've never tried it, give it a shot.

A little lower down under Keyboard settings, you'll see another type of shortcut option: having the keyboard type a full phrase when all you have to do is type a few letters. For example, typing the letters "omw" actually yields "On my way!" Tap Add New Shortcut to do just that, and then enter the phrase and the shortcut that will lead to that phrase. Saving a few letters is rather economical, don't you think?

You can choose to use an international keyboard (as we discuss in Chapter 2), which you enable from Keyboard settings or the International setting — the next setting after Keyboard in the General settings area.

International

The iPad is an international sensation just as it is in the United States. In the International section, you can set the language you type (by using a custom virtual keyboard), the language in which the iPad displays text, and the date, time, and telephone format for the region in question. You can choose a Gregorian, Japanese, or Buddhist calendar, too.

iTunes Wi-Fi Sync

We spend an entire chapter (Chapter 3, to be precise) on syncing. Just know that if you want to sync with iTunes on your computer when you're plugged into power and tapped into Wi-Fi, you can do it here.

VPN settings

After you tap VPN on the General settings screen, you see a control for VPN.

A _virtual private network,_ or _VPN,_ is a way for you to securely access your company's network behind the firewall — using an encrypted Internet connection that acts as a secure "tunnel" for data.

You can configure a VPN on the iPad by following these steps:

1. **Tap Settings⇨General⇨VPN⇨Add VPN Configuration.**

2. **Tap one of the protocol options.**

   The iPad software supports the protocols _L2TP_ (Layer 2 Tunneling Protocol), _PPTP_ (Point-to-Point Tunneling Protocol), and _IPSec,_ which apparently provides the kind of security that satisfies network administrators.

3. **Using configuration settings provided by your company, fill in the appropriate server information, account, password, and other information.**

4. **Choose whether to turn on RSA SecurID authentication.**

   Better yet, lend your iPad to the techies where you work and let them fill in the blanks on your behalf.

After you configure your iPad for VPN usage, you can turn that capability on or off by tapping (yep) the VPN switch inside Settings.

Reset

As little kids playing sports, we ended an argument by agreeing to a do-over. Well, the Reset settings on the iPad are one big do-over. Now that you're (presumably) grown up, think long and hard about the consequences before implementing do-over settings. Regardless, you may encounter good reasons for starting over; some of these are addressed in Chapter 16.

Here are your reset options:

- **Reset All Settings:** Resets all settings, but no data or media is deleted.

- **Erase All Content and Settings:** Resets all settings *and* wipes out all your data.

- **Reset Network Settings:** Deletes the current network settings and restores them to their factory defaults.

- **Subscriber Services:** Here you have options to reprovision (or refresh) your account and reset your authentication code.

- **Reset Keyboard Dictionary:** Removes added words from the dictionary. Remember that the iPad keyboard is intelligent. And, one reason it's so smart is that it learns from you. So when you reject words that the iPad keyboard suggests, it figures that the words you specifically banged out ought to be added to the keyboard dictionary.

- **Reset Home Screen Layout:** Reverts all icons to the way they were at the factory.

- **Reset Location & Privacy:** Restores factory defaults.

Find My iPad

We hope you never have to use the Find My iPad feature — though we have to say that it's pretty darn cool. If you inadvertently leave your iPad in a taxi or restaurant, Find My iPad may just help you retrieve it. All it takes is a free iCloud account.

Well, that's *almost* all it takes. You'll have to turn it on, though, so tap Settings⇨Mail, Contacts, Calendars, and then tap your iCloud account. Or tap Settings⇨iCloud. Either way, make sure Find My iPad is switched to On.

Now, suppose you lost your tablet — and we can only assume that you're beside yourself. Follow these steps to see whether the Find My iPad feature can help you:

1. **Log on to your iCloud account at** `https://www.icloud.com` **from any browser on your computer.**

2. **Click the Find My iPhone icon.**

   If you don't see it, click the icon with a cloud in it that appears in the upper-left corner of the iCloud site. You see a panel with icons that are tied to various iCloud services, including Find My iPhone. (Yes, even though the feature is Find My iPad on the iPad, it shows up as Find My iPhone on the iCloud site. Don't worry; it'll still locate your iPad — and, for that matter, a lost iPhone or iPod touch, and even a Mac computer too.)

   Assuming that your tablet is turned on and in the coverage area, its general whereabouts turn up on a map (as shown in Figure 15-10), in standard or satellite views, or a hybrid of the two. In our tests, Find My iPad found our iPads quickly.

   Figure 15-10: Locate a lost iPad.

   The truth is that even seeing your iPad on a map may not help you much, especially if the device is lost somewhere in midtown Manhattan. Take heart.

3. **At the iCloud site, click the Lost Mode buttons.**

4. **Type a phone number at which you can be reached, as well as a plea to the Good Samaritan who (you hope) picked up your iPad.**

   Apple has already prepared a simple message indicating that the iPad is lost, but you can change or remove the message and substitute your own plea for the return of your tablet.

   The message appears on the lost iPad's screen, as shown in Figure 15-11.

Figure 15-11: An appeal to return the iPad.

To get someone's attention, you can also sound an alarm that plays for two minutes, even if the volume is off. Tap Play Sound to make it happen. Hey, that alarm may come in handy if the iPad turns up under a couch in your house. Stranger things have happened.

Find My iPhone (which finds any iOS device) is now available as a free app in the App Store. Another free app called Find My Friends, as the name suggests, will locate your friends on a map. Just hope that when you find a particular pal, he's not the one who snatched your missing iPad.

After all this labor, if the iPad is seemingly gone for good, click Erase iPad at the iCloud site to delete your personal data from afar and return the iPad to its factory settings. (A somewhat less drastic measure is to remotely lock your iPad by using a four-digit passcode.)

Meanwhile, the person who found (or possibly stole) your iPad cannot reactivate the device to use as his or her own, or to peddle, unless he or she successfully types in *your* Apple ID.

Another new addition: Even if you choose to erase the device remotely, it can still display a custom message with the information needed for someone to return it to you. If, indeed, you ever get your iPad back, you can always restore the information from an iTunes backup on your Mac or PC or iCloud.

We authors are always seeking a happy ending.

16

When Good iPads Go Bad

*I*n our experience, all Apple's iOS devices — namely the iPad, iPhone, and iPod touch — are fairly reliable. But every so often, a good iPad might just go bad. We don't expect it to be a common occurrence, but it does happen occasionally. So, in this chapter, we look at the types of bad things that can happen, along with suggestions for fixing them.

What kind of bad things are we talking about? Well, we're referring to problems involving

✔ Frozen or dead iPads

✔ Wireless networks

✔ Synchronization of computers (both Mac and PC) or iTunes

After all the troubleshooting, we tell you how to get even more help if nothing we suggest does the trick. Finally, if your iPad is so badly hosed that it needs to go back to the mother ship for repairs, we offer ways to survive the experience with a minimum of stress or fuss, including how to restore your stuff from an iTunes or iCloud backup.

Resuscitating an iPad with Issues

Our first category of troubleshooting techniques applies to an iPad that's frozen or otherwise acting up. The recommended procedure when this happens is to perform the seven *R*s in sequence.

1. Recharge

2. Restart

3. Reset your iPad

4. Remove your content

5. Reset settings and content

6. Restore

7. Recovery mode

But before you even start those procedures, Apple recommends you take these steps:

1. **Verify that you have the current version of iTunes installed on your Mac or PC.**

   You can always download the latest and greatest version here: www.apple.com/itunes/download.

2. **Verify that you're connecting your iPad to your computer using a USB 2.0 or 3.0 port.**

   If you encounter difficulties here, we implore you to read the paragraph in the next section that begins with this:

   "Don't plug the iPad's Lightning or dock connector–to–USB cable into a USB port on your keyboard, monitor, or unpowered USB hub."

3. **Make sure that your iPad software is up to date.**

   To check with iTunes on your Mac or PC

   a. *Connect the iPad to the computer, and then click the iPad button just below the Search field.*

   If you use more than one iDevice with this computer, the button will say the number of devices (for example, *5 Devices*) rather than *iPad.* Click the button to display a drop-down list and select the device you want.

   You won't see the button if you've made the iTunes sidebar visible (View⇨Show Sidebar/Hide Sidebar or press ⌘+Option+S on a Mac or Alt+Ctrl+S on a PC). You can select your iPad in the sidebar and follow along, but your screens may look different from the ones in this chapter.

   b. *Click the Summary tab and then click the Check For Update button.*

To check with your iPad

    a. Tap Settings on your Home screen.

    b. Tap General in the Settings list on the left side of the screen.

    c. Tap Software Update on the right side of the screen.

If your iPad requires an update, you receive instructions for doing so. Otherwise, please continue.

If those three easy steps didn't get you back up and running and your iPad is still acting up — if it freezes, doesn't wake up from sleep, doesn't do something it used to do, or in any other way acts improperly — don't panic. The following sections describe the things you should try, in the order that we (and Apple) recommend.

If the first technique doesn't do the trick, go on to the second. If the second one doesn't work, try the third. And so on.

Recharge

If your iPad acts up in any way, shape, or form, the first thing you should try is to give its battery a full recharge before you proceed.

Don't plug the iPad's dock connector–to–USB cable into a USB port on your keyboard, monitor, or an unpowered USB hub. You need to plug it into one of the USB ports on your computer itself. That's because the USB ports on your computer supply more power than the other ports. Although other USB ports *may* do the trick, you're better off using the built-in ones on your computer.

If your computer is more than a few years old, even your built-in USB ports may not supply enough juice to recharge your iPad. It'll sync just fine; it just won't recharge. If it says Not Charging next to the battery icon at the top of the screen, use the included USB power adapter to recharge your iPad from an AC outlet rather than from a computer.

Most *powered* USB hubs, the kind you plug into an AC outlet, will charge your iPad just fine. But *passive* or *unpowered* hubs — ones that don't plug into the wall for power — won't cut it when it comes to charging your iPad.

If you're in a hurry, charge your iPad for a minimum of 20 minutes. We think a full charge is a better idea, but a charge of 20 or minutes is better than no charge at all. And for faster charging in any circumstances, turn off your iPad while it charges.

Restart

If you recharge your iPad and it still misbehaves, the next thing to try is restarting it. Just as restarting a computer often fixes problems, restarting your iPad sometimes works wonders.

Here's how to restart your iPad:

1. **Press and hold the Sleep/Wake button.**
2. **When the red slider appears, slide it to turn off the iPad and then wait a few seconds.**
3. **Press and hold the Sleep/Wake button again until the Apple logo appears on the screen.**
4. **If your iPad is still frozen, misbehaves, or doesn't start, press and hold the Home button for six to ten seconds to force any frozen applications to quit.**
5. **Repeat Steps 1 to 3 again.**

If these steps don't get your iPad back up and running, move on to the third *R:* resetting your iPad.

Reset your iPad

To reset your iPad, merely press and hold the Sleep/Wake button and then press and hold the Home button, continuing to press both for at least ten seconds. When you see the Apple logo, release both buttons.

Resetting your iPad is like forcing your computer to restart after a crash. Your data shouldn't be affected by a reset — and in many cases, the reset cures whatever was ailing your iPad. So don't be shy about giving this technique a try. In many cases, your iPad goes back to normal after you reset it this way.

Sometimes you have to press and hold the Sleep/Wake button *before* you press and hold the Home button. That's because if you press both at the same time, you might create a *screen shot* — a picture of whatever is on your screen at the time — rather than reset your iPad. This type of screen picture, by the way, is stored in the Photos app's Camera Roll album. Find out more about this feature at the end of Chapter 20. A screen shot *should* only happen if you press and release both buttons at the same time, but sometimes pressing and holding both buttons triggers the screen-shot mechanism instead of restarting your iPad.

Unfortunately, sometimes resetting *doesn't* do the trick. When that's the case, you have to take stronger measures.

At this point, it's a good idea to back up your iPad's contents. In iTunes, there's a Back Up Now button in the Backup section of the Summary pane, which identifies when the last backup occurred. On your iPad, look in Settings⇨iCloud⇨Storage & Backup for the Back Up Now button.

Remove content

If you've been reading along in this chapter, nothing you've done should have taken more than a minute or two (or 20 if you tried the 20-minute recharge). We hate to tell you, but that's about to change because the next thing you should try is removing some or all of your data to see whether it's causing your troubles.

To do so, you need to sync your iPad and then reconfigure it so that some or all of your files are *not* synchronized (which removes them from the iPad). The problem could be contacts, calendar data, songs, photos, videos, or podcasts. You can apply one of two strategies to this troubleshooting task:

- ✔ **If you suspect a particular data type** — for example, you suspect your photos because whenever you tap the Photos icon on the Home screen, your iPad freezes — try removing that data first.

- ✔ **If you have no suspicions,** deselect every item and then sync. When you're finished, your iPad should have no data on it.

    If that method fixes your iPad, try restoring your data, one type at a time. If the problem returns, you have to keep experimenting to determine which particular data type or file is causing the problem.

If you're still having problems, the next step is to reset your iPad's settings and content.

Reset settings and content

Resetting involves two steps: The first one, resetting your iPad settings, resets every iPad *setting* to its default — the way it was when you took it out of the box. Resetting the iPad's settings doesn't erase any of your data or media. The only downside is that you may have to go back and change some settings afterward — so you can try this step without trepidation. To reset your settings, tap the Settings icon on your Home screen and then tap General⇨Reset⇨Reset All Settings.

Be careful *not* to tap Erase All Content and Settings, at least not yet. Erasing all content takes more time to recover from (because your next sync takes a long time), so try Reset All Settings first.

Now, if resetting all settings didn't cure your iPad, you have to try Erase All Content and Settings. You find it in the same place as Reset All Settings. (Tap Settings⇨General⇨Reset⇨Erase All Content and Settings.)

The Erase All Content strategy deletes everything from your iPad — all your data, media, and settings. Because all these items are stored on your computer — at least in theory — you should be able to put things back the way they were during your next sync. But you lose any photos or screen shots you've taken, as well as e-mail, contacts, calendar events, playlists, and anything else you've created or modified on the iPad since your last sync.

After using Erase All Content and Settings, check to see whether your iPad works properly. If it doesn't cure what ails your iPad, the final *R,* restoring your iPad using iTunes, can help.

Restore

Before you give up on your poor, sick iPad, you can try one more thing. First, connect your iPad to your computer as though you were about to sync. But when the iPad appears in the iTunes sidebar, click the Restore button on the Summary tab. This action erases all your data and media and resets all your settings.

If your computer isn't available, you can also trigger this step from your iPad by tapping Settings⇨General⇨Reset⇨Erase All Content and Settings.

Because all your data and media still exist on your computer (except for photos you've taken, contacts, calendar events, notes, and On-the-Go playlists you've created or modified since your last sync, as noted previously), you shouldn't lose anything by restoring except possibly e-mail or text messages sent or received since your last backup. Your next sync will take longer than usual, and you may have to reset settings you've changed since you got your iPad. But other than those inconveniences, restoring shouldn't cause you any additional trouble.

Performing a restore deletes everything on your iPad — all your data, media, and settings. You *should* be able to put things back the way they were with your next sync; if that doesn't happen, for whatever reason, you can't say we didn't warn you. That said, you may still be able to restore from an iTunes or iCloud backup as described in this chapter's thrilling conclusion, a scintillating section we call, "Dude, Where's My Stuff?"

Recovery mode

So, if you've tried all the other steps or you couldn't try some or all of them because your iPad is so messed up, you can try one last thing: Recovery mode. Here's how it works:

1. **Disconnect the USB cable from your iPad, but leave the other end of the cable connected to the USB port on your computer.**

2. **Turn off the iPad by pressing and holding the Sleep/Wake button for a few seconds until the red slider appears onscreen, and then slide the slider.**

   Wait for the iPad to turn off.

3. **Press and hold the Home button while you reconnect the USB cable to your iPad.**

   When you reconnect the USB cable, your iPad should power on.

   If you see a battery icon with a thin red band and an icon of a wall plug, an arrow, and a lightning bolt, you need to let your iPad charge for at least 10 to 15 minutes. When the battery picture goes away or turns green instead of red, go back to Step 2 and try again.

4. **Continue holding the Home button until you see the Connect to iTunes screen, and then release the Home button.**

   If you don't see the Connect to iTunes screen on your iPad, try Steps 1 through 4 again.

   If iTunes didn't open automatically already, launch it now. You should see a Recovery Mode alert on your computer screen telling you that your iPad is in Recovery mode and that you must restore it before it can be used with iTunes.

5. **Use iTunes to restore the device, as we describe in the preceding section.**

Okay. So that's the gamut of things you can do when your iPad acts up. If you tried all this and none of it worked, skim through the rest of this chapter to see whether anything else we recommend looks like it might help. If not, your iPad probably needs to go into the shop for repairs.

Never fear, gentle reader. Be sure to read the "If Nothing We Suggest Helps" section, later in this chapter. Your iPad may be quite sick, but we help ease the pain by sharing some tips on how to minimize the discomfort.

Problems with Networks

If you're having problems with Wi-Fi or your wireless carrier's data network (Wi-Fi + 3G or 4G models only), this section may help. The techniques here are short and sweet — except for the last one, restore. Restore, which we describe in a previous section, is still inconvenient and time-consuming, and it still entails erasing all your data and media and then restoring it.

First, here are some simple steps that may help:

- **Make sure that you have sufficient Wi-Fi or 3G or 4G signal strength, as shown in Figure 16-1.**

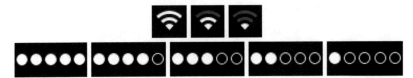

Figure 16-1: Wi-Fi (top) and 3G or 4G (bottom) signal strength from best (left) to worst (right).

- **Try moving around.** Changing your location by as little as a few feet can sometimes mean the difference between great wireless reception and no wireless reception. If you're inside, try moving around even a step or two in one direction. If you're outside, try moving 10 or 20 paces in any direction. Keep an eye on the cell signal or Wi-Fi icon as you move around, and stop when you see more bars than you saw before.

- **Restart your iPad.** If you've forgotten how, refer to the "Restart" section, earlier in this chapter. As we mention, restarting your iPad is often all it takes to fix whatever is wrong.

If you have a Wi-Fi + 3G or 4G iPad, try the following two bullet points.

- **Make sure that you haven't left your iPad in Airplane mode, as we describe in Chapter 15.** In Airplane mode (Wi-Fi + 3G or 4G models only), all network-dependent features are disabled, so you can't send or receive messages or use any of the apps that require a Wi-Fi or data-network connection (that is, Mail, Safari, Maps, and the iTunes and App Store apps).

- **Toggle Airplane mode on and off.** Turn on Airplane mode by swiping upward from the bottom of the screen to bring up Control Center and then tapping the airplane icon. Wait 15 or 20 seconds and then tap the airplane icon again to turn Airplane mode off.

Toggxling Airplane mode on and off like this resets both the Wi-Fi and wireless data-network connections. If your network connection was the problem, toggling Airplane mode on and off may correct it.

Apple offers two very good articles that may help you with Wi-Fi issues. The first offers some general troubleshooting tips and hints; the second discusses potential sources of interference for wireless devices and networks. You can find them here:

```
http://support.apple.com/kb/TS3237
```

and here:

http://support.apple.com/kb/HT1365

If none of the preceding suggestions fixes your network issues, try restoring your iPad, as we describe previously in the "Restore" section.

Performing a restore deletes everything on your iPad — all your data, media, and settings. You should be able to put things back the way they were with your next sync. If that doesn't happen, well, consider yourself forewarned.

Sync, Computer, or iTunes Issues

The last category of troubleshooting techniques in this chapter applies to issues that involve synchronization and computer–iPad relations. If you're having problems syncing or your computer doesn't recognize your iPad when you connect it, here are some things to try.

Once again, we suggest that you try these procedures in the order they're presented here:

1. **Recharge your iPad.**

   If you didn't try it previously, try it now. Go to the "Resuscitating an iPad with Issues" section, earlier in this chapter, and read what we say about recharging your iPad. Every word there also applies here.

2. **Try a different USB port or a different cable if you have one available.**

   It doesn't happen often, but occasionally USB ports and cables go bad. When they do, they invariably cause sync and connection problems. Always make sure that a bad USB port or cable isn't to blame.

   If you don't remember what we said about using USB ports on your computer rather than the ones on your keyboard, monitor, or hub, we suggest that you reread the "Recharge" section, earlier in this chapter.

3. **Restart your iPad and try to sync again.**

   We describe restarting in full and loving detail in the "Restart" section, earlier in this chapter.

4. **Reinstall iTunes.**

   Even if you have an iTunes installer handy, you probably should visit the Apple website and download the latest-and-greatest version, just in case. You can find the latest version of iTunes at www.apple.com/itunes/download.

More Help on the Apple Website

If you try everything we suggest earlier in this chapter and still have problems, don't give up just yet. This section describes a few more places you may find help. We recommend that you check out some or all of them before you throw in the towel and smash your iPad into tiny little pieces (or ship it back to Apple for repairs, as we describe in the next section).

First, Apple offers an excellent set of support resources on its website at `www.apple.com/support/ipad/getstarted`. You can browse support issues by category, search for a problem by keyword, read or download technical manuals, and scan the discussion forums.

Figure 16-2: Search for Sync iPad and you'll see something like this.

Speaking of the discussion forums, you can go directly to them at `http://discussions.apple.com`. They're chock-full of useful questions and answers from other iPad users, and our experience has been that if you can't find an answer to a support question elsewhere, you can often find it in these forums. You can browse by category or search by keyword (Sync iPad, for example, as shown in Figure 16-2).

Either way, you find thousands of discussions about almost every aspect of using your iPad. Better still, you can frequently find the answer to your question or a helpful suggestion.

Now for the best part: If you can't find a solution by browsing or searching, you can post your question in the appropriate Apple discussion forum. Check back in a few days (or even in a few hours), and some helpful iPad user may well have replied with the answer. If you've never tried this fabulous tool, you're missing out on one of the greatest support resources available anywhere.

Last, but certainly not least, before you throw in the towel, you might want to try a carefully worded Google search. It couldn't hurt, and you might just find the solution you spent hours searching for.

If Nothing We Suggest Helps

If you tried every trick in the book (this one) and still have a malfunctioning iPad, consider shipping it off to the iPad hospital (better known as Apple, Inc.). The repair is free if your iPad is still under its one-year limited warranty.

You can extend your warranty for as long as two years from the original purchase date, if you want. To do so, you need to buy the AppleCare Protection Plan for your iPad. You don't have to do it when you buy your iPad, but you must buy it before your one-year limited warranty expires. The retail price is $79, but we've seen it for a lot less, so it might pay to shop around.

Here are a few things you need to know before you take your iPad in to be repaired:

 ✔ *Your iPad may be erased during its repair,* so you should sync your iPad with iTunes before you take it in, if you can. If you can't and you entered data on the iPad since your last sync, such as a contact or an appointment, the data may not be there when you restore your iPad upon its return.

 ✔ Remove any accessories, such as a case or screen protector.

Although you may be able to get your iPad serviced by Best Buy or another authorized Apple reseller, we recommend that you take or ship it to your nearest Apple Store, for two reasons:

 ✔ **No one knows your iPad like Apple.** One of the geniuses at the Apple Store may be able to fix whatever is wrong without sending your iPad away for repairs.

 ✔ **The Apple Store will, in some cases, swap out your wonky iPad for a brand-new one on the spot.** You can't win if you don't play, which is why we always visit our local Apple Store when something goes wrong (with our iPads, iPhones, iPods, and even our laptops and iMacs).

If you've done everything we've suggested, we're relatively certain that you're now holding an iPad that works flawlessly. Again.

That said, some or all of your stuff may not be on it. If that's the case, the following section offers a two-trick solution that usually works.

Dude, Where's My Stuff?

If you performed a restore or had your iPad replaced or repaired, you have one more task to accomplish. Your iPad may work flawlessly at this point, but some or all of your stuff — your music, movies, contacts, iMessages, or whatever — is missing. You're not sunk, at least not yet. You still have a couple of tricks up your sleeve.

Figure 16-3: Select the appropriate backup and click the Restore button.

- ✔ **Trick 1: Sync your iPad with iTunes and then sync it again.** That's right — sync and sync again. Why? Because sometimes stuff doesn't get synced properly on the first try. Just do it.

- ✔ **Trick 2: Restore from backup.** Click the Summary tab in iTunes and click Restore Backup (or, if the sidebar is visible, right-click your iPad in iTunes sidebar and choose Restore from Backup). The Restore from Backup dialog appears and offers you a choice of backups, as shown in Figure 16-3. Select the one you want, click the Restore button, and let the iPad work some magic.

If you have more than one backup for a device, as Bob has for his devices in Figure 16-3, try the most recent (undated) one first. If it doesn't work or you're still missing files, try restoring from any other backups before you throw in the towel.

These backups include photos in Camera Roll, text messages, notes, contact favorites, sound settings, and more, but not media you've synced, such as music, videos, or photos. If media are what's missing, try performing Trick 1 again.

If you aren't holding an iPad that works flawlessly and has most (if not all) of your stuff, it's time to make an appointment with a Genius at your local Apple Store, call the support hotline (800-275-2273), or visit the support web page at www.apple.com/support/ipad.

17

Accessorizing Your iPad

. . . .

In This Chapter

▶ Apple cases, keyboards, and chargers

▶ Apple connection options (camera, TV, and projector)

▶ Earphones, headphones, and headsets

▶ Speakers

▶ Third-party cases

▶ Other protection products

▶ Miscellaneous other accessories

. . . .

*A*nyone who has purchased a new car in recent years is aware that it's not always a picnic trying to escape the showroom without the salesperson trying to get you to part with a few extra bucks. You can only imagine what the markup is on roof racks, navigation systems, and rear-seat DVD players.

We don't suppose you'll get a hard sell when you snap up a new iPad at an Apple Store (or elsewhere). But Apple and several other companies are all too happy to outfit whichever iPad model you choose with extra doodads, from wireless keyboards and stands to battery chargers and carrying cases. So just as your car might benefit from dealer (or third-party) options, so too might your iPad benefit from a variety of spare parts.

The iPads preceding the fourth-generation feature the standard 30-pin dock connector that's been familiar to iPod and iPhone owners over the past decade. If you own either or both of these products, you also know that a bevy of accessories fit perfectly into that dock connector. Heck, you might even try to plug the battery chargers or other iPod/iPhone accessories you have lying around into the iPad. No guarantee that these will work, but they probably will. And you have nothing to lose by trying.

Note: In 2012, Apple switched to a new connector — the Lightning connector. Accessories compatible with the new connector have become pretty much ubiquitous, and there are Dock Connector-to-Lightning Connector cables and adapters from Apple and others so you can use most older accessories with new i-devices.

One thing is certain: If you see a *Made for iPad* label on the package, the developer is certifying that an electronic accessory has been designed to connect specifically to the iPad and meets performance standards established by Apple. Just make sure that the connector matches the specific iPad model you have or that you have an available adapter. Note that not all adapters support video.

We start this accessories chapter with the options that carry the Apple logo and conclude with worthwhile extras from other companies.

Accessories from Apple

You've come to expect a certain level of excellence from Apple hardware and software, so you should expect no differently when it comes to various Apple-branded accessories. That said, you can find a variety of opinions on some of these products, so we recommend a visit to `http://store.apple.com`, where you can read mini-reviews and pore over ratings from real people just like you. They're not shy about telling it like it is.

Casing the iPad

The thing about accessories is that half the time, you wish they weren't accessories at all. You wish they came in the box. Among the things we would have liked to see included with the iPad was a protective case.

Alas, it wasn't to be. No iPad has ever shipped with a case in the box, but you can find cases aplenty just the same. All you need is cash. You read about Apple's here and other cases later in this chapter.

Apple's iPad case, shown in Figure 17-1, is more cover than case, which is probably why it's called a *Smart Cover* instead of a *Smart Case.* Made specifically for iPads, it's ultra-thin and attaches magnetically. Flip the cover open (even just a little), and your iPad wakes instantly; flip it shut, and your iPad goes right to sleep. The case available in numerous bright colors in polyurethane ($39–$49) or leather ($69). Bob says the aniline-dyed Italian leather on his PRODUCT RED Smart Cover is gorgeous and soft as butter.

Courtesy of Apple

Figure 17-1: Apple's Smart Cover for iPad.

Apple's newest entry is the iPad Smart Case, which combines a Smart Cover and a case to protect the back of your iPad. Like the Smart Cover, it too folds into a stand for reading, typing, or watching video. And because it's "smart," it automatically wakes and sleeps your iPad when you open and close it. Smart Cases are all constructed of polyurethane (sorry, no leather this time), and are available in six bright colors for $49.

The Apple iPad Case has a very snug fit, which we generally consider a positive. Not always. If you want to use the Apple iPad Keyboard Dock that we discuss in the next section (and certain other peripherals that use the dock connector), you have to remove the Apple Case to do so. Because of that tight fit, sliding the iPad in and out of the Case is a bit of a nuisance. You'll find that some third-party cases have the same issue.

Whatever case you choose, make sure it is compatible with your favorite accessories.

Apple Wireless Keyboard

We think the various virtual keyboards that pop up just as you need them on the iPad are perfectly fine for shorter typing tasks, whether it's composing e-mails or tapping a few notes. For most longer assignments, however, we writers are more comfortable pounding away on a real-deal physical keyboard, and we suspect you feel the same way.

Fortunately a physical keyboard for the iPad is an easy addition, and because it's the same keyboard that's been bundled with iMacs for years, you may even own one already.

The Apple Wireless Keyboard, as shown in Figure 17-2, is a way to use a decent-enough aluminum physical keyboard without tethering it to the iPad. It operates from up to 30 feet away from the iPad via Bluetooth, the wireless technology we discuss in Chapter 15. Which leads us to ask, can you see the iPad screen from 30 feet away?

Courtesy of Apple

Figure 17-2: The Apple Wireless Keyboard.

If you have an Apple TV connected to your HDTV, you can stream the screen of your iPad to the HDTV by using AirPlay. (See Chapter 8 for the details.) And although you probably can't see it from 30 feet, we've found the Apple Wireless Keyboard is great for using on the couch, where we can easily see the screen.

As with any Bluetooth device that the iPad makes nice with, you have to pair it to your tablet. Pairing is also discussed in Chapter 15.

The Bluetooth keyboard takes two AA batteries. It's smart about power management, too; it powers itself down when you stop using it to avoid draining those batteries. It wakes up when you start typing.

The Wireless Keyboard is small and thin. If you carry a backpack, briefcase, messenger bag, or even a large purse, you almost certainly have enough room for an Apple Wireless Keyboard.

And if your native tongue isn't English, Apple sells versions of the Wireless Keyboard in numerous languages, each still $69.

Not all the function keys on the Wireless Keyboard, will, um, function on your iPad. They're there, though, because (as we note previously), it's the same keyboard Apple bundles with the iMac and sells for other Macs.

Although we have tested a few third-party Bluetooth keyboards, the iPad ought to work fine with any keyboard that supports Bluetooth 2.1 + EDR technology. Bob is currently infatuated with his Logitech Ultrathin Keyboard Cover ($99), which includes iPad (and iPhone) -specific keys, works like a Smart Cover to wake and sleep your iPad, and comes in an ultra thin aluminum enclosure that looks great and matches the iPad perfectly. It's a little more expensive than the Apple Wireless Keyboard, but he says it's worth it.

Finally, you can connect many USB keyboards to your iPad with the iPad Camera Connection Kit (for Dock Connector) or Lightning to USB Camera Adapter discussed in the following section.

Connecting a camera

iPads don't include a USB port or an SD memory card slot, which happen to be the most popular methods for getting pictures (and videos) from a digital camera onto a computer.

All the same, the iPad is a marvelous photo viewer. So, if you take a lot of pictures, Apple's $29 iPad Camera Connection Kit, which we also discuss in Chapter 9, is worth considering for iPads that sport the 30-pin connector (iPad 2s and third-generation iPads). As a reminder, the Kit consists of the two components shown in Figure 17-3, either of which plugs into the 30-pin dock connector at the bottom of the iPad. One sports a USB interface that you can use with the USB cable that came with your camera to download pictures. The other is an SD Card Reader that lets you insert the memory card that stores your pictures.

If you seek the same functionality for your iPad with a Lightning connector, the kit has been separated into two $29 items: a Lightning–to–USB Camera connector and a Lightning–to–SD Card connector.

Courtesy of Apple

Figure 17-3: iPad Camera Connection Kit, Lightning-to-USB Camera connector, and Lightning-to-SD Card connector allow you to import images.

Although the official line from Apple is that this USB adapter is meant to work with the USB cable from your digital camera, we tried connecting other devices. We got an old Dell USB keyboard to work with it. We've gotten other devices to work, too, including readers for non–SD-type memory cards, USB speakers, MIDI keyboards, and more. But don't expect all your USB devices to be compatible: Some require more power than the iPad can provide, and others need software drivers that aren't available on the iPad.

We only hope that despite this helpful accessory, Apple will get around to adding a USB and an SD slot to iPads, but so far it hasn't happened.

Connecting an iPad to a TV or projector

The iPad has a pretty big screen for what it is, a tablet computer, and when it comes to the Retina display, we can't help but give it high praise. But that display is still not nearly as large as a living room TV or a monitor that you might see in a conference room or auditorium. To send iPad content to a bigger screen, you can choose from three connectors:

- ✔ **VGA Adapter cable:** Projecting what's on the iPad's screen to a larger display is the very reason behind the iPad Dock Connector–to–VGA Adapter cable that Apple is selling for $29. You can use it to connect your iPad to TVs, projectors, and VGA displays. What for? To watch videos, slideshows, and presentations on the big screen. Be sure to get the VGA Adapter for your iPad model — choosing the 30-pin or Lightning cable as appropriate.

  VGA (video graphics array) delivers, by today's standards, low-resolution video output, compared, say to the more advanced HDMI (High-Definition Multimedia Interface).

- ✔ **Composite AV Cable:** This is the $39 cable you need to display iPad, iPhone, or iPod touch content on most standard-definition TVs. It connects to the dock connector on the iPad to the so-called composite video port of your TV via a yellow connector. You'll also need to hook up the red and white audio connectors to analog audio ports on your TV or AV receiver. *Note:* It won't work with an iPad with a Lightning connector — even with an adapter.

- ✔ **Digital AV Adapter cable:** The newest addition to the Apple adapter family is the $39 Apple Digital AV Adapter. It uses HDMI, which is pretty much a standard on state-of-the-art HDTVs and other modern gear. And it comes with a nice bonus: You can mirror the display on your iPad on a big screen TV, which is great for demos and presentations. Ed has used this adapter to, among other things, play *Angry Birds* on the bigger TV screen. Bob uses it to watch HD movies in hotel rooms. Both of us think it rocks. Be sure to get the Lightning–Digital AV model for any iPad with a Lightning connector.

Speaking of mirroring the display of your iPad onto a large-screen TV, you can do that wirelessly with iPad as long as you're streaming to another Apple accessory called Apple TV. It's all accomplished through AirPlay, which we discuss in Chapter 8. Apple TV provides a lot of niceties in its own right, even if you don't own an iPad. (But if you don't, why are you reading this book?) For example, you can watch 1080p high-definition TV shows and movies; watch videos on Netflix, Hulu Plus, and Vimeo; listen to music from your iTunes Library on a PC or Mac; and admire photos through iCloud, all for just $99.

Keeping a spare charger

With roughly ten hours of battery life on the Wi-Fi–only iPad and nine hours on models with cellular access, a single charge can more than get you through a typical workday with your iPad. But why chance it? Having a spare charger at the office can spare you (!) from having to commute with one. The Apple iPad 10W USB Power Adapter sells for $29 and includes a lengthy six-foot cord. Again, make sure to get the one with a Lightning cord if you have an iPad with that connector.

And if you're traveling abroad, consider the Apple World Travel Adapter Kit. The $39 kit includes the proper prongs and adapters for numerous countries around the globe, and it lets you juice up not only your iPad, but also iPhones, iPod touches, and Macs.

Finally, if you have an old iPhone or iPod USB power adapter, or almost any other power adapter with a USB port, chances are good it'll work, though it may take longer to charge your iPad.

If you try to charge your iPad with an adapter that doesn't provide enough power, nothing bad will happen. Your iPad will merely display a Not Charging message instead of the battery-with-a-lightning-bolt icon you see when your iPad is connected to a charger with sufficient juice.

Listening and Talking with Earphones, Headphones, and Headsets

You've surely noticed that your iPad didn't include earphones or a headset. That's probably a blessing because the earphones and headsets Apple has included with iPods and iPhones since time immemorial aren't all that good. In fact, Bob referred to them as "mediocre and somewhat uncomfortable" in almost every article he's written about the iPod or iPhone. Ed agrees. For what it's worth, iPhones and iPod touches now include Apple's redesigned — and much improved — EarPods.

Earphones? Headphones? Headsets?

We refer to headphones and headsets several times and thought you might be wondering whether a difference exists, and if so, what it is. When we talk about *headphones* or *earphones,* we're talking about the things you use to listen to music. A *headset* adds a microphone so that you can use it for voice chatting, schmoozing with Siri, FaceTime video chatting, and (in the case of the iPhone or Internet VoIP services such as Skype) for phone calls. So headphones and earphones are for listening, and headsets are for both talking and listening.

Now you may be wondering whether earphones and headphones are the same. To some people, they may be, but to us, headphones have a band across the top (or back) of your head, and the listening apparatus is big and covers the outside of your ears. Think of the big fat things you see covering a radio disk jockey's ears. Earphones (sometimes referred to as *earbuds*), on the other hand, are smaller, fit entirely in your ear, and have no band across the top or back of your head.

Headsets can be earphone style or, less commonly, headphone style. The distinguishing factor is that headsets always include a microphone. And some headsets are designed specifically for use with Apple i-products (iPhone, iPod, iPad) and have integrated Play/Pause and volume control buttons.

One last thing: Some companies refer to their earbud products as headphones, but we think that's confusing and wrong. So in this book, headphones are those bulky, outside-the-ear things, and earphones are teeny-tiny things that fit entirely in your ear.

But the iPad still ships without headphones, so you get to select a pair of headphones, earphones, or a headset that suit your needs and your budget.

That's good, right?

Wired headphones, earphones, and headsets

Search Amazon for *headphones, earphones,* or *headsets,* and you'll find thousands of each are available at prices ranging from around $10 to more than $1,000. Or, if you prefer to shop in a brick-and-mortar store, Target, Best Buy, and the Apple Store all have decent selections, with prices starting at less than $20.

Much as we love the shopping experience at Apple Stores, you won't find any bargains there. Bargain-hunting doesn't matter that much for Apple-branded products because they're rarely discounted. However, you can almost always find widely available non-Apple items such as headphones, earphones, and headsets cheaper somewhere else.

With so many brands and models of earphones, headphones, and headsets available from so many manufacturers at so many price points, we can't possibly test even a fraction of the ones available today. That said, we've probably tested more of them than most people, and we have our favorites.

When it comes to headphones, Bob is partial to his Grado SR60i's, which are legendary for offering astonishingly accurate audio at an affordable price (around $80). He's tried headphones that cost twice, thrice, or even more times as much that he didn't think sounded nearly as good. Find out more at www.gradolabs.com.

Ed goes with sweet-sounding, albeit pricey (about $350) Bose QuietComfort 3 acoustic noise-canceling headphones and Monster Inspiration over-the-ear noise-canceling headphones (about $300).

For earphones and earphone-style headsets, Bob likes the Klipsch Image S4 Headphones and S4i In-Ear Headset with Mic and 3-Button Remote. At around $79 and $99, respectively, they sound better than many similarly priced products, and better than many more-expensive offerings.

Bluetooth stereo headphones, earphones, and headsets

Neither of us has much experience with Bluetooth (wireless) stereo head-phones and headsets, but we thought we'd at least plant the seed. The idea is that with Bluetooth stereo headphones/earphones/headsets, you can listen to music wirelessly up to 33 feet away from your iPad. If this sounds good to you, we suggest that you look for reviews of such products on the web before you decide which one to buy. A search of Amazon for *stereo Bluetooth headset* brought up thousands of items, with prices starting as low as $11.99.

For what it's worth, Bob has a Cardo S-2 Bluetooth stereo headset that he occasionally uses with his iPhone when he walks his dog. He tested it with his iPad, and it worked just fine. The only problem is that the model he has is apparently discontinued. On the other hand, you can find them occasionally on the web for around $70, and Bob says they perform well and sound better than you might expect for a wireless headset. On the other hand, his are more than four years old, so you can probably find something better that costs less.

Listening with Speakers

You can connect just about any speakers to your iPad, but if you want decent sound, we suggest you look only at *powered* speakers and not *passive* (unpowered) ones. The difference is that powered speakers contain their own amplification circuitry and can deliver much better (and louder) sound than unpowered speakers.

Prices range from well under $100 to hundreds (or even thousands) of dol-lars. Most speaker systems designed for use with your computer, iPod, or iPhone work well as long as they have an auxiliary input or a dock connector that can accommodate your iPad.

Desktop speakers

Logitech (www.logitech.com) makes a range of desktop speaker systems priced from less than $25 to more than $300. But that $300 system is the Z5500 THX-certified 505-watt 5.1 digital surround system — surely overkill for listening to music or video on your iPad, which doesn't support surround sound anyway. The point is that Logitech makes a variety of decent systems at a wide range of price points. If you're looking for something inexpensive, you can't go wrong with a Logitech-powered speaker system.

Bob is a big fan of Audioengine (www.audioengineusa.com) desktop speakers. They deliver superior audio at prices that are quite reasonable for speakers that sound this good. Audioengine 5 is the premium product priced at $349 per pair; Audioengine 2 is its smaller but still excellent-sounding sibling priced at $199 per pair. They're available only direct from the manufacturer, but the company is so confident that you'll love them that it offers a free audition for the speaker systems. If you order a pair and don't love them, return them within 30 days for a full refund. Bob knows a lot of people who have ordered them, and so far no one has sent them back.

Bluetooth speakers

Like Bluetooth headsets, Bluetooth speakers let you listen to music up to 33 feet away from your iPad. They're great for listening by the pool or hot tub or anywhere else you might not want to take your iPad.

Both of us have written favorable reviews of the $199.99 wireless Jambox by Jawbone, a rechargeable speaker that offers very good sound despite being able to fit into the palm of your hand. You can connect via Bluetooth or its auxiliary stereo jack. An added bonus: Jambox doubles as a decent-enough speakerphone.

Jawbone has also introduced the Big Jambox. Quick quiz: What do you think that means? Right, a bigger version of the Jambox with bigger sound. Of course, at $299.99, it also carries a bigger price, and it's a bit less portable than its diminutive sibling. And because this isn't a one-size-fits-all society, Jawbone more recently introduced the Mini Jambox, which comes in multiple colors, and commands $179.99.

Ed also likes a big rival to the Big Jambox, the Bose SoundLink Wireless Mobile Speaker, which fetches a similar price.

After reading Ed's review, Bob traveled with a Jawbone Jambox for years and liked it. Then he got Ultimate Ears' Boom Wireless Speaker/Speakerphone ($199.95), of which he says, "blows the doors off the Jambox," and the best-sounding $200 Bluetooth speaker he ever tested.

AirPlay speakers

The newest type of speakers you might choose for your iPad support Apple's proprietary AirPlay protocol, which takes advantage of your existing Wi-Fi network to stream audio and/or video from your iPad (or other compatible i-device) to a single AirPlay-enabled speaker or audio/video receiver.

The biggest differences between AirPlay and Bluetooth speakers are

- Bluetooth can stream music only in a compressed form; AirPlay can stream music (and video) uncompressed. So, a speaker with AirPlay should sound better than a similar speaker with Bluetooth.

- Bluetooth's range is roughly 30 feet; AirPlay's range is up to 300 feet. There's no way to extend Bluetooth's range; Wi-Fi range can easily be extended with inexpensive routers such as Apple's AirPort Express ($99).

- iTunes (on your computer) can use AirPlay to stream audio or video to multiple speakers or audio/video receivers, with individual volume controls for each device; Bluetooth only streams to one device at a time.

Docking your iPad with an extender cable

Because the iPad is much larger than an iPod or iPhone, you can't just dock the iPad into a speaker system designed for the smaller devices. All is not lost if you're partial to those speakers and still want to connect the iPad. CableJive (`http://cablejive.com`), RadTech (`www.radtech.us`), and others sell "dock extender cables," which allow you to use your iPad with any docking device no matter how small its dock. Apple also sells a 30-pin–to–Lightning adapter cable, allowing you to connect an iPad to one of these speaker systems.

This type of cable doesn't work with S-video output, component video, or audio input jacks for recording.

Wrapping Your iPad in Third-Party Cases

Much as we like the Apple iPad Case, other vendors offer some excellent — and as the sidebar "The refrigerator iPad?" points out — some very different options:

- **Abas:** Abas (`www.abas.net`) offers very nice leather cases that won't set you back $689 like the Orbino crocodile-skin case we mention earlier in the chapter.

- **Targus:** Targus (`www.targus.com`) has a full line of iPad cases in a variety of materials and prices. The nice part is that none of them, including the leather portfolio, costs more than $60.

- **Griffin Technology:** Griffin Technology (www.griffintechnology. com) also has a pretty good selection of iPad cases at reasonable prices (that is, none more than $50).

- **iLuv:** iLuv (www.i-luv.com) is yet another case maker with a range of affordable cases fabricated from leather, fabric, and silicone, none of which costs more than $40.

- **Vario:** ZeroChroma (www.zerochroma.com) has Bob's current favorite Vario iPad (and iPhone) case ($69.95). The big attraction is the 16-angle rotating theater stand on the back that folds flush when not in use. Sweet!

- **BookBook:** The BookBook case from Twelve South (www.twelvesouth. com) looks like a fine vintage hardbound book but is actually a very handsome iPad case and stand ($79.99).

- **LifeProof nüüd:** This case may be bulky and relatively expensive, but it is waterproof, dirtproof, snowproof, and shockproof. Bob says his second-generation iPad, which has been dropped several times, and soaked in a spa more than once, would have died long ago without the LifeProof case (www.lifeproof.com). While connecting earphones or docking cables is more of a hassle than with most cases, and it's not cheap ($129.99), Bob says it's a lot cheaper than a new iPad. He's still using it today.

- **The iPad Bubble Sleeve:** From Hard Candy Cases (www.hardcandycases. com), the iPad Bubble Sleeve ($49.95) offers significantly better protection against bumps and scratches than any other case we've seen. If we expected our iPads to be exposed to moderate impacts, this case's rigid exterior and additional shock-absorbing rubber bumpers for the screen make it the case we'd choose.

The refrigerator iPad?

It figured that some outfit would produce a refrigerator magnet mount for your iPad, given how many people consult iPads in the kitchen for, among other reasons, recipes, reminders, and to check out whether it's going to rain. The company in question is Woodford Design (www. woodforddesign.com), and the result of its efforts is the aptly named FridgePad, a mount for any iPad model. You can mount the iPad on a fridge either vertically or horizontally (as long as your fridge door is made of steel or stainless steel) and have full access to ports and buttons. FridgePad costs about $40 and comes in black or silver. We haven't tried it ourselves, but we watched a video online that shows an iPad mounted in FridgePad withstanding repeated slams of a refrigerator door. The company claims the magnet is 25 times stronger than it needs to be.

But Wait . . . There's More!

Before we leave the topic of accessories, we think you should know about a few more products, namely, film protection products that guard your iPad's exterior (or screen) without adding a bit of bulk: the Griffin Technology A-Frame tabletop stand for your iPad, and 2-into-1 stereo adapters.

Protecting the screen with film

Some people prefer not to use a case with their iPads, and that's okay, too. But if you're one of those people (or even if you're not), you might want to consider protective film for the iPad screen or even the whole device. We've tried these products on our iPhones in the past and have found them to perform as promised. If you apply them properly, they're nearly invisible, and they protect your iPad from scratches and scrapes without adding any bulk.

Bob recently discovered the joys of iVisor AG Screen Protector for iPad ($30) from Moshi (www.moshimonde.com) and says it's still the best screen cover he's tested to date. It's easy to apply, resists fingerprints better than Apple's oleophobic screen coating, and features patented technology for a bubble-free installation every time. The best feature, Bob believes, is that if it gets dirty, you just wash it under a faucet, and then air-dry and reapply it (bubble-free, of course).

Another option is from the aforementioned RadTech (www.radtech.us), which offers two types of Mylar screen protectors — clear transparent and antiglare. These screen protectors are somewhat stiffer than the film products, and unlike film, they can be cleaned and reapplied multiple times with no reduction in performance. They effectively hide minor scratches, surface defects, and abrasions, and the hard Mylar surface not only resists scratches and abrasions, but is also optically correct. Finally, they're reasonably priced at $19.95 for a pair of protectors of the same type.

Bob has also tested more traditional film products from invisibleShield by ZAGG (www.zagg.com), BodyGuardz (www.bodyguardz.com), and Best Skins Ever (www.bestskinsever.com) and says, in a nutshell, they're more similar than they are different. If you want to protect your screen with film, get whichever has the price and warranty that suits your needs.

Any or all of these so-called skins (including the iVisor AG, which is the easiest of all to install) can be tricky to apply. Follow the instructions closely, watch videos on the vendors' websites and YouTube, and take your time. If you do, you'll be rewarded with clear film protection that's nearly invisible yet protects your iPad from scratches, nicks, and cuts.

TIP

The last time we checked, Best Buy will apply these skins for you for a small (under $10) fee, which may be a bargain compared to messing things up and having to buy another skin. Ask your favorite electronics retailer if it provides a similar service.

Standing up your iPad

The Griffin A-Frame ($39.99) is so unusual that we just had to include it. As you can see in Figure 17-4, it's a dual-purpose desktop stand made of heavy-duty aluminum. You can open it to hold your iPad in either portrait or landscape mode for video watching, displaying pictures (a great way to exploit the Picture Frame mode, as we describe in Chapter 9), or even reading. In this upright mode, it's also the perfect companion for the Apple Wireless Keyboard (or any other Bluetooth keyboard for that matter). Or close the legs and lay it down, and it puts your iPad at the perfect angle for using the onscreen keyboard.

Photos courtesy of Griffin Technology

Figure 17-4: The Griffin A-Frame is a unique, dual-purpose tabletop stand for your iPad.

Soft silicone padding keeps your iPad from getting scratched or sliding around, and the bottom lip is designed to accommodate the charging cable in portrait mode. Furthermore, it works with many third-party cases, including Griffin's flexible and hard-shell cases, among others.

Bob says, "I really, really like this thing; it's where my iPad resides pretty much any time it's not in my backpack."

The iKlip (www.ikmultimedia.com; $29.99) stand may not look as cool as Griffin's, but it's lightweight and folds flat, as shown in Figure 17-5. Bob says: "I also love my iKlip Studio and rarely leave home without it."

Sharing your iPad with a 2-into-1 stereo adapter

A *2-into-1 stereo adapter* is a handy little device that lets two people plug their headphones/earphones/headsets into one iPad (or iPod or iPhone, for that matter). They're quite inexpensive (less than $10) and extremely useful if you're traveling with a friend by air, sea, rail, or bus. They're also great when you want to watch a movie with your BFF but don't want to risk waking the neighbors or roommates.

Photo courtesy of IK Multimedia
Figure 17-5: iKlip Studio is adjustable, portable, and easy to set up and use.

We call 'em *2-into-1 stereo adapters,* but that's not the only name they go by. Other names you might see for the same device are as follows:

- 3.5mm stereo Y-splitter
- 1/8-inch stereo 1-plug-to-2-jacks adapter
- 1/8-inch stereo Y-adapter
- 3.5mm dual stereo headphone jack splitter
- And many others

You need to know only two things. The first is that 1/8-inch and 3.5mm are used interchangeably in the adapter world (even though they're not really the same).

Some measurements to keep in mind: 1/8 inch = 0.125 inch, whereas 3.5mm = 0.1378 inch. Not the same, but close enough for rock 'n' roll.

The second is that you want to make sure that you get a *stereo* adapter. Some monaural adapters work but pump exactly the same sound into both ears, instead of sending the audio information for the left stereo channel to your left ear and the right stereo channel to your right.

In other words, you need a 1/8-inch or 3.5mm stereo adapter that has a single stereo plug on one end (to plug into your iPad) and two stereo jacks on the other (to accommodate two sets of headphones/earphones/headsets).

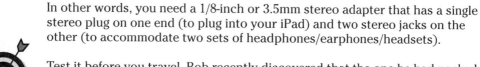

Test it before you travel. Bob recently discovered that the one he had packed made it much louder for one person than the other.

Part VI
The Part of Tens

Enjoy an additional iPad Part of Tens chapter at www.dummies.com/extras/ipad.

In this part...

✔ Explore our ten favorite free apps in the iPad App Store. You'll find clever apps that serve as a repository for sound creations, another for housing great memories, and one that will help you identify the name of an unfamiliar song.

✔ Peruse our ten favorite not-for-free apps for the iPad, including ones that turn your iPad into a goofy photo booth and a baseball reference. Plus you find a couple of addictive games and even an app to control your Mac or PC remotely from your iPad.

✔ Discover hints, tips, and shortcuts that make life with your iPad even better, such as sharing web pages and picking up another trick or two on using iPad's virtual keyboard.

18

Ten Appetizing (And Free) Apps

*K*iller app is familiar jargon to anyone who has spent any time around computers. The term refers to an application so sweet or so useful that just about everybody wants or must have it.

You could make the argument that the most compelling killer app on the iPad is the very App Store we expound on in Chapter 11. This online emporium has an abundance of splendid programs — dare we say killer apps in their own right? — many of which are free. These cover everything from food (hey, you gotta eat) to show biz. Okay, so some rotten apples (aren't we clever) are in the bunch, too. But we're here to accentuate the positive.

With that in mind, in this chapter, we offer ten of our favorite free iPad apps. In Chapter 19, we tell you about our favorite iPad apps that aren't free but are worth every penny.

We show you ours, and we encourage you to show us yours. If you discover your own killer iPad apps, by all means, let us know — our e-mail addresses are at the end of the Introduction to this book — so that we can check them out.

TripCase

We both travel more than most people and are somewhat set in our ways. Before trip, we use our computers to print boarding passes, hotel and rental car details, and any other info we might need while in transit. The printouts are strictly analog, so they don't notify us (or anyone else) of gate changes or flight delays or cancellations. And, of course, they can't remind us to check in. Still, the system works reliably unless we lose our printed documents.

It may be old school, but it's the best we could do until recently. What we wished and hoped for was a single intelligent repository for travel-related information, one that was smart enough to alert us of gate changes, weather delays, flight cancellations, and the like, and one that was easy to configure, convenient to use, and free.

What we found is TripCase, which is all that and more. It's a free app (and website) that organizes details of each trip in one place, with reminders and flight alerts delivered directly to your iPad.

TripCase has a lot to like, but one thing we like best is that it's drop-dead simple to add your travel events — without copying and pasting or even typing. We merely forward our confirmation e-mails — for flights, hotels, rental cars, and other travel-related services — to trips@tripcase.com. TripCase parses the details, creates an itinerary, and sends us an e-mail to confirm that our trip is ready to view in TripCase. We've forwarded confirmations from at least a half dozen travel providers, and TripCase has never failed to interpret them correctly. (And you can always enter details the old-fashioned way — by copying and pasting or typing.)

After TripCase has your info, you can view it in the TripCase app or in any web browser. The app is well-organized, with a timeline view of the itinerary (as shown in Figure 18-1), and details are but a tap away (as shown in Figure 18-2).

TripCase includes an action view with flight alerts, reminders, and other messages. Any way you look at it, TripCase does most of the work for you. For example, if you need to telephone a hotel or an airline, just tap the convenient phone icon (visible for KLM in Figure 18-2) to make the call.

TripCase can even help you locate an alternate flight based on your original reservation should your flight be cancelled or delayed. And it reminds you to check in and print boarding passes 24 hours before each flight. Sweet!

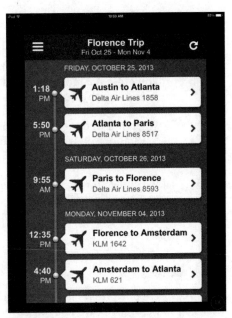

Figure 18-1: The Timeline view shows you everything you need in the order you're likely to need it.

TripCase's motto is "stress-free travel," and while it may not make travel stress-free, it definitely makes it less stressful.

One last thing: TripCase is an iPhone app but one that's so good and works so well on an iPad that we just couldn't omit it for not being a native iPad app (yet).

Shazam

Ever heard a song on the radio or television, in a store, or at a club and wondered what it was called or who was singing it? With the Shazam app, you may never wonder again. Just launch Shazam and point your iPad's microphone at the source of the music. In a few seconds, the song title and artist's name magically appear on your iPad screen.

In Shazam parlance, that song has been *tagged*. Now, if tagging were all Shazam could do, that would surely be enough. But wait, there's more. After Shazam tags a song, you can

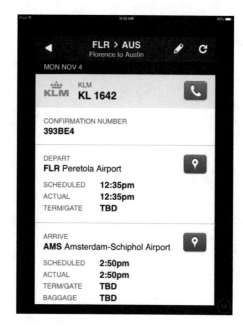

Figure 18-2: Tap any item in the timeline to see its details.

- ✔ Buy the song at the iTunes Store

- ✔ Watch related videos on YouTube

- ✔ Tweet the song on Twitter if you set up Twitter in Settings

- ✔ Read a biography, a discography, or lyrics

- ✔ Take a photo and attach it to the tagged item in Shazam

- ✔ E-mail a tag to a friend

Shazam isn't great at identifying classical music, jazz, show tunes, or opera, nor is it adept at identifying obscure indie bands. But if you use it primarily to identify popular music, it rocks (pun intended). It has worked for us in noisy airport terminals, crowded shopping malls, and even once at a wedding ceremony.

NFL Mobile

Ed is an avid football fan who routinely peeks at his iPad while watching games on TV, to follow his favorite team (the New York Giants), to follow his fantasy team, and to stay on top of the latest scoops and scores. The digital arm of the National Football League designed its NFL Mobile app to appeal to the legions of folks who live and breathe the sport.

You can watch highlights of games or check out other featured videos, organized under themes like Top 5 Catches, Drive Of The Week, and Can't Miss Plays. You can also listen to audio broadcasts of games (in English or Spanish). And you can exchange tickets, purchase team apparel, or buy other NFL paraphernalia — hey, in case you haven't noticed, football is big business.

During an actual game, you can chart the action inside an animated graphic of an NFL stadium.

Although the app is free, Verizon customers who shell out $5 per month can watch Thursday Night Football (via NFL Network), Monday Night Football (ESPN), and Sunday Night Football (NBC). You can also watch NFL Network at all times, and NFL RedZone on Sunday afternoons, which shows action across the league when teams enter scoring territory.

Movies by Flixster

We like movies, so we both use the Flixster app a lot. Feed it your zip code and then browse local theaters by movie, showtimes, rating, or distance from your current location. Or, browse to find a movie you like and then tap to find theaters, showtimes, and other info, as shown in Figure 18-3. Another nice feature is the capability to buy tickets to most movies from your iPad with just a few additional taps.

Figure 18-3: Find out showtimes, watch the trailer, or get more info on the director or cast with a single tap.

We appreciate that we can read reviews, play movie trailers, and e-mail movie listings to others with a single tap. We also enjoy the movie trailers for soon-to-be-released films and DVDs. Other free movie showtime apps are out there, but we like Flixster the best.

IMDb Movies & TV

While we're on the subject of the silver screen, we couldn't resist opening IMDb, shorthand for Internet Movie Database (owned by Amazon). And what a database it is, especially for the avid filmgoer. This vast and delightful repository of all things cinema is the place to go for complete cast/crew listings, actor/filmmaker bios, plot summaries, movie trailers, critics' reviews, user ratings, parental guidance, famous quotations, and all kinds of trivia.

You can always search for movies, TV shows, actors, and so on by typing a name in the search box in the upper-right corner of the screen. Or tap Browse at the lower left to find current movies by showtimes, what's coming soon, or box office results. You can browse TV recaps, too, or find people born on the day you happen to be looking and poking around the app. It's also fun to check out the Trending Celebrities on IMDb. The recent roster included Aaron Paul, Scarlett Johansson, Bryan Cranston, Charlie Hunnam, Jennifer Lawrence, Miley Cyrus, Joseph Gordon-Levitt, Chloe Bennet, and on and on.

One piece of advice to movie buffs: Avoid the IMDb if you have a lot of work to do. You'll have a hard time closing the curtain on this marvelous app.

Netflix

Flixster, IMDb, and now Netflix. You've no doubt detected a real trend by now, and that trend is indeed our affection for movies and TV shows. If you love TV and movies, too, you're sure to be a fan of the Netflix app. Over time, Netflix, the company that built its reputation by sending DVDs to subscribers through the mail, started streaming movies over the Internet to computers, TVs, and other consumer electronics gear. You can now add the iPad to that list.

From the iPad, you have more or less instant access to thousands of movies on demand. And although these titles aren't exactly current blockbusters, we know you'll find plenty of films worth seeing. You can search by *genre* (classics, comedy, drama, and so on) and *subgenre* (courtroom dramas, political dramas, romantic dramas, and so on).

What's more, Netflix has started producing its own shows, including *House of Cards* featuring Kevin Spacey, which Ed binged on.

Although the app is free, as are the movies you choose to watch on the fly, you have to pay Netflix streaming subscription fees that start at $7.99 a month. You also need an Internet connection, preferably through Wi-Fi, although Netflix works on 3G and 4G models as well.

Remember what we've told you about streaming movies over 3G or 4G and be mindful of your data plan.

DVD Netflix subscribers might also quibble about the fact that you can't manage your DVD queue inside the app.

Comics

Comics is actually three apps rolled into one. First and foremost, it's a fantastic way to read comic books on a 9.7-inch touch-screen. Second, it's a comic bookstore with hundreds of comics and comic series from dozens of publishers, including Arcana, Archie, Marvel, Devil's Due, Digital Webbing, Red 5, Zenescope, and many more, including hundreds of free comics. (See Figure 18-4.)

Figure 18-4: Comics lets you shop for and read (d'oh!) comics on your iPad.

Finally, this app provides a great way to organize the comics you own on your iPad so that you can find the one you want quickly and easily.

The free Comics app gives you access to hundreds of free comics, or you can use the built-in store to purchase comics, usually $0.99 to $2.99 per issue.

New releases are available every Wednesday, so visit the store often to check out the latest and greatest offerings. Both the store and your personal comic collection are well organized and easy to use. And reading comics in Comics is a pleasure you won't want to miss if you're a fan of comics or graphic novels.

Our technical editor, Dennis, a true comic aficionado, says we should mention that this app can read only comics — free or paid — from the app's built-in store. Although the store offers tens of thousands of titles by hundreds of publishers, his point is that you can't use this excellent app to read comics acquired elsewhere or scanned at home.

Epicurious Recipes & Shopping List

We love to eat. But we're writers, not gourmet chefs, so we'll take all the help we can get when it comes to preparing a great meal. And we get a lot of that culinary assistance from Epicurious, which easily lives up to its billing as the "Cook's Companion." This tasty recipe app comes courtesy of Condé Nast Digital.

Tap the Control Panel button in the upper-left corner of the screen to get started, and you can find a yummy recipe in no time. Tap Featured inside the Control Panel (if it's not already highlighted) to find recipes that have been lumped into categories, often timed to the season. Around the time we were writing this book, recipe collection categories included Oktoberfest Dishes, Halloween Treats, Veggie Thanksgiving, Kid-Friendly Mains, Decadent Desserts, and more. To which we say, "Yum." Some recipes carry reviews.

If you tap Search inside the Control Panel instead, you can fine-tune your search for a recipe by food or drink, by main ingredient (banana, chicken, pasta), by cuisine type, and by dietary consideration (low-carb, vegan, kosher, and so on), among other parameters.

When you discover a recipe you like, you can add it to a collection of Favorites, e-mail it to a friend, pass along the ingredients to your shopping list, summon nutritional information, or share it on Facebook and Twitter.

If you want to sync favorite recipes on your iPhone and iPad through a personal Recipe Box on Epicurious.com, that'll cost you $1.99 as an in-app purchase.

Bon appétit.

Evernote

Before we even talk about the Evernote iPad app, let's take a quick look at the problem Evernote resolves for us: storing our little bits of digital information — text, pictures, screen shots, scanned images, receipts, bills, e-mail messages, web pages, and other info we might want to recall someday — and synchronizing all the data among all our devices and the cloud.

Evernote (www.evernote.com) is all that and more, with excellent free apps for iOS, Mac OS X, Android, and Windows, plus a killer web interface that works in most browsers.

You can create notes of any length on your iPad by typing, dictating, or photographing. You can add unlimited tags to a note, and create unlimited notebooks to organize your rapidly growing collection of notes.

You can even annotate images and PDFs in Evernote notes, using another free app from Evernote called Skitch, which we also recommend without hesitation.

Getting words and images into Evernote couldn't be much easier, but the info will be useless if you can't find it when you need it. Evernote won't let you down, with myriad options for finding and working with your stored data. In addition to the aforementioned tags and notebooks, Evernote offers searching and filtering (Tags and Notebooks) options to help you find the note you need, as shown in Figure 18-5.

Two other nice touches are worth noting:

Figure 18-5: Evernote's main screen only hints at how easy it is to create and find notes.

- ✔ Notes are automatically tagged with your current location (as long as you create them on your iPad or other location-enabled device), so you can filter by Places.

- ✔ You can attach reminders to notes and receive notification on the date and time you chose. Best of all, you'll be notified on your iPad as well as on your other iDevices, Macs, PCs, and on the Evernote website!

Our two favorite features are that Evernote syncs notes with all your devices and the cloud automatically and that everything we've mentioned so far — creating, organizing, and syncing notes — is free.

Bob likes Evernote so much that he recently upgraded to the premium plan ($5/month or $45/year), primarily to increase his monthly upload limit from 60MB to 1GB and to get the capability to search for text in PDFs.

Pandora Radio

We've long been fans of Pandora on other computers and mobile devices, so we're practically delirious that this custom Internet radio service is available *gratis* on the iPad. And you can play Pandora music in the background while doing other stuff.

Pandora works on the iPad in much the same way that it does on a Mac or PC. In the box at the upper left, type the name of a favorite artist, song title, or composer via the iPad keyboard, and Pandora creates an instant personalized radio station with selections that exemplify the style you chose. Along the left panel of Figure 18-6, you see some of the eclectic stations Ed created. Tapping QuickMix at the top of the list plays musical selections across all your stations.

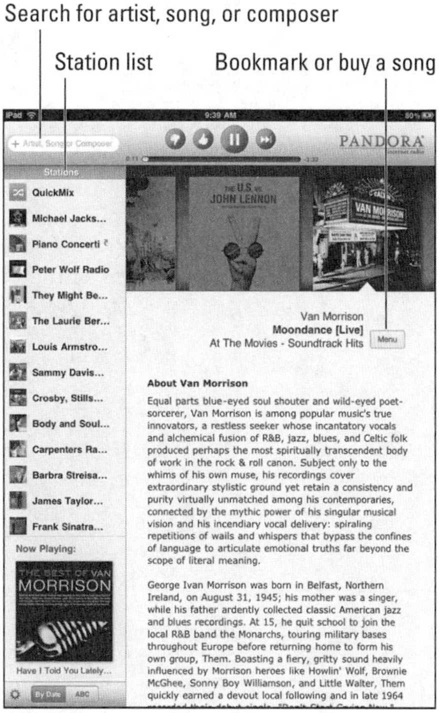

Suppose that you type **Beatles**. Pandora's instant Beatles station includes performances from John, Paul, George, and Ringo, as well as tunes from other acts.

And say that you type a song title, such as **Have I Told You Lately**. Pandora constructs a station with similar music after you tell it whether to base tunes on the Van Morrison, Rod Stewart, or another rendition.

Search for artist, song, or composer

Station list   Bookmark or buy a song

Figure 18-6: Have we told you lately how much we like Pandora?

Pandora comes out of the *Music Genome Project,* an organization of musicians and technologists who analyze music according to hundreds of attributes (such as melody, harmony, and vocal performances).

You can help fine-tune the music Pandora plays by tapping the Thumbs Up or Thumbs Down icon at the top of the screen above the album covers associated with the music you've been listening to during the current session.

Pandora also takes advantage of the generous screen real estate of the iPad to deliver artist profiles. (Refer to Figure 18-6.) You may see ads, too.

If you tap the Menu button below an album cover of the currently playing song, you can bookmark the song or artist that's playing or head to iTunes to purchase the song or other material from the artist directly on the iPad (if available).

Before we leave the realm of the free apps, we'd like to remind you of an eleventh freebie — a free app so wonderful that we wrote a whole chapter (that would be Chapter 10) about it. The app is iBooks.

19

Ten Apps Worth Paying For

• •

*I*f you read Chapter 18, you know that lots of great free apps are available for your iPad. But as the old cliché goes, some things are worth paying for. Still, none of the ten for-pay apps we've chosen as some of our favorites are likely to break the bank. As you're about to discover, some apps in this list are practical, and some are downright silly. The common theme? We think you'll like carrying these apps around on your iPad.

Bill Atkinson PhotoCard

Who is Bill Atkinson? He had a hand (or both hands) in the first Macintosh computer, as well as in the MacPaint and HyperCard Mac applications. Today he's a world-renowned nature photographer, which brings us to his app. Bill Atkinson PhotoCard is a free app that lets you create gorgeous high-resolution postcards and send them via either e-mail or the U.S. Postal Service. Sending postcards by e-mail is free, and so is the app.

But the reason we love it is that you can have printed postcards sent via USPS for $1.50 and $2.00 per postcard, depending on how many print-and-mail credits you purchase. The 8.25-x-5.5-inch postcards are, in a word, stunning. Printed on heavy glossy stock on a state-of-the-art HP Indigo Digital Press and then laminated for protection, they're as beautiful as any postcard you've ever seen.

You can use one of the 200 included Bill Atkinson nature photos, as shown in Figure 19-1, or you can use any picture in your Photos library. You can add stickers and stamps, as shown in Figure 19-1, and you can even add voice notes to e-mailed cards.

If you're still uncertain, download the app (it's free) and try it. Send an e-mail postcard or two to yourself. After you've seen how gorgeous these cards can be and how easy the app is to use, we think you'll spring for some print-and-mail credits and take your iPad on your next vacation.

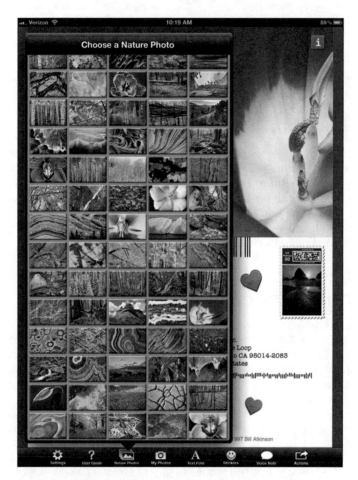

Figure 19-1: Your postcard can feature one of Bill Atkinson's gorgeous nature photos.

Words with Friends HD

This brings us to perhaps the only time in this whole book that your authors had a disagreement. Both of us love word games and puzzles, but Bob loves Words with Friends HD, whereas Ed prefers the real thing: namely, SCRABBLE.

Social media is all the rage these days, but most multiplayer iPad games are either boring or not particularly social. Words with Friends HD ($2.99), on the other hand, is the most social game Bob has found — and a ton of fun, too. It's kind of like playing SCRABBLE with a friend, but because it's turn-based, you can make a move and then quit the app and do other stuff. When your friend makes his next move, you can choose to be notified that it's your turn by sound, onscreen alert, and/or a number on the Words with Friends icon on your Home screen.

Bob says: "Try the free version (Words with Friends HD Free), and I'm sure you'll be hooked. Then challenge me if you like; my username is `boblevitus` (although I often have the maximum 20 games going, so keep trying if I don't accept your challenge right away)."

ArtStudio for iPad

Do you fancy yourself an artist? We know our artistic talent is limited, but if we were talented, ArtStudio for iPad is the program we'd use to paint our masterpieces. Even if you have limited artistic talent, you can see that this app has everything you need to create awesome artwork.

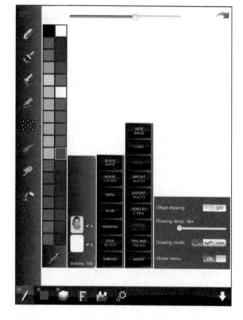

We were embarrassed to show you our creations, so instead, we whipped up a composite illustration (see Figure 19-2) that shows all the ArtStudio for iPad's tools and palettes at once.

Here are just some of ArtStudio for iPad's features:

✔ Offers 25 brushes, including pencils, a smudge tool, bucket fill, airbrush, and more. Brushes are resizable and simulate brush pressure.

✔ Allows up to five layers with options, such as delete, reorder, duplicate, merge, and transparency.

✔ Provides filters, such as blur, sharpen, detect edges, sepia, and more.

Figure 19-2: ArtStudio for iPad's tools from left to right: brushes, colors, layers, special effects, file management options, and settings.

Don't believe us? AppSmile.com (`www.appsmile.com`) rated it 5 out of 5, saying, "This is what Photoshop Mobile wishes it had been." SlapApp.com (`www.slapapp.com`) also rated it 5 out of 5 and said, "I've dabbled in quite a few painting and drawing apps and this one has 'em all beat by a long shot." And by all means, check out what talented artists can do with ArtStudio for iPad at `www.flickr.com/groups/artstudioimages` and `www.artistinvermont.com`.

One last thing: The app was only $0.99 when we bought our copies — a "special launch sale" price. The price has gone up, but even at the new price, a whopping $5.99, it's still a heck of a deal for a thoughtfully designed and full-featured drawing and painting app.

Beware of rip-offs in the iTunes App Store, such as the similarly named Art Studio HD — For Your iPad. That one's a bad knock-off from developer Party Sub Productions that has garnered mostly 1-star ratings. Don't be fooled — the app you're looking for is ArtStudio for iPad, from Lucky Clan. Note that Art and Studio run together to form a single word; if you search for the single word *ArtStudio,* you'll find it.

Pinball Crystal Caliburn II

Good pinball games require supremely realistic physics, and Crystal Caliburn II ($3.99) nails it. The way the ball moves around the tables and interacts with bumpers and flippers is so realistic that you'll think you're at an arcade. It's so realistic, in fact, that you can shake the table to influence the ball's movement.

Another hallmark of a great pinball game is great sound effects, and this game doesn't disappoint. The sounds the ball makes when it bounces off a bumper, is hit with a flipper, or passes through a rollover are spot-on and totally authentic.

If you like pinball, we think you'll love Pinball Crystal Caliburn II on your iPad. LittleWing (the developer) recently released an iOS version of its original pinball hit, Tristan, that also sports realistic physics and sounds and is also a lot of fun.

Art Authority for iPad

We've already admitted to being artistically challenged, but that only applies to making art. We both appreciate good art as much as the next person, or even more. That's why we're so enthusiastic about Art Authority, only $4.99.

Art Authority is like an art museum you hold in your hand; it contains more than 50,000 paintings and sculptures by more than 1,000 of the world's greatest artists. The works are organized into eight period-specific rooms, such as Early (up to 1400s), Baroque, Romanticism, Modern, and American. In each room, the artworks are subdivided by movement. The Modern room, for example, has works of Surrealism, Cubism, Fauvism, Dadaism, sculpture, and several more.

You find period overviews, movement overviews, timelines, and slideshows, plus a searchable index of all 1,000+ artists and separate indices for each room.

Since we first wrote about this app, developer Open Door Networks has added an Art Near Me feature that lets you search for art in your vicinity, and the developer released another version with artworks and rooms optimized for the Retina display. It looked great before and even better today. If you love art, check it out.

Solar Walk — 3D Solar System

We like to gaze at the heavens, but we often have no clue what we're looking at. This handsome animated $0.99 guide to the night sky from Vito Technology — it was refreshed to take advantage of the Retina display — will delight astronomy students and really anyone fascinated by outer space, even if purists scoff that Pluto, no longer considered a planet, is included in the model of the solar system.

From the start, you're taken on a virtual tour through the galaxy to the Earth. You can search planets, satellites, stars, and more and travel through time and space with a Time Machine feature. Animated movies cover topics such as Earth's Cycles, Solar Eclipse, and The Moon Phases.

What's more, the app can exploit 3D, provided you supply your own *anaglyph*-style cyan-red 3D glasses. And if you hook the iPad up to a 3DTV using an HDMI adapter (see Chapter 17), you can get a true sense of the depth and sheer size of the solar system in 3D, while controlling what you see on the screen through the iPad.

Of course, without 3D, you can use AirPlay to mirror what's on the iPad screen on the bigger TV screen, provided you have an Apple TV.

Action Movie FX

With Action Movie FX, it's a breeze to add big-budget Hollywood-style special effects to video you shoot with your iPhone. Action Movie FX comes from producer J. J. Abrams's Bad Robot Productions, best known for TV shows such as *Alias* and *Fringe* and feature films including *Star Trek* and *Super 8*. We expected it to be pretty good and it is — it may well be the most fun app we've ever used to make videos with an iPad.

The free version features eight big-budget movie effects, such as Missile Attack, Avalanche, and Meteor from Outer Space, as well as Phaser Fight and Photon Torpedoes from Abrams's epic theatrical release *Star Trek into*

Darkness. In other words, Action Movie FX lets you add Hollywood-style special effects to your videos so you can "destroy" people, places, pets, and other stuff in a variety of fun and interesting ways.

Making a video with Action Movie FX couldn't be easier. Just launch the app, select the scene you want to use, tap Start, and shoot a minimum of five seconds of video. It's better if the footage is of someone or something that will remain still, unlike Bob's dog Zeke, the slightly blurry miniature vizsla in Figure 19-3.

Figure 19-3: An alien bursting out of Bob's dog.

When you've finished filming, you can adjust the timing as well as resize and reposition the special effects. When you're satisfied with your creation, your masterpiece appears after a bit of processing; you can then share it, save it to your Camera Roll, trash it, adjust its timing again, or shoot another video.

Figure 19-4: A jet taking out several vehicles on a quiet street.

The free effects are great, but we found ourselves wanting more and have purchased most (if not all) of the ten currently available FX packs for $0.99 each. They're mostly great, but our absolute favorites are *The Jet* (shown in Figure 19-4) and *Alien Burst* (refer to Figure 19-3).

The videos are HD, and look great in a text message or an e-mail displayed on any device. The videos look fabulous on your iPad, but also look surprisingly good on a bigger display such as the one on a Mac, a PC, or an HDTV.

Finally, you just can't beat the price — your first eight effects are free. But we're betting that you'll like it enough to pop for one or more $0.99 FX packs. Either way, we're pretty sure you'll have as much fun as we have adding special FX to your videos.

Facetune for iPad

You don't really think those drop-dead gorgeous models are really that drop-dead gorgeous, now do you? They had "work done." And the portraits that show these men and women in their very best light were doctored, touched-up, made to look perfect.

The $3.99 Facetune app can make you look perfect, too — okay, we'll amend that to say it promises to make you look better. (As Bob and Ed know, you've got to work with what you've got.)

After uploading a photo or taking pictures inside the app using the camera on your iPad, you can tap Facetune controls shown in Figure 19-5. Facetune smooths away wrinkles, whitens teeth, changes the contours of your face, makes it look like you've got a full head of hair (when you don't), and even defocuses the image so that any imperfections in your face don't show as well.

In other words, it all adds up to perfection.

Figure 19-5: Facetune can make Ed look better.

60 Minutes

As news junkies, we have long appreciated _60 Minutes,_ CBS's venerable TV news magazine. CBS Interactive's $4.99 companion app to the series brings the latest _60 Minutes_ segments to your iPad so that you can watch at your convenience. The _60 Minutes Overtime_ segments that provide weekly behind-the-scenes looks at how the various stories came together are also available.

But the best part to us is the "Classics" section that features more than 250 hand-picked stories, covering the 40-plus-year history of the show. Interview subjects include Coretta Scott King, Johnny Carson, Ayatollah Khomeini (see Figure 19-6), Jodie Foster, Ronald and Nancy Reagan, Oprah Winfrey, Barack Obama, and many more.

Figure 19-6: Bringing *60 Minutes* history to your iPad.

You can search shows by topic (newsmakers, politics, science, business, sports, entertainment, nature), by decade, and by correspondent, letting you zero in on some of the finest work from Ed Bradley, Harry Reasoner, and Mike Wallace. Andy Rooney is here too, as is the famous *60 Minutes* stopwatch.

Parallels Access

If you're like most of the iPad community, you mostly use your iPad for consumption purposes: watching movies, listening to music, playing games, browsing the web. You engage less often in "productive-type" activities on the iPad, mostly because it lacks a physical keyboard. As a result, you still schlep a laptop with you on the road even though you also carry the iPad.

Parallels, a company best known for letting you run "virtualized" versions of Microsoft Windows on Macintosh computers, may eliminate the need to carry the extra machine. Its Parallels Access iPad app ties into a subscription service that lets you tap into your home or office PC remotely, whether it's a Windows PC or a Mac.

What sets Parallels Access apart from other apps that provide remote access to computers is that you can get to and use *all* the programs that reside on your PC or Mac, including the proprietary software that your company may employ. Moreover, you can interact with those applications on the tablet as if each were designed for the iPad, and even use a browser running Adobe Flash on the iPad.

You start any PC or Mac "desktop" application on the iPad from a familiar-looking launcher screen with icons for the apps you use most often. Such a screen is shown in Figure 19-7. You can add or remove icons to this launcher screen.

Parallels, as the company puts it, "applifies" PC/Mac programs so that the software is modified on the tablet to display iPad-style buttons for actions such as copy/paste/select.

Figure 19-7: Parallels Access lets you run programs on a Mac or PC from the iPad.

And touch gestures on the iPad substitute for mouse moves on your computer. For example, tapping is like clicking with a mouse; two-finger tapping is equivalent to a right-click. Hold your finger against the display in an Excel spreadsheet, say, and an iPad magnifying glass appears.

You can also use your voice to dictate text remotely onto the home or office computer. And listen to music on the iPad that resides on your faraway computer, too — no, the folks back home or in the office will not hear what you're hearing; the app is set up so as not to disturb them.

Parallels Access can't completely make up for the lack of a physical keyboard on the iPad. But the onscreen Mac or Windows keyboards that appear within the app display any dedicated special keys that are unique to Mac or Windows keyboards.

The Parallels Access app itself is free to download, as is the "agent" program you must install on each Mac or PC that you choose to access. But you must pay $79.99 per year, per remote computer, for the required subscription that makes it all possible.

20

Ten Hints, Tips, and Shortcuts

fter spending a lot of quality time with our iPads, it's only natural that we've discovered more than a few helpful hints, tips, and shortcuts. In this chapter, we share our faves.

Saving Time and Keystrokes with Keyboard Shortcuts

Keyboard shortcuts are a way to have your iPad automatically type a phrase when you type the shortcut. For example, when we type **vty** followed by the spacebar, our iPads type **Very truly yours**. In other words, we type a 3-letter shortcut, and our iPads replace it with a 14-letter phrase in the blink of an eye.

How long would it take you to type **Dictated to and scent from my iPad; please blame Siri for any missed steaks** on your iPad's onscreen keyboard? And would you type it without mistakes? It took a fraction of a second to type our shortcut for this phrase (**dict**), and another fraction of a second for the iPad to expand it (to **Dictated to and scent from my iPad; please blame Siri for any missed steaks**).

So, shortcuts save you time and keystrokes.

Another advantage is that you'll always spell things correctly (so long as you spell them correctly when you create the shortcut and phrase).

You can even use shortcuts to automatically correct the spelling of words you commonly mistype. Say you often type **taht** when you mean to type **that**. Here's how to create, edit, and enjoy your iPad's convenient little keystroke savers. Start by creating a shortcut:

1. **Tap Settings➪General➪Keyboard.**

2. **Tap Add New Shortcut.**

3. **Type the phrase and the shortcut you want to trigger it.**

   For example, say you want the phrase "I'll call or text you as soon as I am free," to appear when you type the shortcut **cty**, as shown in Figure 20-1.

4. **Tap Save.**

After you create a shortcut, just tap its name to change (edit) it.

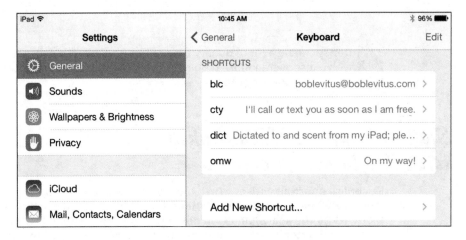

Figure 20-1: Here are some shortcuts and phrases we've created.

After you create and edit 'em, here's how you use 'em:

To insert a phrase, type its keyboard shortcut. Say the shortcut is **cty**, as shown in Figure 20-1. If you stop after you type **y**, the phrase appears below the cursor, as shown in Figure 20-2. To insert the phrase, press the spacebar on your iPad keyboard; to ignore it, tap the gray *x* to the right of the phrase.

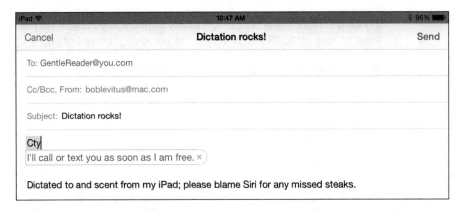

Figure 20-2: Type a space to insert the phrase, "I'll call or text you as soon as I am free."

One last thing: You can use the same technique to create keyboard shortcuts like this on an iPhone or iPod touch. Although you can't easily sync or share your shortcuts, you can create and use them on any device running iOS 5 or later.

One more last thing (this time we mean it, but we just had to include this tip-within-a-chapter-full-of-tips): You can create keyboard shortcuts such as these in OS X since at least version 10.6 (Snow Leopard). Just launch the System Preferences app, click the Language and Text (Snow Leopard) or Keyboard (Lion or later) icon, and click the Text tab (Snow Leopard) or Keyboard Shortcuts tab (Lion or later).

Auto-Correction Is Your Friend

Here are three related tips about Auto-Correction that can also help you type faster and more accurately.

Auto-apostrophes are good for you

First, know that you can type **dont** to get to **don't**, and **cant** to get to **can't**. We've told you to put some faith in the iPad's Auto-Correction software. And that applies to contractions. In other words, save time by letting the iPad's intelligent keyboard insert the apostrophes on your behalf for these and other common words.

We're aware of at least one exception. The iPad can't distinguish between *it's* and *its*. (*It's* is the contraction of *it is,* and *its* is the possessive adjective and possessive pronoun.) So if you need, say, e-mails to important business clients to be grammatically correct, remember that Auto-Correction doesn't get it (or *it's* or *its*) right all the time.

In a similar vein, if you ever *need* to type an apostrophe (for example, when you want to type *it's*), you don't need to visit the punctuation and numeric keyboard. Instead, press the Exclamation Mark/Comma key for at least one second, and an apostrophe magically appears. Slide your finger onto it and then lift your finger, and presto — you've typed an apostrophe without touching the punctuation and numeric keyboard.

Make rejection work for you

Along those same lines, if the Auto-Correction suggestion isn't the word you want, instead of ignoring it, reject it. Finish typing the word and then tap the *x* to reject the suggestion before you type another word. Doing so makes your iPad more likely to accept your word the next time you type it and less likely to make the same incorrect suggestion again.

If you're using a physical keyboard (for example, Apple's Keyboard Dock or any Bluetooth wireless one), you can reject an autosuggestion by pressing the Esc key.

Here you thought you were buying a tech book, and you get grammar and typing lessons thrown in at no extra charge. Just think of us as full-service authors.

If you hate auto-correct, turn it off

Some people, like our editor Rebecca, for example, don't care for auto-correct and turn it off. If you hate it too, here's how to get rid of it: Tap Settings⇨General⇨Keyboard and tap the Auto-Correction switch to Off.

Settings⇨General⇨Keyboard is also where you enable or disable other keyboard-related features, including Auto-Capitalization, Check Spelling, Enable Caps Lock, and the "double-tapping the spacebar will insert a period followed by a space" shortcut. See Chapter 15, where we dive into settings.

Viewing the iPad's Capacity

When your iPad is selected in iTunes, you see a colorful chart at the bottom of the screen that tells you how your media and other data use your iPad's capacity.

By default, the chart shows the amount of free space on your iPad, along with colored bands that represent the audio, video, photo, apps, documents, books, and such on your iPad. What you may not know is that when you hover your cursor over the chart, an overlay appears with the number of items of that type that are stored on your iPad, and how much space those items consume in megabytes (MB) or gigabytes (GB), as shown in Figure 20-3 for Photos.

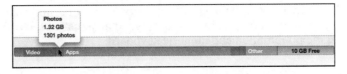

Figure 20-3: Hover over the colorful chart, and you'll see the details in an overlay.

The Way-Cool Semi-Hidden Audio Scrub Speed Tip

Here's the situation: You're listening to a podcast or audiobook and trying to find the beginning of a specific segment by moving the Scrubber bar — the little red line representing the playhead — left and right. The only problem is that the Scrubber bar isn't very precise, and your fat finger keeps moving it too far one way or the other. Never fear — your iPad has a wonderful (albeit somewhat hidden) fix. Just press your finger on the Scrubber, but instead of sliding your finger to the left or right, slide it downward toward the bottom of the screen. (See Figure 20-4.) As you slide downward, the scrubbing speed changes like magic, and the Scrubber bar moves in finer and finer increments. Furthermore, the speed is displayed below the Scrubber bar

Drag to here for half-speed scrubbing.

Drag to here for quarter-speed scrubbing.

Elapsed time   Scrubber   Remaining time

Drag to here for ultra-fine scrubbing.

Figure 20-4: Press the Scrubber bar, and slide your finger downward to change the scrubbing rate.

(Half-Speed Scrubbing in Figure 20-4) and updates in real time. So when you slide your finger downward an inch or so, the speed changes to roughly half-speed scrubbing. Drag another inch or so, and it changes to quarter-speed scrubbing. Keep dragging, and it changes to very fine scrubbing.

This scrub trick is easier to do than to explain, so give it a try.

Tricks with Links and E-Mail Addresses

The iPad does something special when it encounters an e-mail address or a URL in e-mail messages. The iPad interprets character sequences that look like web addresses (URLs), such as `http://www.`*`websitename`*`.com` or `www.`*`websitename`*`.com`, and any sequences that look like e-mail addresses, such as *`yourname@yourmailhost`*`.com`. When the iPad sees what it assumes to be a URL or an e-mail address, it makes that text appear as a blue link on your screen.

Assault on batteries

Because this is a chapter of tips and hints, we'd be remiss if we didn't include some ways that you can extend your battery life. First and foremost: If you use a carrying case, charging the iPad while it's in that case may generate more heat than is healthy. Overheating is bad for both battery capacity and battery life. So take the iPad out of the case before you charge it. The Smart Cover isn't actually a case, so if you use one of those, you're good to go.

If you're not using power-thirsty 3G, 4G, or Wi-Fi networks, or a Bluetooth device (such as a headset), consider turning off the features you don't need in Settings. Doing so could mean the difference between running out of juice and seeing the end of a movie.

Activate Auto-Brightness to enable the screen brightness to adjust based on current lighting conditions. Using this setting can be easier on your battery. Tap Settings⇨Brightness, and then tap the On/Off switch, if necessary, to turn it on.

Turn off Location Services (tap Settings⇨Location Services) globally or for individual apps with the On/Off switches. Figuring out your precise location takes its toll on your battery, so you may want to disable Location Services for apps you don't use very often.

Push notifications are notorious juice-suckers as well. Disable them (tap Settings⇨Mail, Contacts, Calendars⇨Fetch New Data⇨Push On/Off switch) and watch your battery life improve dramatically. You can disable push notifications for other apps via Settings⇨Notifications.

If you tap a URL or an e-mail address like the ones just shown, the iPad launches Safari, takes you to the appropriate web page for a URL, and starts a new e-mail message for an e-mail address. So don't bother with copy and paste if you don't have to — tap those blue links, and the right thing will happen every time.

Here's another cool Safari trick, this time with links. If you press and hold a link rather than tapping it, a little floating text bubble appears and shows you the underlying URL. In addition, it offers the following options, as shown in Figure 20-5:

Figure 20-5: Press and hold a link to find additional actions you can take.

- ✔ **Open:** Opens the page.

- ✔ **Open in New Tab:** Opens the page while stashing the current page in one of the nine available tabs, as we describe in Chapter 4.

- ✔ **Add to Reading List:** Adds the page to your Reading List, as we describe in Chapter 4.

> ✔ **Copy:** Copies the URL to the Clipboard (so that you can paste it into an e-mail message, save it in Notes, or whatever).

TIP

You also see the underlying URL if you press and hold a URL in Mail with buttons to open or copy it. Having this information in Mail is even more useful because it enables you to spot bogus links without switching to Safari or actually visiting the URL.

Finally, here's one last Safari trick. If you press and hold most images, a Save Image button appears in addition to the four other buttons (see Figure 20-6). Tap Save Image, and the picture is saved to the Camera Roll on the Albums tab of the Photos app. Tap Copy, and it's copied to the Clipboard so that you can paste it into an e-mail message or document created in another app (such as Apple's Pages or Keynote).

Figure 20-6: Save images you want to find easily later.

Share the Love . . . and the Links

Ever stumble onto a web page you just have to share with a buddy? The iPad makes sharing dead simple. From the site in question, tap the Action icon, which looks like a little rectangle with an arrow sprouting from it. Just tap the Message, Mail, Twitter, or Facebook button to share the link via e-mail, iMessage, or post it to your Facebook wall or Twitter stream. See Figure 20-7. With iOS 7 and a fourth-generation iPad or later or iPad mini, you can also use AirDrop to share your link. See Chapter 13 to find out how to use AirDrop.

Figure 20-7: Share links with your friends.

Type a short message body (or don't), supply your pal's e-mail or iMessage address if necessary, and then tap the Send or Post button.

Choosing a Home Page for Safari

You may have noticed that there's no option to specify a home page in the iPad version of Safari, though that popular option exists on Mac and PC versions of Safari (and, for that matter, every other web browser in common use today). Instead, when you tap the Safari icon, you return to the last site you visited.

The trick is to create an icon for the page you want to use as your home page. This technique is called creating a *Web Clip* of a web page. Here's how to do it:

1. **Open the web page you want to use as your home page and tap the Action button (it looks like a little rectangle with an arrow sprouting from it at the top of the screen).**

2. **Tap the Add to Home Screen button.**

   An icon that will open this page appears on your Home screen (or one of your Home screens if you have more than one).

3. **Tap this new Web Clip icon instead of the Safari icon, and Safari opens to your home page instead of the last page you visited.**

You can even rearrange the icons so that your Home Page icon, instead of or in addition to the Safari icon, appears in the Dock (the bottom row that appears on

Figure 20-8: The B.L. Dot Com icon now appears to the left of Safari in the Dock.

every Home screen), as shown in Figure 20-8. Just drag your Home Page icon down into the Dock.

Consider moving the Safari icon from the Dock onto one of your Home screens so that you never tap it by accident. Finally, remember that the Dock has room for six icons, even though it has only four by default. If you like, place both Safari and your new Home Page icon in the Dock so that you can tap either one depending upon your needs.

Storing Files

A tiny Massachusetts software company — Ecamm Network — sells a piece of OS X software, PhoneView ($29.95), which lets you copy files from your Mac to your iPad and copy files from the iPad to a Mac, as shown in Figure 20-9. (No Windows version is available.) Better still, you can try the program for a week before deciding whether you want to buy it. Go to www. ecamm.com to fetch the free demo.

The big deal here is that while automatic backups protect most of the files on your iPad, there's no way to manipulate them. They're backed up and restored, but heaven help you if you want to extract one or more individual iMessages, specific songs, videos, notes, or other types of data from your iPad. The bottom line is that there's no easier way than PhoneView.

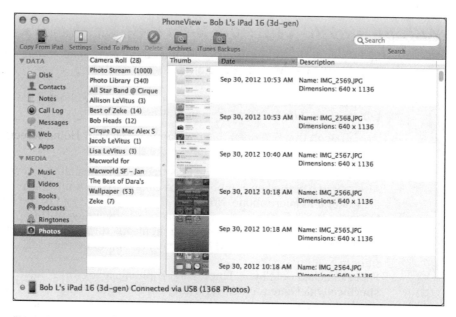

Figure 20-9: Store all your files with PhoneView.

In a nutshell, here's how PhoneView works. After downloading the software to your Mac, double-click the program's icon to start it. Then do one of the following:

✔ **To transfer files and folders to the iPad** (assuming that you have room on the device), click the Copy to iPad button on the toolbar and then select the files you want to copy. The files are copied into the appropriate folder on the iPad. Alternatively, you can drag files and folders from the Mac Desktop or a folder into the PhoneView browser.

✔ **To go the other way and copy files from your iPad to your computer,** highlight the files or folders you want to be copied and then click the Copy from iPad button on the toolbar. Select the destination on your Mac where you want to store the files, and then click Save. You can also drag files and folders from the PhoneView file browser onto the Mac Desktop or folder. Or you can double-click a file in the PhoneView browser to download it to your Mac's Documents folder.

If you need access to the files on your iPad or if you want to use your iPad as a pseudo–hard drive, PhoneView is a bargain.

Bob says: "I use Printopia, also from Ecamm ($19.95), to print from my iPad to several of our non-AirPrint printers. It works great and costs a lot less than a new AirPrint-enabled printer."

Making Phone Calls on the iPad

Many people, including us, have compared the iPad to an iPhone on steroids. Only the iPad isn't actually a phone.

Don't let that stop you from making or even receiving phone calls on the tablet.

Come again?

You read right. You *can* make and even receive phone calls on your iPad. After all, two of the key components to calling are built into the iPad: a speaker and microphone. Now all you have to do is head to the App Store to fetch a third component, an app that takes advantage of *VoIP*, or *Voice over Internet Protocol*. In plain-speak, that means turning the iPad into a giant iPhone. And yes, you can find more than one app to do the trick.

We've checked out Skype, Line2, and Truphone, all of which have a version specifically designed to take advantage of the large iPad screen. The apps themselves are free although you have to pay for calls to regular phones. Here are the details:

- **Line2:** We especially like Line2 although it costs $9.95 per month. It can receive calls through Wi-Fi or a cellular data network (if you have an iPad with 3G or 4G). It boasts such features as visual voice mail (like the iPhone) and conference calling. And it taps right into your iPad contacts list.

- **Skype:** Skype's app permits free Skype-to-Skype calls, instant messages, and video chats; calls to regular phones around the world cost pennies per minute.

- **Truphone:** This app permits free Wi-Fi calls to Truphone and Google Talk users. Other rates are cheap.

Taking a Snapshot of the Screen

True confession: We threw in this final tip because, well, it helps people like *us*.

Permit us to explain. We hope you've admired the pictures of the iPad screens that are sprinkled throughout this book. We also secretly hope that you're thinking what marvelous photographers we must be.

Well, the fact is, we couldn't take a blurry picture of the iPad using its built-in (and little-known) screen-grab feature if we wanted to.

Press the Sleep/Wake button at the same time you press the Home button, but just for an instant. The iPad grabs a snapshot of whatever is on the screen.

The picture lands in the Camera Roll of the Photos app. From there, you can synchronize it with your Mac or PC, along with all your other pictures, or e-mail it to yourself or anyone else. And from there, the possibilities are endless. Why, your picture could wind up just about anywhere, including in a *For Dummies* book.

You can also show what's happening on your iPad's screen on an HDTV in real time. All you need is a television that has at least one HDMI port and the $39 Apple Digital AV Adapter for iPads with a 30-pin connector, $49 for iPads with a Lightning connector, or $99 Apple TV to connect your iPad to the TV.

Index

• *D* •

● *N* ●

• *T* •

About the Authors

Edward C. Baig writes the weekly Personal Technology column in *USA TODAY* and is a regular on *USA TODAY* podcasts and videos. Ed is also the author of *Macs For Dummies,* 11th Edition (John Wiley & Sons, Inc.) and co-writer of *iPhone For Dummies.* Before joining *USA TODAY* as a columnist and reporter in 1999, Ed spent six years at *Business Week,* where he wrote and edited stories about consumer tech, personal finance, collectibles, travel, and wine tasting, among other topics. He received the Medill School of Journalism 1999 Financial Writers and Editors Award for contributions to the *"Business Week* Investor Guide to Online Investing." That followed a three-year stint at *U.S. News & World Report,* where Ed was the lead tech writer for the News You Can Use section but also dabbled in numerous other subjects.

Ed began his journalist career at *Fortune* magazine, gaining the best basic training imaginable during his early years as a fact checker and contributor to the Fortune 500. Through the dozen years he worked at the magazine, Ed covered leisure-time industries, penned features on the lucrative "dating" market and the effect of religion on corporate managers, and was heavily involved in the Most Admired Companies project. Ed also started up *Fortune*'s Products to Watch column, a venue for low- and high-tech items.

Bob LeVitus, often referred to as "Dr. Mac," has written or co-written over 70 popular computer books, with millions of copies in print. His titles include *OS X Mavericks For Dummies, iPhone For Dummies, Incredible iPhone Apps For Dummies,* and *Microsoft Office 2011 For Mac For Dummies,* all for John Wiley & Sons, Inc.

Bob has also penned the popular Dr. Mac column for the *Houston Chronicle* for more than 15 years and has been published in pretty much every magazine that ever used the word *Mac* in its title. His achievements have been documented in major media around the world. (Yes, that was him juggling a keyboard in *USA TODAY* a few years back!)

Bob is known for his expertise, trademark humorous style, and ability to translate techie jargon into usable and fun advice for regular folks. Bob is also a prolific public speaker, presenting more than 100 Macworld Expo training sessions in the United States and abroad, keynote addresses in three countries, and Macintosh training seminars in many U.S. cities.

Dedications

I dedicate this book to my beautiful wife, Janie, for inspiring me in myriad ways every day I am with her. And to my incredible kids: my adorable little girl, Sydney (one of her first words was *iPod*), my little boy, Sammy (who is all smiles from the moment he wakes up in the morning), and my "canine" puppy daughter Sadie (who thankfully hasn't chewed on the iPad yet). My kids are already hooked on the iPad. This book is also dedicated to the memory of my "canine" son, Eddie, Jr., and my late parents, Samuel and Lucille Baig. I am madly in love with you all. — Ed Baig

Every book I've ever written and every book I will ever write is dedicated to my wife of almost 30 years, Lisa, who has taught me more about everything I know than anyone on the planet. Every book I've written has also been dedicated to my awesome (adult) kids, Allison and Jacob, who love their iPhones and iPads almost as much as I love them (my kids, not my gadgets). This book, however, is dedicated to my young cousin, Jack Wagner, who is my only relative who loves iPhones, iPads, and other gadgets more than both of my kids put together. This one's for you, cousin Jack! — Bob LeVitus

Authors' Acknowledgments

Special thanks to everyone at Apple who helped us turn this book around so quickly: Katie Cotton, Natalie Kerris, Natalie Harrison, Teresa Brewer, Trudy Muller, Keri Walker, Jennifer Bowcock, Simon Pope, Tom Neumayr, Christine Monaghan, and everyone else who lent a hand from the mothership out in Cupertino. We couldn't have done it without you and apologize to anyone we left out.

Big-time thanks to the gang at Wiley: Bob "Incredibly laidback again for this edition" Woerner, Rebecca "Remarkably mellow yet again" Senninger, Andy "The Boss" Cummings, and our incredible technical editor Dennis R. Cohen, whose suggestions and observations helped immensely (even the ones we ignored). Finally, thanks to everyone at Wiley we don't know by name. If you helped with this project in any way, you have our everlasting thanks.

Ed adds: Thanks to my agent Matt Wagner for again turning me into a *For Dummies* author. Matt had the right instincts to push this book, even back when we were calling the first edition of this book Project X For Dummies. I'd also like to thank Jim Henderson, Geri Tucker, Nancy Blair, Jefferson Graham, Eli Blumenthal, and all my *USA TODAY* friends and colleagues for your continuing support and encouragement of such projects. Most of all, thanks to my loving family for understanding my nightly (and weekend) disappearances as we raced to get this project completed on time. You are quite simply the greatest.

And Bob says: Extra special thanks to Carole "Swifty" Jelen, my literary agent for going on 25 years. I don't say this often enough, but you rock, Carole!

Publisher's Acknowledgments

Executive Editor: Bob Woerner

Project Editor: Rebecca Senninger

Senior Copy Editor: Barry Childs-Helton

Technical Editor: Dennis R. Cohen

Editorial Assistant: Anne Sullivan

Sr. Editorial Assistant: Cherie Case

Cover Image: © iStockphoto.com / enjoynz